NONVIOLENCE AND EDUCATION

In current global politics, which positions China as a competitor to American leadership, in-depth understandings of transnational mutual engagement are much needed for cultivating nonviolent relations. Exploring American and Chinese professors' experiences at the intersection of the individual, society, and history, and weaving the autobiographical and the global, this book furthers understanding of their cross-cultural personal awareness and educational work at universities in both countries. While focusing on life histories, it also draws on both American and Chinese intellectual traditions such as American nonviolence activism, Taoism, and Buddhism to formulate a vision of nonviolence in curriculum studies.

Centering cross-cultural education and pedagogy about, for, and through nonviolence, this volume contributes to internationalizing curriculum studies and introduces curriculum theorizing at the level of higher education. Hongyu Wang brings together stories, dialogues, and juxtapositions of cross-cultural pathways and pedagogies in a powerful case for theorizing and performing nonviolence education as visionary work in the internationalization of curriculum studies.

Hongyu Wang is Professor, School of Teaching and Curriculum Leadership, Oklahoma State University-Tulsa, USA.

STUDIES IN CURRICULUM THEORY
William F. Pinar, Series Editor

Wang	Nonviolence and Education: Cross-Cultural Pathways
Hurren/Hasebe-Ludt (Eds.)	Contemplating Curriculum: Genealogies/Times/Places
Pinar (Ed.)	International Handbook of Curriculum Research, Second Edition
Latta	Curricular Conversations: Play is the (Missing) Thing
Doll	Pragmatism, Post-Modernism, and Complexity Theory: The "Fascinating Imaginative Realm" of William E. Doll, Jr., Edited by Donna Trueit
Carlson	The Education of Eros: A History of Education and the Problem of Adolescent Sexuality Since 1950
Taubman	Disavowed Knowledge: Psychoanalysis, Education, and Teaching
Pinar	What Is Curriculum Theory? Second Edition
Tröhler	Languages of Education: Protestant Legacies, National Identities, and Global Aspirations
Hendry	Engendering Curriculum History
Handa	What Does Understanding Mathematics Mean for Teachers? Relationship as a Metaphor for Knowing
Joseph (Ed.)	Cultures of Curriculum, Second Edition
Sandlin/Schultz/Burdick (Eds.)	Handbook of Public Pedagogy: Education and Learning Beyond Schooling
Malewski (Ed.)	Curriculum Studies Handbook—The Next Moment
Pinar	The Wordliness of a Cosmopolitan Education: Passionate Lives in Public Service

Taubman	Teaching By Numbers: Deconstructing the Discourse of Standards and Accountability in Education
Appelbaum	Children's Books for Grown-Up Teachers: Reading and Writing Curriculum Theory
Eppert/Wang (Eds.)	Cross-Cultural Studies in Curriculum: Eastern Thought, Educational Insights
Jardine/Friesen/Clifford	Curriculum in Abundance
Autio	Subjectivity, Curriculum, and Society: Between and Beyond German Didaktik and Anglo-American Curriculum Studies
Brantlinger (Ed.)	Who Benefits from Special Education?: Remediating (Fixing) Other People's Children
Pinar/Irwin (Eds.)	Curriculum in a New Key: The Collected Works of Ted T. Aoki
Reynolds/Webber (Eds.)	Expanding Curriculum Theory: Dis/Positions and Lines of Flight
McKnight	Schooling, The Puritan Imperative, and the Molding of an American National Identity: Education's "Errand Into the Wilderness"
Pinar (Ed.)	International Handbook of Curriculum Research
Morris	Curriculum and the Holocaust: Competing Sites of Memory and Representation
Doll	Like Letters in Running Water: A Mythopoetics of Curriculum
Westbury/Hopmann/Riquarts (Eds.)	Teaching as a Reflective Practice: The German Didaktic Tradition
Reid	Curriculum as Institution and Practice: Essays in the Deliberative Tradition
Pinar (Ed.)	Queer Theory in Education
Huebner	The Lure of the Transcendent: Collected Essays by Dwayne E. Huebner. Edited by Vikki Hillis. Collected and Introduced by William F. Pinar

For additional information on titles in the Studies in Curriculum Theory series, visit www.routledge.com/education.

NONVIOLENCE AND EDUCATION

Cross-Cultural Pathways

Hongyu Wang

NEW YORK AND LONDON

First published 2014
by Routledge
711 Third Avenue, New York, NY 10017, USA

and by Routledge
2 Park Square, Milton Park, Abingdon, Oxfordshire OX14 4RN

First issued in paperback 2016

Routledge is an imprint of the Taylor & Francis Group, an informa business

© 2014 Taylor & Francis

The right of Hongyu Wang to be identified as author of this work has been asserted by her in accordance with sections 77 and 78 of the Copyright, Designs and Patents Act 1988.

All rights reserved. No part of this book may be reprinted or reproduced or utilized in any form or by any electronic, mechanical, or other means, now known or hereafter invented, including photocopying and recording, or in any information storage or retrieval system, without permission in writing from the publishers.

Trademark Notice: Product or corporate names may be trademarks or registered trademarks, and are used only for identification and explanation without intent to infringe.

Library of Congress Cataloging-in-Publication Data

Wang, Hongyu.
Nonviolence and education : cross-cultural pathways / by Hongyu Wang.
    pages cm. — (Studies in curriculum theory series)
  Includes bibliographical references and index.
  1. Nonviolence—Cross-cultural studies. 2. Education—Curricula—Cross-cultural studies. I. Title.
  HM1281.W35 2014
  303.6′1—dc23
  2013033310

Typeset in Bembo
by Apex CoVantage, LLC

ISBN 13: 978-1-138-28712-9 (pbk)
ISBN 13: 978-0-415-83469-8 (hbk)

Dedicated to

the four participants in this study, who inspired me onto pathways of nonviolence education

and

Doctor Tang Qiang, who restored my trust in organic healing.

CONTENTS

Preface   *xi*
Acknowledgments   *xv*

0 Pathways of Surprise, Stillness, and Spirituality   1

1 The Past Leading to the Present: Cross-Cultural Engagements   16

2 Beyond the Category: Cross-Cultural Imaginations   42

3 From Drama to Peace: A Hermit in a Cosmopolitan City   71

4 Serendipity: We Teach What We Are   105

5 Following the Flow: An Organic Approach to Research   134

0 A Playful Curriculum of Nonviolence in a Zero Space   156

References   *187*
Index   *201*

PREFACE

This book is based on a life history, qualitative study of four university professors' cross-cultural pathways. When I started this research during my sabbatical leave in China in September, 2009, I had no idea what it would lead me to. To my astonishment, it turned out to be one of the most spiritual experiences in my life. As a result, I became fully committed to nonviolence education, inspired by the life stories of the four professors in their cross-cultural engagements situated in history, culture, and educational contexts.

Two Chinese professors, one male and one female, and two American professors, one male and one female, from different generations participated in this study. This book tells these professors' extraordinary stories of encountering a culture different from their own and how such engagements influenced their educational work. Specifically, the Chinese professors' engagement with American/Western thought and culture and the American professors' engagement with Chinese thought and culture are narrated. Their stories are also situated in the context of the intellectual and cultural history of China–US engagement, with my autobiographical voice woven in when applicable. While Chinese immigrants' stories are more often heard in the North American educational field, Americans' lived experiences in China must also be heard to achieve the *mutuality* that is necessary for forming constructive relationships between the self and the other globally (Aoki, 2005). It is at the site of mutuality that non-dualistic engagement with difference becomes possible in cross-cultural and intercultural education.

Nonviolence has emerged as a central thread of cross-cultural pathways and pedagogy. Here nonviolence is defined as unity between the body and the mind within the self and compassionate relationships between the self and the other that can be extended to the group, the nation, and the global (and further to the ecological relationship between humanity and nonhuman beings, which is not the focus of this book). Defined in this way, nonviolence is a *positive* force, not merely the negation of violence—as the term "non-violence" seems to imply. For this reason, I choose the term "nonviolence" over "non-violence" to indicate that nonviolence not only curbs violence but is a primarily positive energy that is situated in the interconnectedness of life. Nonviolence is often associated with being *passive* or with passive resistance, but its inner *strength* is unyielding and it can endure attack from both inside and outside and further convert negative drives into life-affirmative energies.

Nonviolence is not discussed much in the field of curriculum studies, while scholars focus more on critical analysis of violence. However, focusing only on violence without offering a positive direction may reinforce the message of violence and cannot unravel its mechanism. This book highlights the role of nonviolence that promotes inner peace and organic relationality and treats internally the root of violence, pointing in the direction of transforming relational dynamics toward a "mutual contribution to sustainably shared flourishing" (Hershock, 2012, p. 257) in an educational community enriched by difference.

Nonviolence education is sometimes discussed in peace studies, which has become a field of study since World War II, but is usually perceived as a means to improving intergroup and international dynamics (Wang, 2013b). While my inquiry is historically and culturally situated, it is each professor's engagement in his or her unique pathway that is the center of attention, not intergroup relationships. The site of education, I argue, is ultimately individual personhood, not politics between groups and nations, even though personal growth influences and is influenced by relational situations at both the local and the global levels. Closely connecting the individual and the global is much needed in today's education because we live in a world where a global economy, Internet connections, and transnational mobility loom large, potentially subsuming individuality and diversity. Furthermore, nonviolence is not instrumental but an ontological way of life, uniting the means, the end, and the content of education.

At the heart of cross-cultural engagement—and essential to nonviolence—is how to deal with difference. In the past several decades, various approaches to identity and difference have emerged and now coexist in the Western academy, ranging from erasing differences in order to achieve universality, which runs the risk of reinforcing uniformity, to radicalizing the otherness of the other, which makes it difficult to bring the self and the other back into organic relationality. My interactions with the four participants have taught me a nonviolent approach to difference: respecting and engaging difference through mutuality and compassion without reifying and objectifying difference. Figuratively drawing a zero space of nonviolence that is inclusive, playful, and full of positive energy, I envision that engaging difference in such a space can release individual, relational, and curriculum creativity for realizing the best part of human aspiration, hope, and possibility.

The data sources for this study include interviews, observations, artifacts, documents, and ongoing dialogues collected from the fall of 2009 to the summer of

2012. Multiple analytic lenses are adopted in critically, deconstructively, and dialogically narrating and discussing participants' stories. The analytic frame for each story emerges from the particular nature of both the participant's stories and of the interaction between the participant and the researcher. The process of doing this study has led to an organic approach that integrates logic, intuition, and revelation, and blends Western qualitative research methodology and Chinese scholarly tradition. Organic research as an emergent process is also nonviolent, following the twists and turns of pathways to curve through multiple languages and cultures. Such an approach not only acknowledges the role of tensionality, contradictions, and ambiguity in intercultural, cross-cultural, and international education, but it also attempts to bring tensionality back to an organic whole. The means and the end of research are integrated through nonviolence.

Higher education is chosen as the site for this study because of its transnational nature, and research in higher education also needs more exploration of professors' (and students') cross-cultural personhood that goes beyond the current model of knowledge, skill, or competency-oriented global citizenship. However, nonviolence is a vision that can be embraced at all levels of education, and I am currently working with school teachers to enact it in their work, against the structural violence of standardization and accountability, which will be portrayed in the near future.

Overview

Chapter 0 introduces this book. Chapters 1–4 focus on individual participants, situating their stories in the intellectual and social history of cross-cultural engagements between China and the USA. I chose to start with David in Chapter 1 for a simple reason: He has the least similarity to me along cultural and gender lines. I believe that the openness to the other who is dramatically different from the self is a fertile ground for cultivating insights, wisdom, and ethical responsibility. I also situate David's stories in the intellectual history of his field and the cultural context of Chinese–American exchanges. Fen's stories follow David's in Chapter 2. As a female philosopher and administrator who had never traveled to the USA, Fen's engagement with Western thought was based mainly upon her readings rather than face-to-face interactions. To correspond with the intellectual nature of her stories, I sketch Chinese intellectual engagements with the West, especially during the New Culture Movement period in the 1910s and the 1920s, which was not only a turning point for the nation but also an important period for Fen's intellectual work. Gendered tales about public intellectuals and leadership are also presented in this chapter. Song's stories in Chapter 3 form an interesting contrast to David's as both professors are in the field of China Studies although their specialties are different. The influences on Song of the Cultural Revolution in China and of American culture and politics are narrated and analyzed. In Chapter 4, Teresa's voice as an educator—"we teach what we are"—comes through clearly, and I elaborate a pedagogy of nonviolence. Throughout these chapters, I discuss these participants' contributions to an educational vision of nonviolence.

The analysis and writing styles of these chapters are somewhat different, and these differences come from both the nature of the participants' stories and the nature of my interaction with them. Chapter 1 adopts an interpretative approach that highlights David's turning points in and transformative pathways of cross-cultural engagements in the contexts of cultural and intellectual history. In Chapter 2, in addition to an interpretive analysis, I use a post-structural lens to highlight contradictions in Fen's work and life, since ambiguity comes forward as a striking feature of her stories. Chapter 3 experiments with a combination of a dialogue format and the post-structural "juxtaposition" (Miller, 2005) of double stories to present both resonance and dissonance in the mutual engagement between Song and me. Chapter 4 also uses double texts for presenting Teresa's teaching stories and my stories, but my own stories are also doubled as they are about both the cross-cultural learning self and teaching self.

Chapter 5 tells research stories. An organic flow characterizes this study, although it is full of interruptions, contradictions, and surprising turns. Identifying defensive, disruptive, deconstructive, and dialogical moments in research relationality and living creatively with these tensions, I propose an organic approach to qualitative research that integrates logic, intuition, and revelation. This approach is a result of integrating Western methodology and Chinese scholarly tradition. Furthermore, the discussion addresses the turns and curves of a cross-cultural study in dancing with language, translation, and subjective positioning.

The last chapter is again titled Chapter 0 to synthesize the life histories of the four participants and envision the curriculum dynamics of nonviolence through engaging cultural differences. Such nonviolent dynamics go beyond liberal, pluralist, critical, or post-structural approaches to difference because difference is neither suppressed, nor separated, nor essentialized, nor radicalized but is considered an organic part of the web of human life. This chapter identifies major themes in the participants' stories, uses a diagram to portray a playful curriculum of nonviolence in a zero space, and intends to inspire both individual and communal quests for education about, through, and for nonviolence.

Although the voice of nonviolence speaks through a study that mainly involves two nations, it belongs to the best part of the human heritage across national, cultural, and spiritual boundaries. Human and ecological survival is at stake in today's world, and it is time for us as educators to embrace nonviolence and spread its effects throughout educational networks. Anything we do to contribute to nonviolence work will help in creating a culture of nonviolence. As a fundamental educational task that we must take on, creating curriculum about, for, and through nonviolence points the way to a future that we have not been able to imagine. Now, please turn the pages, listen to these professors' stories, and imagine a curriculum of nonviolence yourself . . .

ACKNOWLEDGMENTS

First of all, I cannot express how much gratitude I have for the four participants in this study who have inspired me beyond my imagination. Their extraordinary and moving life stories have touched my life as an educator in profound ways. Nonviolence education has become my long-term commitment as a result of this study.

My heartfelt thanks to Dr. Bill Pinar for his generous support of this book project, his deep care for my ideas in their emergence during the process of my research and writing, and his profound influence on my life. It is a tremendous honor that this book finds a home in his book series. Dr. Bill Doll's generative mentorship and nonviolence pedagogy also speak through this book in visible and invisible ways, and it will be my labor for another day to explore his pedagogical life history.

Dr. Rosa Hong Chen, Dr. Jon Smythe, and Liesa Smith read the whole manuscript and provided valuable and detailed suggestions: I cannot thank them enough for their care, encouragement, and generative questions. The book is better because of their input. Liesa also did a second-round grammar check on the manuscript, which makes me feel confident in the academic language of the book. I am indebted as well to my students in two doctoral seminars who read the book manuscript: Their engaged discussions have greatly contributed to my revision of the manuscript. I wish to thank Dr. Peter Hershock at the East–West Center for his enlightening comments from a philosophical viewpoint on my initial formulation of nonviolence. Thanks also goes to Dr. Petra Munro Hendry and Dr. Jackie Bach for inviting me to the Curriculum Camp as a campfire speaker, and to Dr. Michael P. O'Malley and Dr. Brian D. Schuhtz for inviting me to the Professors of Curriculum meeting to speak about nonviolence and education, which helped me to achieve more insights.

I have participated in a Jungian-oriented dream group in Tulsa for a couple of years, and the group members have supportively listened to my ideas about nonviolence since my first meeting with them. When I was writing the last words of the book, these friends brainstormed ideas at the dinner table in my house and helped me find a recursive ending. Thank you Marilyn Clarke, Susan Singh, Jenna Cassells, and Diana Bost (who just passed away in June, 2013) for teaching me the craft of dream-reading and the wisdom of the subconscious. Particularly, thanks goes to Susan for sharing the book *Engage: Exploring Nonviolent Living,* which is helpful for my teaching.

The anonymous reviewers of my book proposal provided critical insights and upon one reviewer's advice, I drew a diagram to symbolize a zero space of nonviolence that my students considered helpful for understanding what it is. I am very grateful to Editor Naomi Silverman for her support of this book project, her timely responses to all my inquiries, and her wisdom on many relevant issues. My thanks also goes to all the other staff at Routledge to craft the manuscript into a book. My grammar editor in Stillwater, Frances Griffin, has gracefully worked on the manuscript and patiently taught me some of the nuances and complexities of the English language. I cannot thank her enough for all her timely, detailed, and wonderful work.

I am also thankful that Oklahoma State University granted me a sabbatical leave to do the fieldwork for this book. I wish to thank the Hopkins-Nanjing Center for Chinese and American Studies, where I studied in the 1991–1992 academic year, for leading me onto my cross-cultural pathways. I thank my colleagues and friends in the Special Interest Group on Confucianism, Taoism, and Education at the American Educational Research Association for their insights into nonviolence and peace education: Xin Li, Jing Lin, Mei Wu Hoyt, Heesoon Bai, Avraham Cohen, Tianlong Yu, and Jenna Min Shim. I thank my colleagues and friends Kathryn Castle, Pam Brown (now our Department Chair), Gretchen Schwartz (now at Baylor University), and Seungho Moon for their wonderful work in the Curriculum Studies Project at OSU, which supports nonviolence education. I also greatly appreciate that Professor Feng Shengrao and Professor Huang Fuquan invited me to teach a two-week class at South China Normal University in December 2010, which adds a valuable dimension to my cross-cultural teaching.

In addition, I would like to acknowledge my long-time Chinese friends Bao Yanfeng, Zhu Huailan, Luo Jincao, and Wang Xia, among others, for their sustained friendship and their contribution to my cross-cultural journey. My mother, Lin Shuduan; father, Wang Hezeng; sisters Wang Hongmei, Wang Hongkun, and Wang Hongyan; and my third aunt, Wang Shaoling, have contributed to shaping what I am today, and I would not have found the inner voice of nonviolence without their love, support, and respect for my own pathway. And with deep affection, I thank my nephew, David Man, for the awesome time I have spent with him every year since his birth. He has taught me the meanings of play, love, and interconnectedness in his childhood.

I came a full circle in reconnecting with Ke Zuqiang, whom I met more than 20 years ago in Shanghai. Our marriage is a wonderful gift of life. The process of writing this book coincided with our shared time together; without his affectionate company, this book would not be the same. His loving presence in my life provides a safe harbor that anchors my work in nonviolence education.

I dedicate this book to the four participants in this study and to doctor Tang Qiang who helped restore my confidence in the art of natural healing (see the conclusion of this book).

0
PATHWAYS OF SURPRISE, STILLNESS, AND SPIRITUALITY

>Was not war in the interest of democracy for the salvation of civilization a contradiction of terms, whoever said it or however often it was repeated?
>(Jane Addams, 1922 [2002])

>If nonviolence is the law of our being, the future is with woman.
>(Mahatma Gandhi, Quoted in Eknath Easwaran, 1972 [1997])

>It is no longer a choice between violence and nonviolence in this world; it is nonviolence or nonexistence.
>(Martin Luther King, Jr., 1960)

November, 2009. Sitting in a hotel in a southern city in China, I was in the middle of transcribing an interview with Teresa, one of my research participants. This hotel on campus had a traditional Chinese cultural flavor in its architecture and interior design, and I enjoyed my stay in it. All of a sudden, everything came together in my mind in a moment of revelation with Teresa's voice from the recorder still lingering in my ear. I quickly stopped the tape recorder to write down the title of this book and its chapter layout. The structure of the book has remained true to this initial idea with minor revisions. What came as a surprise has stayed.

Surprise has appeared throughout this life-history, qualitative study of four university professors—two Americans and two Chinese; two women and two men—as all of them have brought critical moments, when I least anticipated them, to my new awareness. The purpose of my study was to understand how university professors' life experiences contribute to their cross-cultural engagements and how such engagements influence their work in universities to inform transnational and intercultural education. I focused on Chinese professors' engagement with Western thought and culture and American professors' engagement with Chinese thought and culture, and for that purpose, I selected participants in humanities and the social sciences whose educational work might be more related to cross-cultural thought and experiences than professors in the natural sciences or engineering. The fact that two participants, an American professor, David, and a Chinese professor, Song, were both in the field of China studies and graduated from different prestigious American universities was an unplanned coincidence, providing two different lenses for cross-cultural engagements in the same field (yet with different specialties), a field closely related to the theme of my study. It was a pleasant surprise.

Four months of sabbatical leave allowed me to travel back to China to do this research. My original plan was to select comparable participants in the USA after my return from the sabbatical. But the study in China has generated such rich, complicated, and inspirational materials that it forms an independent book, focusing a bit more on the Chinese side of the stories.

Surprise has also come from my participants' interruptions into my presumptions. Fen, for example, a Chinese professor, insisted that she did not think in terms of Chinese or Western thought, which directly challenged my explicit category of China/West and my implicit category of Western thought as liberal philosophy (see Chapter 2). Their lives and teachings also questioned conventions of pedagogy, including new conventions. For instance, Teresa's teaching in a Chinese university formed an interesting contrast to the notion of culturally relevant teaching in the American multicultural education mainstream. She did not try to change her teaching style per se according to pre-assumed cultural patterns, but her teaching was successful with Chinese students (see Chapter 4).

The biggest surprise for me, however, is how I have discovered the central thread of nonviolence through participants' stories and my own life history. As a result of this study, I have sensed a deeper integration of cross-cultural personhood[1] within myself and embraced nonviolence education as a "curriculum vision" (Doll & Gough, 2002), which is both transcendent and intimate. While the dramatic changes in China I saw during the time of this study were both exciting and overwhelming, it was the internal work rather than the external affairs that set me on "a voyage out" (Pinar, 1979 [1994]) to risk what is taken for granted and to listen to the inner voices of the other and of the self.

Incidentally and intentionally, my academic tour (lecturing in different universities and interviewing participants for this study) followed the same trajectory as my leaving home in the north and traveling to the south when I studied and worked in China. For several months, I was re-experiencing the past in places I used to know but no longer recognized, in a journey of letting go my previous attachments while integrating the cross-cultural fragments inside of me, a journey of listening to the whisper of that little girl who longed for nonviolence and peace as she grew up and moved from place to place, finally landing in the American South for her doctoral studies. The whisper was subsumed under the noise of the relentless pursuit of "progress" in China (or worldwide) and my own determination to pursue academic excellence. Now as a middle-aged woman, revisiting places where I went to school, college, and graduate school and where I worked, listening to my participants' powerful voices, reflecting on my own disillusion first with the Chinese socialist ideal and then the American ideal of democracy, the voice of nonviolence finally broke through the surface and rang like a bell in my ear.

Surprise is also accompanied by stillness. When unexpected interconnections are made through surprising discoveries, stillness can follow. "Stillness speaks" its own language (Tolle, 2003) and we need to listen to it well. Sometimes the intensity of thoughts and feelings can lead to stillness when deeply experienced relatedness pacifies the turbulence of mind and brings moments of peace. One early morning during my research, I went out for a casual walk and somehow ended up in front of the library on campus, a library I used to enter when I studied there. I was no longer a student and did not have a library card, so I could not get in, but facing the entrance was a swing. I sat on the swing, watching folks coming in and out of the library: A moment of stillness washed over me. I could have just sat there for hours, swinging.

That moment happened after I had experienced internal turmoil in revisiting a university important to me. The intense re-experiencing of places, people, and the past surprisingly led to the pause of stillness that gently opened up the knots of my heart to let go of old attachments. In working through intensity to reach stillness, my interaction with participants, particularly with Song, played an important role (see Chapter 3). After all the drama Song experienced both in the USA and China, he achieved a sense of inner peace from which he was able to play with language, culture, and thought, and his humorous play eased the tension in me. Moments of clarity washed away my clinging longings to see the landscape anew. Walking in the stillness of my mind, I saw grass become greener, flowers become more colorful, air become more refreshing, and people become more friendly. The world became fuller internally and externally.

Stillness indicates the dissolution of boundary, which opens the door to experiencing the energy of life, whether it is the flow of nature, or the vitality of the arts, or the passion and vigor of intellect. Naming both the beginning and ending chapters in this book as Chapter 0 is my play with such a generative stillness, which is open to possibilities, possibilities that defy any rigid definition but carry the vital source of life. I use the term "zero" in the Buddhist sense of emptiness and the Taoist circle[2] of *yin–yang* dynamics. The Buddhist teaching of no-self requires us to practice seeing all things as empty, or having no essence, because they exist in the web of relationships through particular patterns. Emptiness—zero—holds "a relational pattern of interdependence" (Hershock, 2005, p. 19). In such a non-dualistic viewpoint, emptiness is also full. Coming from zero, we also go back to zero, but it is not a stagnant zero in which nothing happens; it is an ongoing process of birth, life, death, and rebirth.

Tao Te Ching says in Chapter 42: "*Tao* gives birth to one, one gives birth to two, two gives birth to three, and three gives birth to a myriad of things." The singular one comes from *Tao* and must be sustained by the dynamics of two opposing cosmic forces (*yin* and *yang*) to give birth to a myriad of things. In this sense, *Tao* is both still and dynamic, as the circle of the *Taiji* symbol demonstrates. In my earlier work, I defined curriculum as a third space that transforms cultural, gendered, and psychic conflicting doubles to generate new educational possibilities (Wang, 2004). While I still value the notion of the third in going beyond dualism and living with multiple differences, I no longer privilege the third in negotiating conflicts but come back to a more fundamental notion of zero—empty, still, and dynamic—which includes, yet goes beyond, the role of the third through its deeply rooted sense of interdependence across differences and diversity (Wang, 2010a).

Through stillness, one reaches spirituality. Here spirituality is a broad concept, a contrast to materialism; in Chinese philosophy and culture, spirituality is not necessarily a religious idea, although it does not exclude religions. Teresa's story is threaded by her faith in God, whose message is love, and it is love that supports her openness to cultural differences. Dwayne Huebner (1993 [1999]) argues that the myth of redemptive violence—"that the world can be corrected and redeemed through power" (p. 407)—rather than the redemptive love essential to spirituality prevails in school education. Love also springs from stillness. As Tolle (2003) says, "You feel a oneness with whatever you perceive in and through stillness. Feeling the oneness of yourself with all things is true love" (p. 5). For me, the mysterious interconnectedness I have experienced in life, beyond any individual person or any particular event, which is also immanent in the particular, is spirituality. Those intensely experienced moments of deeper integration during my study highlighted the significance of the spiritual in life. And I prefer to symbolically express this interconnectedness as zero, which hosts the all-encompassing energy of life and leaves room for alternative openings. When interaction, interplay, and cross-cultural dynamics happen in a zero space, one can play more freely and creatively.

This sense of play can be strangled by the deadly seriousness of scientific reason, which has had its overwhelming triumph for the last several centuries in the West, and moral reason, which has controlled China for a thousand years. Derrida's project to deconstruct modern Western philosophy is to see through the fragility of its foundation to deconstruct "the apparent firmness, hardness, durability, or resistance" of systems and institutions (Derrida, 1990 [2002], p. 10), a hardness that is forged by the logocentrism of scientific reason, a hardness Song sees as the problem of the West in its desire for only *yang* without *yin* (see Chapter 3). Modern Chinese intellectuals' project to challenge Chinese traditions in the New Culture Movement in the 1910s and 1920s—and still ongoing—was to liberate humanity from the confinement of a deadening moral system. The material comfort and technological advances that modern society has been able to achieve have not been able to heal the moral and spiritual crises of both the East and the West. We need to be more playful in education to transcend the rigidity of reason.

The pathways of surprise, stillness, and spirituality indicate that cross-cultural journeys are always "in-the-making" (Miller, 2005, p. 227), not something given. In this brief introduction I highlight the pathways of my study in its surprising turns, integration in stillness, and pursuit of spirituality. The following chapters will demonstrate my participants' marvelous journeys of surprise, stillness, and spirituality. In different ways, all of them told me like David said: "My past prepared me for the present in such a way that has been beyond what I could have anticipated." David explained that he had not chosen to become a leader in Chinese–American educational exchanges, but life had simply taken him onto such a path (see Chapter 1). This sense of becoming and emergence leading to a different consciousness is the motif of *currere* (Pinar, 1994, 2004; Pinar & Grumet, 1976), unfolding the path of each professor in being educated and educating others.

Currere is about the autobiographical pathways of educational experiences that temporally and spatially situate and transcend the evolution of self to open new possibilities. Its purpose is to "release from the past, release from arrest, release into movement" (Pinar, 1976 [1994], p. 45), or in other words, to cultivate new consciousness. As a word, *currere* is the Latin root of curriculum, referring to the running of the course. Such a running was the discursive performing act of my participants when they narrated their life stories, although I am authoring their tales in this book. Their autobiographical voices also intersect with my own autobiographical voice as a cross-cultural university professor. The *currere* of cross-cultural pathways performed in this way is a mixed genre creating a web of interconnections and disjuncture to depict a dynamic and complex picture. The aspiration of this book is to inspire educators to reach a new consciousness of education in our transnational, intercultural, global society.

Cross-Cultural Studies in Education

Autobiographical studies of going across the borders of race, gender, class, and sexuality in education—to name a few—have expanded dramatically in the past several decades in the field of curriculum studies. When culture is defined in a broad sense, works related to multiple identities—however identity is defined—can be seen as "cross-cultural." This book, however, focuses specifically on Chinese–American dialogues in the context of higher education. East/West engagement has had a long history, as David Geoffrey Smith (2008) points out, but because of Western scientific reason's victory during the past several centuries, such a link has become invisible. In recent decades, Western scholars, especially in the fields of philosophy, religion, literature, history, and sociology, have begun to pay more attention to what Eastern traditions can offer to rethinking human life in its contemporary complexity, turbulence, and simultaneous connections and fragmentation (e.g., Allan, 1997; Hall & Ames, 1987; Hershock, 2005; Ko, 1994; Loy, 1988; 2009; Tu, 1979).

The field of education, however, has lagged behind in this area, and only recently have educational scholars in the West devoted more effort to opening up East/West dialogues at the level of educational thought (e.g., Bai, Scott, & Donald, 2009; Eppert & Wang, 2008; Li, 2005; Smith, 1996). There are also a few qualitative narrative inquiries of Chinese immigrants' cross-cultural lives and subjectivity (e.g., He, 2000; Li, 2002), including Xin Li's (2002) poetic rendering of Chinese women immigrants' stories in North America. More in-depth works in the area of cross-cultural and transnational *mutual* engagement, including American engagement with China, is needed, especially in the current context in which China has recently emerged as a competitor in the global setting and is sometimes perceived by the American public as a threat to American superpower leadership in the world. Intercivilizational dialogues such as between American and Chinese cultures, which have dramatic differences on multiple dimensions, are imperative in contemporary education. The recent movement toward the internationalization of curriculum studies in the American curriculum field (Pinar, 2003a, 2003b) intends to promote scholarly conversations within and across national and regional borders, challenging both narrow nationalisms and the homogenizing tendency of globalization.

My study joins in such dialogues and conversations by exploring daily intercultural and cross-cultural encounters through diverse channels. Studying both American professors' and Chinese professors' engagement with the other culture affirms the reciprocity of exchanges at the level of life, thought, and culture, and it is at this site of *mutuality* that the promise of intercultural conversations for the well being of all participants lies. Different pathways of engagement are discussed, ranging from the stories of participants who had in-depth life experiences in the counterpart culture to those who had no direct experience, from the mode of activism to the mode of meditation, and from the site of teaching to the site of administrative work. In contemporary American and Chinese universities, border crossing within and across national or cultural boundaries happens every day at various sites, including college classrooms, international exchange programs, and in the virtual world. It is this sense of everyday encounters and mutual engagements of individual persons that is crucial to "learning *from* the other" (Todd, 2003, p. 1) and "creating transnational spaces" (Gough, 2003, p. 68) for collaboration between and among different localities.

There have been many discussions about globalization and higher education, and here I can only briefly mention several issues related to my study. First, in these discussions, the focus has often stayed on macro, socioeconomic, institutional levels, including the role of markets, new forms of online universities, and educational structures and systems (see Hershock, Mason, & Hawkins, 2007; Odin & Manicas, 2004). Second, new courses and new programs in global learning have been developed (e.g., Stearns, 2009) and an emphasis on developing students' global competency (e.g., Anderberg, Norden, & Hansson, 2009) has recently emerged. Third, critiques of globalization through multiple lenses have been ongoing since its contemporary inauguration.

It is important to address structural issues at the macro level, but it is equally important to understand the interaction between global transformation and personal transformation, since what is unfolding at the global level regarding simultaneous integration and multiplicity also unfolds at the level of an individual person, who is the site of education. The search for unity at the global level not only has the potential to subsume individuality and diversity, but it may also provide an illusory sense of wholeness to the individual that denies the otherness within the individual and social differences in the outside world. Therefore, it is important to probe the depth of personhood and "interbeing" (Thich, 1989 [2009]) in order to negotiate a productive dynamic of the global, the local, and the personal. It is an essentially educational task to work at the intersection between the autobiographical and the global.

Both knowledge and competency in global education and global learning are necessary, but personal growth is more than the addition of knowledge, behavior, and ability. Adding global citizenship to the list of qualities that students need to develop in a global society as if it were a separate quality can hardly address the complexity of the influences of globalization on individual persons. William F. Pinar (2009) argues for the significance of autobiography over identity politics in the worldliness of cosmopolitanism that privileges the meanings of lived experience for situated personhood. Ronald Barnett (2009) privileges being and becoming over knowing in the higher education curriculum. In my study, the site of *being/personhood* at the intersection of macro and micro levels is privileged in order to demonstrate the dynamics of cross-cultural pathways.

In more critical approaches to globalization and education, neoliberalism and the commercialization embedded in globalization have been the target of critiques (see the special issue of the *Journal of Curriculum Theorizing,* December, 2010). While it is important to question the colonizing and commercializing tendency of globalization, we cannot stop short at critique; we must also understand the educational potentiality of cross-cultural and intercultural encounters and make educative use of such potential to shift the tide of globalization towards "a new kind of global [and intercultural] dialogue regarding sustainable human futures" and "a new kind of imaginal understanding within human consciousness" (Smith, 2003, p. 35). My participants' diverse pathways of cross-cultural engagements walk toward such a new kind of imaginal understanding.

For this study, I use a life history approach because it is situated at the intersection of the individual, society, and history. As Ivor Goodson (1998) points out, life history goes deeper than life stories to make historical, cultural, and social links with personal experiences to depict a bigger picture so that we can take one step back from the present in order to reconstruct the present. My participants' trajectories of cross-cultural engagements carry the weight of collective histories, as we will see in later chapters, and illuminate our current efforts towards the internationalization of curriculum studies that resists the uniformity tendency of globalization but promotes cross-cultural and international conversations on education, curriculum, and pedagogy. Considering the importance of personhood situated in history, place, and culture and the interdependent relationships between the personal and the (global) communal in Chinese educational philosophy (Wang, 2009), a life history approach embodying an integrated, organic research perspective (see Chapter 5) for studying Chinese–American cross-cultural lives seems a good fit.

I chose higher education as the research site because instructors' direct engagements with another country usually happens at the university level, not at the K–12 level, although this is dramatically changing, as more and more public school teachers go abroad with their students for international exchanges. Another consideration was related to the lack of curriculum theorizing works at the level of higher education. The primary site of American curriculum studies has been K–12 schools, and by extension, teacher education. During recent decades, teacher subjectivity and teacher lore have become an important research topic. Curriculum studies in higher education, however, has been marginalized between the field of higher education and the field of curriculum and instruction, and when it has a place, it is primarily concerned with curriculum development and design. The 1970s reconceptualization movement in American curriculum studies has seldom been introduced at the higher education level (other than in teacher education). Introducing the lens of curriculum theorizing to understand professors' cross-cultural personhood at universities, this study involves multiple disciplines such as history, political science, philosophy, and literary criticism and promises an interdisciplinary contribution to the field of higher education.

It is worthwhile to say a few words about the term "cross-cultural" before I move to the details of my study. Aoki (1981 [2005]) critiques the use of "cross-cultural" in the identity-oriented imaginaries of East and West as separate and essentialized entities, and understands "conversation as a bridging of two worlds by a bridge, which is not a bridge" (p. 228). He evokes the image of a non-bridge bridge to set into motion the demarcation of boundary and calls for dwelling in an inter-space in which the tensionality of conjunction and disjuncture upholds the emergence of newness. Inspired by his effort to deconstruct the East/West binary, I nevertheless think crossing and dwelling are interdependent. Without crossing into another world and coming back, an inter-space does not embody what exists on the other side; without dwelling on the bridge, crossing pushes away the interactive potentiality of an in-between space. To allow newness to emerge, both crossing and dwelling are necessary, as you will see from my participants' life histories. In today's mobile society in which migration, immigration, and globalization continue to disrupt the homogeneous picture of locality, crossing can happen within the border without a person's setting foot in a foreign land, while dwelling can gesture towards what is beyond the existing landscape. In this book, cross-cultural and intercultural are interdependent terms and cannot exist separately from each other.

Participants and Data Collection

Because of the nature of this study, the selection of participants was purposeful with the help of friends and Internet searches. I intended to have a balance of gender and nationality, and participants needed to be present in China when I was there during my sabbatical leave. Ideally, I also wanted two participants from the same country to have a different degree of engagement with the counterpart country. I imagined having difficulty in locating American participants in China because few American professors were teaching in Chinese universities regularly, and when they did teach there, they usually came and left during the summer. Fortunately, I was able to find four participants who matched or nearly matched my criteria. However, the two female participants happened to have fewer experiences with the counterpart cultures than the two male participants. While there is a gendered imbalance in this aspect, my own engagement with American culture has been extensive, and since a strong autobiographical voice is present in this study, I hope that it serves as a complementary contribution.

I first briefly introduce these participants' backgrounds and then explain more about the process of selection and data collection. I follow the order of their appearance in the later chapters. (All the names of people and places are pseudonyms.)

David was in his mid-40s in 2009 when I interviewed him. He was an American professor, born in a cosmopolitan city in the Northeast, and an administrator of a bicultural center in China. His first encounter with China was when he was a high school student. He spent eight months in China with his father, who taught in a Chinese university in the early 1980s. This experience was influential during his formative years. When he went back to China on a fellowship after graduating from a program related to China in a prestigious American university, he witnessed the 1989 student movements, which had a huge influence on him. Carrying the burning question of "why democracy did not happen in China," he continued with his graduate studies and finished his Ph.D. in China Studies. Ever since 1989, he has been passionately involved in promoting intercultural exchanges.

Fen was also in her mid-40s, a Chinese professor and an administrator in a Chinese university. She was born in northern China and was the only one among her classmates who went to university. She became a professor in a comprehensive Chinese university with a three-year experience of working as a part-time journalist during her early career. As a college dean in a comprehensive university, she had multidisciplinary expertise and taught in different fields including literature and philosophy. She was the only participant who had not lived abroad and had not had any direct encounter with Western culture, so her understanding of Western thought came through reading and study. She has authored numerous academic books and articles related to Western thought. Her teaching philosophy was influenced by constructivism, although I did not have a chance to observe her teaching.

Song was in his mid-50s, a Chinese[3] professor in a Chinese university. He had lived through the Cultural Revolution (1966–1976), through countryside reformation life as a teenager and factory life as a worker. He went to college in 1977 when the college entrance exam was restored. When his work in a tourist college offered him an opportunity, he came to the USA as an exchange instructor, and then became a student and finished his Ph.D. in political science at a prestigious American university in the Northeast. After his graduation, he worked in an American university in the Midwest. After 10 years as a professor, he gradually became disillusioned with his faith in the American ideal and returned to China. When I interviewed him, he was living a hermit-style life, teaching in a Chinese university and practicing meditation daily.

Teresa was in her mid-60s, an American professor teaching English in a Chinese university. She had not known much about China until she traveled there to teach English in 2000. Invited by an exchange program, she continued to teach for several years. Initially teaching only English, later she began to teach other classes such as American history and culture, teaching methods, and community service. As an activist, she also initiated a project for helping a Chinese school with children with disabilities. Teresa ventured into another culture without much prior knowledge. She was the only one among the four participants whose teaching I had a chance to observe in 2009. She was also the only one who told me her love stories and about her religious faith, in addition to her professional work, which gave me a more holistic picture of her life history.

In China, finding a Chinese participant through only an email request to do in-depth interviews and observations would be very rare if not impossible. I failed to get any response when I contacted professors I did not know, so personal networks had to be used one way or another. My initial contact with Fen was mediated by a third person. I met Song, who had lived in the USA for 20 years, when he was making the decision to go back to China. He actually volunteered to participate when I told him about my plan, although it took me several tries to locate him in China when I began this study. I found Teresa with the help of a Chinese professor at her university and located David's information through an Internet search. The two Americans accepted the invitations once I contacted them through email, although David warned me from the beginning that he might not have enough time for the interviews.

I obtained the IRB approval for this three-year research. The major time line for data collection was the fall semester of 2009, but I also requested an extension of the IRB permission through Oklahoma State University twice in order to finish the third interview with Fen and other follow-up procedures, so the study officially ended in June of 2012. The data included interviews, documents and writings, teaching observations, teaching artifacts (including syllabi, students' evaluations, and teaching materials), and email updates of recent activities. These materials were collected over a three-year period. I also kept a research journal that recorded my ideas and feelings throughout the research process as well as critical reflections of my research subjectivity. All participants signed consent forms and gave me permission to use the data; I asked them to verify the accuracy of interview transcripts and shared the drafts of book chapters with them.

I interviewed David three times, each time for about one hour. His passion for the topic sustained his continuing conversations with me, even though originally he did not expect that his schedule would allow such a long period of time for each interview. But I did not have a chance to observe his teaching. I collected some of his scholarly writings in order to understand more of his intellectual history, as I did with Fen and Song. Considering the concerns about revealing participants' identities, my reading of all participants' scholarly writings is used for deepening my understanding, but I don't directly quote their writings.

Because of Fen's busy administrative schedule, I was able to finish only two interviews with her in 2009, and each interview lasted about one and a half hours. I returned to China to finish the third, follow-up, interview with her during the summer of 2011. I did not have a chance to observe her teaching, but she gave me her writings about teaching along with her reading list for a feminist literature class. She provided a few scholarly publications for me as well. In order to prepare for the third interview, I read as many of her published journal articles as I could find. Since she never lived abroad, I focused more on her intellectual engagement than I did with the other participants.

My interviews and interactions with Song produced the longest interview transcriptions. I interviewed Song four times, up to three hours each time. We also had many informal conversations after the formal interviews. In addition, I had a telephone follow-up interview with him for more than an hour. I did not have a chance to observe his teaching, however, since he had lost interest in the content of his teaching and preferred that I not observe it. I also read part of his published writings. During the winter of 2011, I was able to meet and talk with him informally and asked further questions.

I interviewed Teresa three times (ranging from one and a half hours to more than two hours) and also observed her teaching twice, including one time when I took the bus with her to a branch campus of her university. On the bus, she showed me the students' profiles she had asked them to create in English. She also gave me or emailed me teaching materials, students' evaluations, and PowerPoint presentation slides of cultural and activist events she initiated or was involved in. She not only responded to my follow-up questions but also gave me updates throughout the process on her subsequent activities in China.

Originally, teaching was what I wanted to focus on in understanding how these participants' cross-cultural engagements influenced their pedagogy in the classroom. Although all of them teach, I did not have a chance to observe all of them teaching for multiple reasons. As I listened to their fascinating stories, my focus shifted to their multidimensional roles as educators who educate not only in the classroom. While I highlight Teresa's teaching activities in Chapter 4, I include these participants' educational work broadly, including educational leadership, cross-cultural educational exchange, pedagogical activism, or meditative self-education. Their stories in both juxtaposition and intersection have so much to offer us for rethinking the meaning of education in today's globalized, transnational, and conflict-ridden society.

Important Aspects of Nonviolence and Education

While I have learned many things from participants' stories, it is the message of nonviolence that speaks to me the most. Foregrounding each participant's own perspectives and journeys, I highlight the central thread of nonviolence across their pathways. In order to situate the stories of the four participants in the next few chapters, I would like to briefly discuss the notion of nonviolence here, although this notion emerged and was articulated *during and after* my study, not before.

Nonviolence as a term, according to Michael Nagler (2004), is a literal translation of the Sanskrit word *Ahimsa,* which means "the absence of the desire, or intention, to harm" (p. 44). What is missed in the English translation is the fundamentally positive quality in the Sanskrit abstract noun. Especially when it is spelled "non-violence" in the English language, it usually indicates the negation of (physical) violence, but nonviolence is a positive force that actively engages all parties through the interconnectedness of life. There is an internal mechanism in nonviolence that goes against all forms of violence—not just physical forms—through a process of transforming fear, anger, or hatred into life-affirmative energies.

Both violence and nonviolence are broad concepts, involving physical, intellectual, emotional, cultural, political, and other dimensions (Wang, 2010a). In education, we have discussed violence much more than nonviolence, but I am afraid that critiquing violence without embracing nonviolence may lead to reinforcing rather than dissolving violence. Philosophically and spiritually, nonviolence as a notion and a practice—not doing harm to the other—has existed for thousands of years in different traditions throughout the world (Smith-Christopher 2007; Nagler 2004). As an antidote to violence, nonviolence not only heals the wound but also promotes a relational dynamic that does not lead to violence in the first place. Nonviolence builds a loving, compassionate, and constructive community in which nonviolent relationality contributes to cultivating creative expressions of individuality.

Politically, nonviolence is widely recognized because of anticolonial and civil rights movements in the contemporary age, particularly the nonviolence movements in India led by Gandhi, the American civil rights movement, and the recent nonviolent uprisings against dictatorships in different parts of the world. In political contexts, nonviolence refers to using nonviolent means in collective struggles against colonization, dictatorship, or social injustice. Nagler (2004), however, argues that practicing nonviolence from above has also had a long history in the USA (such as William Penn's nonviolent governing leading to 70 years of peaceful association between the colonists and the Delaware Indians in the late 1600s) and in the world (such as Emperor Ashoka's nonviolent ruling by Buddhist principles in ancient India). He further advocates nonviolence as an integrative power to be educationally cultivated. Therefore, nonviolence is not only multidimensional but also can be enacted from multiple directions, and education is an important site for its cultivation.

Understood in a broad, multidirectional way, several aspects of nonviolence are particularly important and informative to education. First, a sense of interconnectedness is the cornerstone of nonviolence. Second, nonviolence initiates and sustains relational dynamics that draw out the most humane side of humanity to rise above hatred and aggression. Third, a nonviolent relationship with the other goes hand in hand with a nonviolent relationship with the self. Fourth, the means and end are united through nonviolent principles, which do not use any form of coercion but that never compromise the position of noncooperation with any form of violence. Fifth, a playful spirit of nonviolence decenters the hard core of domination and transcends categorical thinking. I discuss these aspects briefly as follows.

First, the underlying basis of nonviolence is the mutual embeddedness of everything and everybody in the cycle of life. Heesoon Bai and Avraham Cohen (2008) argue that violence comes from a dualistic, objectified consciousness that separates the self from the other (and fragments the self, I would add here) and from the world. They call for a non-dualistic and intersubjective consciousness that integrates matter/mental, body/mind, and self/other to reach a sense of interconnectedness that can dissolve violence against the human and ecological other. Healing the wound cut by dualism, nonviolence cultivates the intellectual, the social, the moral, and the spiritual imagination for organic relationships in a local, national, international, and planetary community. As Jing Lin (2006) envisions, "Education is a calling to teach people to live interdependently with a deep respect for all" (p. 9). Such a social and ecological sense of interdependence is essential for enacting nonviolent dynamics.

Second, the power of nonviolence lies in the relational dynamics that transcend a win-or-lose mentality to situate the relationship between the self and the other—individually or collectively—as mutually beneficial in the picture of the whole. While dealing with social and cultural differences becomes important in contemporary education, Peter Hershock (2009) draws upon the Buddhist notion of non-duality to argue for "a concerted shift from considerations of how much we are the *same* or *different from* each [sic] another to how we might best *differ for* one another" (p. 160; emphasis in the original). Then the task of education becomes creating conditions for such relational dynamics of "differing for" rather than "differing from." The belief in nonviolence is also a belief in human capacity for compassion and love that can dissolve aggression and hatred, and the purpose of nonviolence education is to cultivate the best potentiality within everyone and transform the aggressive side of humanity into productive activities so that we can learn and grow nonviolently. To enact such a relational dynamic requires not only going beyond ego to connect with others but also the courage to stop aggression and curb the destructive tendencies of both the self and the other.

Third, not doing violence to oneself is also important for forming a nonviolent relationship. Nonviolence requires cultivating inner peace as an important step. To be able to interact with the other nonviolently, including both friendly others and hostile others, one must engage in the inner work of transforming anger, hatred, fear, and greed into constructive relational orientations. Often such an inner work requires psychic and social unlearning and involves rigorous emotional work.

Being able to negotiate conflicts within makes it possible to negotiate conflicts in the outside world, while the inner work and the outer work are usually intertwined and mutually enhance each other. Inner peace and outer peace go hand in hand (Lin, 2006; Wang, 2013a). Engaging in nonviolent inner work leads to balance, integration, and wholeness in the process of individuation, in the Jungian term (Jung, 1969; Mayes, 2005; Taylor, 2009). Educators' "work from within" (Pinar, 1972) becomes crucial here. Nagler (2004) affirms the importance of the individual person in nonviolent work: "the human individual is always the source, and individuality the ultimate beneficiary, of nonviolence" (p. 200). The relational orientation of nonviolence does not diminish but enhances modes of individuality that ultimately serve the well-being of all individuals.

Fourth, the key to enacting nonviolence is to use nonviolent means to transform the nature of relationality. Nonviolent principles of relying on lived experiences, persuasion, emotional resonance, personal examples, or collective pursuits of peace operate not only at the conscious level but also at the subconscious level to influence the whole person. In pedagogical situations, educators have a unique opportunity to practice nonviolence from an authority position and thus to model how to establish nonviolent relationships. Nonviolent means, however, do not shy away from challenging the taken-for-granted assumptions to undo violence in various forms. Gandhi insists that his noncooperation against colonialism is rooted in love, love not only for people who are with him, but also for people who are against him, because nonviolence believes that the whole world is one family (Easwaran, 1972 [1997]). Inner strength is required for carving out compassionate understandings and commitments while challenging all forms of violence (including pedagogical violence).

Fifth, the spirit of playfulness in nonviolence enables the process of seeing through any narrow sense of boundary to reach a higher-level sense of interconnectedness. When we don't take any category too seriously, the fluidity, flexibility, and fun aspects of life can be opened up to bring conflicts back into the organic whole. Play transcends dualism and bridges separateness, and in so doing, heals the divide cut open by violence and releases the imagination for nonviolent relationality. A sense of playfulness is essential to William E. Doll, Jr.'s (1998) three-S curriculum (Science, Story, and Spirit), which follows the flow of interplay with texts and among participants to keep curriculum alive.

All my participants have demonstrated certain aspects of nonviolence in their cross-cultural engagements and educational work, and their life histories helped me formulate these five aspects. For example, enacting constructive relational dynamics in David's work, challenging categorical thinking in Fen's work, cultivating playful non-duality and inner peace in Song's life, and a pedagogy of nonviolence in Teresa's teaching, all powerfully speak to the importance of nonviolence in intercultural and international educational encounters. Even though the majority of the participants did not use the term "nonviolence" directly, it is the coming together of these aspects and my interactions with the participants that has inspired the central thread of this book. Nonviolence is a vision that we work towards rather than something already actualized, and such a vision of education through and for nonviolence can inspire many educators' individual and collective work in creating a better world with our students.

In short, nonviolence, as the calling of our time, is the visionary work of curriculum studies for achieving organic interconnectedness within and across the individual, the national, and the international to create sustainable pathways for individuals, societies, and ecological communities. Attending to this call, can we engage in our daily educational work nonviolently?

Notes

1. As I explain in my earlier book (Wang, 2004), the notion of identity is not a widespread concept in China. What is close to the Western notion of self development or identity construction is the Chinese concept of personal cultivation, which refers to a process of cultivating the best potential within each individual person through social, cultural, and cosmic relatedness (See Wang, 2004, Chapter 3). Here I use the term "cross-cultural personhood," rather than "cross-cultural identity" or "self," to refer to the process of cultivating the best potential of humanity across different cultures and blending it into one's inner landscape as I or my participants travel back and forth between China and the USA. But sometimes I use the term "identity" or "self" or "subjectivity" when it is a more appropriate term to refer to my participants' stories.
2. In my Internet search for visual representations of nonviolence and peace, a circle is almost always included in the symbol across different traditions, locally and internationally, including the iconic image of Gandhi's wheel and the universal symbol of nonviolence. The similarity of the shapes and symbolic meanings of zero and circle has certainly contributed to my choice of zero. Mathematically, as Bill Doll points out in his class, zero is an important number, full of possibilities; for instance, a number line would not exist without zero. But the role of zero is usually neglected as "nothing."
3. Song became an American citizen while he was in the USA, so legally he was a Chinese American. But while living in China during the time of my study, his cultural identity was much more aligned with being Chinese. So, for this study I count him as a Chinese professor.

1
THE PAST LEADING TO THE PRESENT

Cross-Cultural Engagements

I found David as a participant through an Internet search of bicultural institutes in China where American professors teach Chinese students. Actually, I found another potential participant, but our schedules conflicted, so I had to find a replacement. The brief description of David and his substantial experiences in China on the Internet attracted my attention. As I began to interview him, it turned out that the depth and breadth of his engagements with China were much more extensive than I had ever imagined. It was a pleasant surprise.

The fact that David was a busy administrator bothered me a bit since I knew that time would be an issue. It was indeed an issue. When I first met him in his office, David showed a great deal of interest in my study, but when I said I wanted to do three one-hour interviews, he replied that he probably would not be able to have an hour at a time with me, perhaps half an hour, or maybe 20 minutes. But once he started to talk, his passion prevented him from stopping at 20 or 30 minutes. And it was his passion for what he had been doing for more than two decades—building bridges between China and the USA through study and educational exchange—that ran deep throughout his life history. "I love what I am doing," David said repeatedly, and his commitment and devotion were evident in his stories. He finished three one-hour interviews with me despite his overbooked schedule.

David had made great contributions to Chinese and American educational exchange. His long-time engagement with China had been both dramatic and gradual. In this chapter, I discuss those defining moments and transformative pathways in David's cross-cultural experiences in the context of the shifting lenses of China studies in the USA and their contributions to his pedagogy of cross-cultural mutual learning.

Defining Moments and Turning Points

David was born in 1965 in a cosmopolitan city in the northeastern part of the USA. His formative years as a child were influenced by the international orientation of the city and of his parents. His father was a professor at a well-known university, and his mother was an exile from a European country under communist control. David spent almost every summer in Europe, where his grandparents lived, and he was bilingual with dual citizenship. He described his parents as having international minds, so he had grown up comfortable with international settings. David commented, "If I have any issue with adjusting to a place, that would be those places not cosmopolitan." But his early experience was very Europe-focused and Asia was not in the picture. His earliest exposure to Asia was slides of Hong Kong, Japan, and Taiwan taken by his father in the early 1950s.

The early cosmopolitan experiences made it easier for David to venture into another culture and take full advantage of that experience in China when he was a teenager. There was no hesitation on his part to go to China when such an opportunity appeared, even though he knew little about China, which was portrayed mostly negatively in the USA in the early 1980s. As we will see in later chapters, David's early childhood exposure was unique among the participants. It is informative here to briefly compare David's openings to another culture with Alan Watts' exposure to Asian cultures. As a leader in the US countercultural movement in the 1960s, Watts made an intentional break during his teenage years with his rigid upbringing (Watts, 1972; Wang, 2009). While the foundation for David's encounter with China was firm and organic, Watts departed from his own tradition in a rebellious way. Watts did not like the denial of sensuality and the body in fundamentalist Christianity that had set the tone of his childhood life. It was his deep dissatisfaction with the mainstream of his time that turned his attention to alternative horizons that promised him a different world. Here we see two contrasting modes of opening to differences: For David, it was a continuity of a cosmopolitan pathway; for Watts, it was a discontinuity of an existing pathway and the quest for a new alternative.

For David, the foundation of his childhood life eased his dramatic encounter with China into a natural extension of his youthful adventure in life. But there were milestones in the process, since China was so different from the USA and Europe. He located two turning points in his life: The first was eight months of living in China as a teenager; the second was his encounter with the Chinese student movements in 1989 when he was a young foreign instructor in a Chinese university.

Teenage Adventure in China

David's father started to have some Chinese students in graduate seminars in the early 1980s after the China–US relationship returned to a normal diplomacy in

1979. The students invited his father to go to China, who began to think: Why not go to a country different from England or France? Their neighbor, a great Chinese historian, was so excited about the invitation that he walked over to urge: "You have to go. This is a most exciting time. China is changing." This historian's passion made a great impression on David, as he could see so clearly that this person cared very much about China. Accepting the invitation was a risk on his father's part, not only politically but also because the living conditions in China at that time were quite difficult. But his father decided to take the risk and go.

David was in high school at that time and his parents let him choose whether or not to go. As he laughingly put it, "Staying at high school, bored, or going to China. That was not much of a choice." He took off his senior year and went to China with his parents and two of his sisters. He enrolled in Xinhua Secondary School (pseudonym) a year back in order to avoid being with students who were preparing for the national college entrance examination. He described this experience as "absolutely the biggest, the most dramatic thing I've ever done in my life." Even the travel was difficult. They took a detour through Switzerland, Greece, and India in order to reach Beijing, and from there went to the city where they lived. At that time there were very few American academics and probably only 30 foreigners altogether in that city.

It is interesting to note here that it is not unusual for youth to be open to another thought and another culture. Quite a few pioneers in introducing Buddhism to the West were young when they began their engagement with Eastern thought. For example, the founder of the Buddhist Lodge in London, Christmas Humphreys, encountered Buddhism when he was 17; another Buddhist pioneer, Ananda Metteyya, read *The Light of Asia* in 1890 when he was 18 (Humphreys, 1968), and Alan Watts (1972) declared himself a Buddhist when he was 15. In a sense, youth is an age of exploration into all kinds of different possibilities. If family or educational institutions do not try to constrain youth's creative energy, they may be freer to tap into new potentiality. Dwayne Huebner (1967 [1999]) suggests, "Perhaps it would be more appropriate to ask what prevents creativity than to ask how one learns to be creative" (p. 134).

David described his initial encounter with China as "a pleasant surprise" because as much as he had tried to learn about China before they went there, what he knew was only from books, which could not match the richness of the culture that he experienced firsthand. The experience was "endlessly fascinating, and always challenging," as everything was so different. The image of China in the USA was quite limited and often negative. All Chinese were imagined as uniform. But when David arrived in China, he could see that a lot more than uniformity was going on. As Paochin Chu (1991) relates, the American attitude towards China between 1957 and 1982 was gradually changing from hostile to conciliatory. Not until the late 1970s and the beginning of the 1980s could Chu publically talk about China without being treated with "stiff faces and frozen civility" (p. 174). David arrived in China during this period when two countries and two peoples began to be open to each other. Like David, France H. Conroy (1991) wondered whether the Communist party members in China would appear as all the same rather than unique individuals, and during his visit, Conroy was delighted to encounter individual persons who showed their own singular personalities. In cross-cultural encounters, face-to-face interaction with the other is important for unlearning preconceived notions, which are usually stereotypical.

David's experiences at Xinhua Secondary School had a huge impact on him. First, he was immersed in learning Chinese, with the teaching of a tutor and the help of his classmates who accompanied him on the road between home and school. Everybody spoke Chinese at school. It was experientially-based learning, as his classmates taught him Chinese by pointing to what was surrounding him: This is street, this is bridge, this is car, etc. The intimate link between language and culture implies the necessity of learning another language in order to understand another culture in depth. David had this unique opportunity to learn the Chinese language through his experiences, and he tried to take full advantage of it. Later he also introduced such experiences to American students by setting up exchange programs.

Second, he immediately became the center of attention at school. For the first two months, whenever there was a break, he was surrounded by classmates who asked him questions:

> I think it helped that I was a fairly mature 17-year-old, so I was not too alarmed by that kind of attention and I was not bothered by things that were different. I was just fascinated by almost everything that happened every day. For me it was endless. And I really liked the people who I got to know. They were very intelligent and very good people. The question was always, "Do you carry a gun?" "Do you smoke marijuana?" "How many times do you beat up your teachers?" "Is it too scary to be outside of the house in America?" There was this whole vision of America as a scary place and everybody was exploited and violent and there were problems everywhere. . . . And we had a lot of trust built. They were so interested in everything, and they were always trying to learn more, to learn language.

So to a great degree, David and his Chinese peers were mutually fascinated by each other's cultures, although stereotypes of each other—Chinese as uniform and Americans as violent—largely promoted by politics and the media of that time in both countries were evident. They learned from each other and helped each other, and intercultural trust was developed through these interpersonal experiences despite the initial stereotypes. David was singled out at school as a foreigner, a powerful experience for a teenager. David seemed to handle that amount of attention well. Living in a stranger's land as a foreigner, David lived existentially the stance of a stranger who saw the world as if for the first time and experienced himself through another dimension to generate new understandings, new awareness, and new relationships (Greene, 1973; Kristeva, 1991; Wang, 2002). For Dwayne Huebner (1985 [1999]),

> Education is a call from the other that we may reach out beyond ourselves and enter into life with the life around us. . . . Education is the lure of the transcendent—that which we seem is not what we are for we could always be other. (p. 360)

David lived with a transcendent vision of education throughout his life.

What is also interesting is that David did not perceive pain in this stance of the stranger but approached it as the site of learning opportunities. Donna Porche-Frilot (2002) questions the notion of the stranger based upon her painful experiences of "being the other" as a "colored girl" in Louisiana schools. And she asks whether welcoming the metaphor of the stranger "affirm[s] Western culture's propensity to reify otherness, to iconize human differences, and hence, create valuated categories of humanity?" (p. 302). So the relationship between the self and the stranger/ the other is not easy to define, depending on the specific dynamics in a particular context of power relationships. While acknowledging the profound effect of racism on "people of color," I also think David's cosmopolitan experiences in his early childhood and his constant contacts with different cultures had already cultivated a sense of comfort with the stranger or with himself being positioned as the stranger. David and his classmates in their mutual strangeness provided each other new opportunities for growth, and trust and friendship were built across differences.

Third, cultural difference became the foreground due to cross-cultural encounters. One dramatic example was the male/female relationship, which was very different between China and the USA when David came to China. The code of forbidden intimacy between boys and girls in China—even the smallest gesture of a small gift exchange would lead to the teacher's scolding—was not something David was familiar with, but he quickly learned the code and respected the boundary.

Fourth, the contrast between American and Chinese living standards was shocking, but the students' hard-working mentality made a lingering impact on David:

> But the great impression I had at the time was that their conditions were so basic, and there was almost no heat anywhere. Many of students lived in dormitories and they lived in incredibly crowded dormitories, not well-kept, not very clean. There was an enormous pressure at school to get basic things done, and not many were properly clothed, and this was the best school in the province. And they were from the city, and they, by my standard, were incredibly poor, and yet they were studying all the time. I remember that they studied in the cold, and their fingers were kind of purple or cracked sometimes. It had a huge impact on me as a student. One reason that I have a Ph.D., I think, was because of that.

He had a great admiration for the students' commitment to learning. And he also enjoyed the simple entertainments his Chinese peers devised for fun, made up from almost nothing. He visited his Chinese peers' families and sometimes the homes of his parents' friends, and was continually amazed by how the Chinese managed to make the best out of the basic living conditions: a small living space full of people, no indoor plumbing, and poor sanitary conditions. The contrast between American life and Chinese life was sharp, but he was not driven away. Not many Americans could have had such an appreciation if they had gone to China in the early 1980s.

Fifth, David's self-confidence increased as a result of dealing with difficult situations. On most occasions, Chinese people took care of them very well, but on rare occasions they had to handle issues on their own. David was the one who helped his family to get through difficulties. He remembered one occasion vividly:

> I remember on one occasion, we've gone on a trip to Xian. I cannot remember the reasons, but we ended up in Xian train station—the only time—but did not have tickets to get back to [the city where we lived]. Almost every time things were arranged for us, but that time nobody was with us; and in those days, you probably remember, getting a ticket was very difficult. You know there was such an incredibly long line of people, everybody pushing each other trying to get to the front. And you know it was completely outside the range of my experiences, but I had been in China long enough and my Chinese was OK and could function for me to buy the tickets. And my dad could not do any of this, so he sent me to get tickets. I was already very big, tall, so I did not feel physically threatened, but it was a different [kind of difficulty], sort of pushing my way to come forward for the tickets. . . . It built a lot of confidence.

His story reminded me of the time when I was waiting outside the ticket office in a crowd to buy a train ticket in the early 1990s. When I got a chance to push my way into the office, I lost one of my shoes and ended up finding it upstairs, carried up by the crowd, even though I bought my ticket downstairs! But David could find what was positive about the situation and was proud of himself for accomplishing things he would never have imagined in his comfortable home in the USA. Dealing with situations like these and playing the role of being an adult when necessary contributed positively to his sense of self.

After three decades, David spoke about his experience in China as a teenager enthusiastically, with fondness and vivid memories. It was definitely a turning point, which channeled him onto cross-cultural pathways. Yet as much as he felt that he was compelled to do so, he also chose to walk that path. His opening to China in that formative year was dramatic, but it was also a natural extension of his cosmopolitan mindset. His open-mindedness, cultivated in a cosmopolitan family in a cosmopolitan city, played an important role in his ability to adventure into a culture that is dramatically different from his own and to learn the most from his experiences. The difficult living conditions in China did not turn him off but inspired him to commit his life to cross-cultural learning and intercultural education.

From his accounts, we can see that he respected his Chinese peers and appreciated Chinese attitudes towards life in general, even though China and the Chinese people, in the American public imagination at that time, were largely portrayed as backward, authoritarian, and antidemocratic. He could easily have adopted a stance of "we are better than you are" after witnessing the living and political climates in China. I have known Americans who came back from China with a reinforced notion of "we are better." But David saw and admired the resilience of the Chinese people and the younger generation's willingness to learn and to change. His teenage adventure set the stage for his later cross-cultural engagement.

Encountering the Student Movements in 1989

The second turning point for David was initially exciting but turned into a traumatic[1] experience. When he graduated with a B.A., he got a fellowship for teaching English in China. He went to a normal university in central China where he was involved in a lot of extracurricular activities and made many Chinese friends. In December of 1988, students started all kinds of groups—they called them "salons"—to talk about various ideas. David found it exciting and felt that these students were like the May Fourth generation in 1919, which was a part of the broader New Culture Movement in China that questioned traditional Chinese culture and called for the formation of a new culture adopting Western science and democracy to revitalize China. He was not alone in experiencing the 1989 movement as the "new May Fourth" (Cunningham, 2009; Mitter, 2004). As I will discuss in more detail in Chapter 2, the May Fourth movement set a milestone in China–West engagement and transformed the Chinese political, social, and cultural landscape. David saw what was happening in 1988 and 1989 as similar to what had happened 70 years earlier.

David described these students as

> intellectually curious and idealistic, that I almost had not experienced in any other time, in any other place. And often under the miserable conditions, they got together to have coffee, tea and very cheap snacks in a very cold room, and somebody got up to talk about Nietzsche, or Laozi; then another guy said, "Well, that is interesting, but it makes me think about love," and then they talked about that for a while . . .

These discussions covered numerous topics, many of which involved social and political issues, such as social inequalities and lack of political freedom. As an American, David could not directly participate, but his observations convinced him that China seemed close to real change. It was exhilarating to watch the press in the city unprecedentedly begin to criticize the political and social system (since the press was always under the control of the Communist Party) and to see that for a while students controlled the campus broadcasting system. Some communist party members also showed support. It was an "amazing moment, youthful, idealist moment for change," and a shaping moment for David. While the city where David lived was far away from Beijing, the converging forces throughout the country during that time grew so powerfully that they led to the eruption of large-scale student demonstrations in the capital. In April and May of 1989, student demonstrations in Tiananmen Square rocked the nation and quickly spread to other parts of the country. Then the bloodshed on June Fourth shocked the world. It took David years to recover from the shock.

As a young college professor at that time who was close in age to his students, David was as passionate as they were about the possibilities of change. The crackdown led to a sense of hopelessness. He recognized that what he had experienced was different from what those students who were directly involved and suffered from the crackdown either physically or emotionally had experienced, but he had been so fascinated with what was happening before the crackdown and so invested along with his students that he also suffered from a terrible sense of loss afterwards, and from which he developed a burning desire for a better understanding of China.

David considered what happened in 1989 as part of his life rather than history, and said, "That is why I felt like to some extent I did not make any decision about the career of what I am doing; I was in the situations [that led me to today]." In a sense, it was not a career that he chose, but a calling that he answered. For years, that experience was crystallized as a burning question for him: Why not democracy in China? In the international setting, the Berlin wall collapsed the following year, and then the Soviet Union dissolved. Global communism quickly collapsed, and many Eastern European countries, including the country where his mother came from, threw out communism. So why not China?

Interestingly, he talked about these two defining moments of his life in China in the first interview. As he told these stories, I suspected that he was reliving the experiences with certain intensity. While both moments could have turned other Americans away from China, David turned the other way around and built his work and life around China studies and American–Chinese educational exchange. His calling was to engage people with differences in exchange, and he loved to bring people together cross-culturally. Both moments had shaped his cross-cultural pathways, and, without planning on my part or his part, he was compelled to tell both dramas in the first interview because of their significance in his life.

Transformative Pathways

Following those two turning points, David's studies and work were centered on his interest in China, and he pursued a career of creating possibilities for

Chinese–American interactions and connections through programs in which people from both sides could come together to study, work, and learn from each other. He told me, "I've always enjoyed what I am doing now, which is organizing things and getting people involved . . . to arrange things so people can have interesting experiences, to create opportunities for people to make connections." The administrator position for the bicultural institute in China allowed him to do what he loved to do. Even as a master's level student, he initiated an exchange program to bring American students to China to study Chinese language and culture.

As David reflected on those years of studying at university and of working after his graduation with a Ph.D., he perceived them as part of a gradual process of deep learning. Here I trace these years of transformative pathways and discuss his studies and working experiences separately even though the two are intimately related.

College and Graduate Studies

After his experience in the Chinese secondary school, David went to a well-known American university where he could learn about China. After graduation, he went to China as an English instructor and encountered the student movement in 1989. Afterwards, he went on to an M.A. program at Middle Path University (pseudonym), which was not located on the mainland of either the USA or China. He was pleased with his choice because it provided him an emotional distance from the intensity of his experiences in China. During his studies there, he applied for a grant and was able to set up an exchange program to take American undergraduate students to a Chinese university during the summer. While providing American undergraduate students a unique opportunity to learn about China on site, he also had chances to interact with Chinese scholars, one of whom particularly influenced him. He decided to do a historical study for his thesis and finished it in China. Then he returned to the US mainland to finish his Ph.D. program in China Studies. These periods of studies about China followed his turning points and channeled his dramatic experiences towards a process of gradual change and transformation in which he refined his focus.

When David went to his undergraduate university, he quickly found that his Chinese accent, obtained in southern China, was not welcome, and the simplified Chinese language[2] he had learned in mainland China did not match the complicated Chinese language system used in his program. His professors tried to change his southern accent, which was very frustrating.[3] The initial experience was so difficult that he moved away from his interest in China for a year, but then he came back. He did not know, as an undergraduate student, that some of his professors were world-renowned experts. Nor did he know that the university had a long history of engagement with China. But he was impressed enough that he kept and still keeps the lecture notes of his professors. At that time, China studies as a field was a small community, and he got the best education he could find.

When he went to a graduate school as a master's level student, he carried his burning question "why not democracy in China?" and wrote papers related to what had happened in 1989. He first chose political science but felt quite lost; however, in the second semester he found a niche in history. He had been interested in history since his early childhood when his parents took him to historical sites in different places and always asked him interesting questions. He had a natural curiosity about history, but he also felt that history was a good way to empathize with people in different places. There were Chinese scholars at that university, and one of them made a remark that served as a sort of wake-up call for him to look at issues in a different way: "Look, you've got to look at issues along a historical framework." He was pulled back from his focus on what happened in 1989 to study Chinese intellectuals at the turn of the 20th century. Such an intellectual dive into historical understandings gave him both emotional distance and an opportunity to intellectually contextualize his personal questions.

By the time David returned to the US mainland to continue his doctoral studies, the field of China Studies in the USA was expanding. He had an opportunity to study with many well-known experts, and he had to study both Chinese (including classical and modern Chinese) and Japanese as languages. His doctoral program was intellectually challenging and demanding. He referred to the incredibly long list of readings:

> I think it was helpful to go through [the list], but what frightened me about graduate school was that I kind of lost touch with the rest of the world, [because I was] so deeply into all these things that took all my attention. I had been doing all these readings.

For five years David was immersed in his studies of Chinese history in graduate school and did not go to China. On one hand, he enjoyed the rigorous studies; on the other hand, he felt he had no idea about what was happening in the real world of China. Learning through "lived experience" (Aoki, 2005; van Manen, 1990) was very important to David. Creating opportunities for participants to engage in cross-cultural lived experience became the landmark of David's public work in education later.

As I kept probing how he dealt with his burning question in graduate school, he commented that the question "first of all, at one level, was too easy to answer, and at another level, it is not the core question." He further realized that even the question of why China did not embrace democracy was still framed in the presumption of a Western perspective in which democracy was considered the norm that everybody else should follow. His professors also advised him that it was good to have a personal drive, but one needed to "frame the question [as] analytically worthy and valuable to the broader field." Taking another step away from the topic that had driven him, he shifted his focus to the more underlying issue of how power functions, particularly how intellectuals have historically been subject to the imposed transformation of thought and emotion from authority. It was an original project that nobody else had undertaken in a substantial way. He did a lot of archive work and wrote an excessively long dissertation.

He further elaborates these intellectual shifts:

> As a thinker, a more sophisticated approach is to question the assumptions of my own questions. I need to think through the issues related to Chinese political culture. I still work on Chinese political culture, but I just no longer have a simple question to ask: it is not just about democracy. . . . I don't have ideas about easy changes that can be made, and it is very complicated. We need a much broader, deeper understanding of the realities of the problems. I try to understand all the different aspects to it. As a historian, I am also working on all kinds of different aspects of stories of change and how such development can occur.

Achieving a certain distance from experience, studying it from a broad view, connecting it with historical and general concerns, David has been able to craft his experiences into scholarship that speaks to a wider audience. Experience itself does not necessarily lead to insights and wisdom; the individual must undergo a painstaking process of working through personal and cultural materials to achieve clarity about the situation. It is clear from David's intellectual trajectory—self-initiated with the help of his professors, colleagues, and peers—that the process of confronting his own intense thoughts and feelings had channeled his passion into a long-lasting commitment to transformative cross-cultural studies and work as a scholar, a professor, and an activist. Both dwelling in Aoki's (1981 [2005]) intercultural non-bridge bridge (p. 228) and crossing national borders are important in David's stories.

The Public Work of Cross-Cultural Engagements

David asserted at the end of our third interview that "no one does history without a moral center to it. . . . [After] a long time I am still interested in society searching for a better life, or a more just life." Such a moral commitment to justice and a better life ran through his public work and summarized the central thread that wove together his teaching, his leadership, and his tireless dedication to exchange programs.

David enjoyed teaching. He had taught various courses in various settings in both the USA and China, including Chinese history, world history, law history, and English as a secondary language. His first formal academic job as an assistant professor was teaching Chinese history in a small department at a southern liberal arts college. He admitted that he experienced a bigger culture shock in the American South than in China, but he loved teaching there. In reflecting on his teaching, he did not think that cross-cultural experiences changed his teaching methods, but his ability to present China in an embodied approach, rather than presenting it as an alien place, made a difference to his students. For those Americans who didn't know much about China, David found it important to invite them into the landscape of another culture without orientalizing it:

> One should not study China because it is somehow so different from somewhere else, [but because] it is a part of the world, it is very important, very interesting, and there is a lot you can learn from that. . . . The most important thing was that I could show China to my students in a comfortable way: I could talk in that language; I could use the language; I could write characters on the board; I could use the words. I made them—students complained about this—remember Chinese names; if you can remember French names, you can learn Chinese names. I put Chinese characters on the sheet so they would be familiar with it. I think the biggest thing I brought from my experiences with China was that comfort level to say: Look, this is not an exotic place, China is not exotic, and China is another part of the world you should know as a world citizen.

David was aware of Said's (1979 [1994]) works on Orientalism and of the need to not generalize China in a prejudiced way. As a historian, he could provide specific details, which can prevent a generalized image that obscures the richness and complexity of reality. In order for students to experience real, complicated, and rich reality, he felt that it was very important to bring students to China. Furthermore, he insisted that students needed to learn the Chinese language, even though it was difficult, because of the intimate link between language and culture. His teaching about another language/culture is an act of translation (Edgerton, 1996) in multiple senses—linguistic, transnational, and intercultural. Through the labor of translation, he invites his students to translate curriculum rather than treating another culture as an object of learning. Such a labor requires dwelling in linguistic, temporary, and cultural differences on the part of both teacher and student.

For David, the teacher mediated between students and the world they were unfamiliar with in order to help them experience a different life not as something exotically strange or utterly other but as something that is part of the world, something that can become an intimate part of the self despite its difference. He did not approach difference as negative, or something to be erased, but as a learning opportunity for further growth. However, he did not see difference as radicalized to the degree of being located in the Levinasian "unknowable" (Todd, 2003, p. 3). In order to counteract the tendency of the self to assimilate the other, the post-structural discourses emphasize the otherness of the other (Bernstein, 1991; Derrida, 1992; Levinas, 1987). But when such an emphasis goes to the extreme, it runs the risk of distancing the self and the other to such a degree that it becomes difficult to weave the self and the other back into the whole. By contrast, David's way of making connections across differences for himself and for his students was to experience the bridge, not to see differences as separate, and to understand what is strange as a part of the bigger picture.

David felt the need to break down prejudices and barriers through bringing students to China, and that was exactly what he tried to do in that southern university. With the collaboration of a colleague who was also a China scholar, he really pushed the agenda and started the Study in China program, which brought students to Chinese cities during the summer. He felt fortunate to be able to pursue such programs at a small university, an opportunity that allowed him to explore new things. He personally ran those programs and spent almost half of his six-year appointment at that university in China. David and his colleagues built a one-year language program out of a four-year undergraduate program and offered well-designed classes, internships, and opportunities for research and travel. They also brought Chinese students to the American university so that it became a mutual exchange program between a Chinese university and an American university. The program was nationally recognized, and David and his colleagues also got a national grant to run a spoken Chinese program in China.

All these activities were "endlessly" exciting and interesting for David. He was proud of his current leadership position at the bicultural institute located in China, which furthered his work in educational exchanges by bringing Americans and Chinese together: "I think I am in a very privileged position to try to carry this institute forward and play my part and I want to hand it on to somebody else to keep it going." He also felt privileged to learn from wonderful scholars and students at the institute.

It was a mission, or a calling, for David to bring people cross-culturally together to create a more just society. He commented from time to time that his past experiences had prepared everything for his present work: "I feel like everything I had been doing in my whole career was leading up to doing this." Teaching as a vocation and the spiritual calling of teachers have been discussed from various angles in education (Durka, 2002; Huebner, 1999; Palmer, 1998 [2007]). While David's work went much beyond teaching, he was also an educator in a broad sense, and his devotion to the mission of intercultural and cross-cultural understanding was an answer to the calling from the moral center in his life.

David also pointed out that, different from the two turning points when the world looked completely different, what he was currently doing in China was a "steadier, deeper kind of learning . . . and I am humbled by the fact that there is always more to learn." To a great degree, whether directly teaching or not, his public work of cross-cultural engagement itself was a mode of teaching, and he was learning all the time as well. Transformative pathways and turning points all illuminate David's life journey of learning from another culture dramatically different from his own and his pathway of becoming a cross-cultural educator who brought people from diverse backgrounds together to learn from each other.

In general, a public intellectual is defined as a scholar who actively participates in public affairs and engages social change with "the moral conscience of his society" (Mills, 1958 [1963], quoted in Brouwer & Squires, 2003, p. 203). Even though there have been discussions about the decline of public intellectuals in the USA or in the West in general (Posner, 2003; Shambaugh, 2009), it is clear to me that David acted as a public intellectual whose scholarship was connected to his practice in intercultural education and cross-cultural exchanges. In the following section, I briefly situate David's stories in the context of American intellectual engagement with China historically.

Stories in Context

China studies as a field is related to systematic studies of China from its language to its philosophy, history, religion, culture, society, politics, literature, and folklores, among many other areas, and it exists in both European and American academics. Because of its interdisciplinary nature, it is difficult to portray the history of China Studies, so I offer only some brief comments about the general background. In the West, in general, the emergence of China studies was related to the Jesuit missionaries in the late 16th century who introduced Christianity to China while at the same time bringing Chinese philosophy, aesthetics, and ethics back to the West in their writings (Oldmeadow, 2004; Smith, 2008). The 17th and 18th centuries marked Western intellectuals' great interest in China, and the influence of Confucian thought on the Enlightenment thinkers is well recognized. The high regard for the Chinese civilization faded at the end of the 18th century when the West considered the Chinese political system backward and at odds with European democracy and shifted its attention to Indian religions and thought (Oldmeadow, 2004; Smith, 2008). By the middle of the 19th century, China had been defeated in the Opium Wars by the Western allied military force and its door had been bombed open. China was forced to open some port cities to the West. The past glories of Chinese civilization and what the West had learned from China were mostly forgotten.

However, such a general neglect did not prevent some European and American scholars from showing interest in Taoism after the decline of Confucian influence in the West. Ironically, such an interest coexisted with the Western imperialist encroachment in China after the mid-19th century. As Karl-Heinz Pohl (2003) points out, World War I marked "a turning point" (p. 472) in the reception of Taoism because the devastation of war asked for "a pacifistic and spiritual reorientation" (p. 473). In the first part of the 20th century, Western thinkers as diverse as Martin Buber, Hermann Hesse, Bertold Brecht, Martin Heidegger, and Carl Jung were influenced by Taoism one way or another. However, such scholarship and connections did not have a great impact in this period, which was marked by general ignorance in the West about China (Pohl, 2003).

The more popularized version of influence came after World War II when the New Age Movement (beginning in the late sixties following the Beat Generation and the Hippies) used Zen/Taoism to achieve their own ends in the USA, although at best theirs was a trivialized form of Taoism. In other words, the crisis mentality at that time was associated with the reception of Taoism in the American and European contexts. In recent decades, the philosophical connections between deconstruction and Taoism has been made (Deng, 2005; Shepherd, 2007). In science, quantum physics and chaos and complexity theory also show links with Taoist principles (Capra, 1975 [2010]; Walter, 1994). David Geoffrey Smith (2008) traces how East and West have interacted and mutually influenced each other since long before the 1600s and argues that forgetting the mutual engagement between East and West is to deny the West's own history:

> *In spite of* the exclusionary disposition of Euro-American sensibility, an engagement between East and West has *always already* been in effect for over 2,000 years, . . . most of the operating assumptions of the West are *already* inhabited by Asian influences, [and] those who persistently criticize occidental interest in things oriental merely contribute to a logic of denial that itself is a denial of the West's own history. (p. 24; emphasis in the original)

Since David's field was history, I situate a more detailed discussion of the contemporary intellectual history of China studies in this field. For understanding American studies of Chinese history, Paul A. Cohen's new edition (2010) of his 1984 critical study, *Discovering History in China: American Historical Writing on the Recent Chinese Past*, offers important insights. In 1984, Cohen summarized three major approaches to studying Chinese history in the postwar era (1945–1980s)—the impact-response approach, the tradition-modernity approach, and the imperialism approach—and proposed an alternative: a China-centered approach. In its reissue in 2010, Cohen further discusses the limitations of the China-centered approach.

Cohen (1984 [2010]) argues that the conceptual frameworks most influential in the 1950s and 1960s among American historians who studied China, the impact-response and tradition-modernity approaches, and an opposing framework, the imperialism approach, were all laden with Western-centric assumptions, which could not capture the Chinese reality of the recent past.

The impact-response approach assumes that the changes in China since the Opium Wars were responses to the Western impact rather than an internal transformation. Such an approach implies that "China was incapable of making its own history, that it needed the West to do so for it" (p. xvi). Cohen points out that this approach ignores the interior social and economic changes that were already under way in China before the Opium Wars and distorts historical reality to an excessive degree. To depict pre-Western-contact China as stagnant and unchanging, waiting to be changed by the West, betrays the underlying assumptions of Western superiority over Chinese inferiority. Moreover, those aspects of Chinese history not directly connected with the Western presence were considered unimportant and thus trivialized.

The tradition-modernity approach pictures a dichotomous world in which traditional Chinese values and institutions are perceived as obstacles to achieving modernization. The modernization theory takes the Western modern society as the model for analyzing non-Western societies. China was able to overcome the grip of tradition and become "modern" only through "revolution from without" under the Western influence. A variety of approaches in studying Chinese history from the tradition-modernity dyad existed, from denying Chinese agency altogether to acknowledging the synthetic nature of the Chinese intellectual life of the previous two centuries. Cohen argues that to the degree that the Western language and framework of modernization is used—forced—upon China's history, the analytical models of change remain closed and cannot describe the dynamic picture of the recent Chinese past. There is an inherent ethnocentrism in modernization theory, so it is necessary to pursue alternative modes of descriptions.

The imperialism approach charges that modernization theory masks American imperialism (Cohen, 1984 [2010]). This approach sees imperialism as the major moving force in Chinese history from the Opium Wars through World War II and maintains, specifically, that "imperialism distorted and reconstructed the Chinese economy" (p. 125). The opposite side of the debate argues that imperialism had a minimal impact on the Chinese economy. Cohen points out that the semicolonialism in the Chinese situation was more complicated than the situation in fully colonized countries and that the last Chinese dynasty was the result of the Manchu invasion and conquest in the 17th century. Further, seeing imperialism as the master key to an entire century of Chinese history is reductive and falls into the China-responding-to-the-West model in another form, and thus neglects Chinese internal dynamics and mechanisms in making its own history. Moreover, the imperialism approach does not question modernization theory itself as a Western construct.

After questioning these three approaches of American scholarship to recent Chinese history as embedded in the Western framework one way or another, a framework that neglects to address the interior and internal dynamics of the Chinese situation, Cohen (1984 [2010]) describes a China-centered approach, which highlights Chinese experiences from Chinese perspectives. Such an approach, emerging in the 1970s, is linked with the historical context of American society and the intellectual life of that time. The disillusion with American supremacy in the global setting led intellectuals to depart from using Western norms to study non-Western societies, and historiography became other-centered rather than Western-centered.

What Cohen describes is a set of tendencies rather than a single approach, but it is an approach that Cohen explicitly called China-centered. This approach searches for the Chinese storylines addressing Chinese problems that were important from Chinese viewpoints. It pursues a view of the reality experienced by Chinese participants rather than defined by outsiders, internal changes rather than comparisons between China and the West. Furthermore, this approach examines regions or provinces or other smaller units, and thus yields a more differentiated understanding of China. Another feature of the China-centered approach is that "it sees Chinese society as being arranged hierarchically in a number of different levels" (Cohen, 1984 [2010], p. 172) so that all levels, rather than only the top level, should be studied. All these features of the China-centered approach adopted by American historians shed light on the internal Chinese structures, systems, and changes from various locations and at various levels, and as a result present a far more dynamic, complicated history, a history that does interact with external forces such as Western modernity, but a history that cannot be reduced to the Western influence.

It is clear to me that such a development in American historical scholarship on China is not an isolated phenomenon, but is closely associated with the Western intellectual world, which became increasingly critical of its own ethnocentric biases after the 1970s and subsequently moved towards postmodern discourses in the 1990s. More than two decades after his first formulation of these four approaches, Cohen (1984 [2010]) also acknowledges the limitations of the China-centered approach based on new studies about China. For instance, the ethnic diversity and tensions within China and Chinese migration to other parts of the world question a nation-based approach that does not address the crucial role of mobility, multiplicity, and dispersion. He also further complicates the roles of historians along the line of cultural outsider/insider, recognizing that an outsider researcher precisely due to distance may have certain advantages that direct participants or insider researchers do not have. He credits the influence of postmodernism for these shifts, and sees the postmodern scholarship that emerged in the early 1990s as holding forth "the hope of a future scholarship that will be less distortive and oppressive, more self-aware and self-critical" (p. xx).

Furthermore, Cohen (1984 [2010]) discusses the need to weaken the West's "long-standing perception of China as the quintessential 'other'" because "historical approaches that place excessive emphasis on such differences are apt to generate unfortunate distortions, even caricatures, of one sort or another" (p. liii). Cohen believes that transcultural, universal human dimensions must be addressed along with cultural differences to have a fuller picture of the Chinese past. He also acknowledges that other historians hold a different viewpoint: Jacques Gernet, for instance, believes that missionaries in China found "a different kind of humanity" (quoted in Cohen, 1984 [2010], p. lxiv). I wonder whether there is a need to cast a sharp distinction between commonality and difference. Is it possible that commonality and difference are mutually embedded within each other and that whether we see the universal or the different is dependent upon the angle of perceiving through a kaleidoscope in a particular setting? If we are not preoccupied with finding either difference or similarity as the bridge to make meaningful connections, then either commonality or difference or both can become the basis for mutual understanding.

Reading about American studies of China and its evolution is an interesting experience for me: I knew so little about it but my participant brought me to this unfamiliar landscape. To see the image of the (cultural) self in the mirror of the other is hardly pleasant. However, I am not surprised, considering the power relationships between China and the West since the Opium Wars, to see the historical intellectual objectification—intentional or unintentional—of China into a static image of the other, the other in the sense of being different from the Western norm, the other that the West attempts to remake according to its own image. In his historical analysis of Western perceptions of China for the past 400 years, historian Jonathan D. Spence (1992) also locates the post Opium War period as the time when "the very obvious weakness of China bred contempt rather than admiration" (p. 84) in the West, even though there was not a lack of admiration before. However, Spence argues, "there have been so many twists and turns along the way to depicting China during the last four hundred years" (p. 90) that a broad generalization of cognitive imperialism cannot hold. It seems to me that it is more interesting to understand a particular construct in a particular historical period than to make a generalization, and if objectification happened, what were the historical, social, and intercultural factors that contributed to such an objectification.

Objectification is reflected not only in biases but also in the romanticized or idealistic presentation of China, such as in the initially positive American responses to the Cultural Revolution in the 1970s, which was a disaster for China and the Chinese people (Chan, 1991; Harding, 1991). The distance and the limited access to information contributed to those positive responses, but they were also linked to a more critical stance towards the American self-image in the 1970s. David also told me an interesting story about another American who went to the same city where David went as a teenager in the early 1980s. That American had a romantic notion of the Chinese as honest and less materialistic and went to China to look for a socialist paradise. He left his bicycle unlocked outside of his apartment. The bicycle was stolen, but he could not believe it, so he bought another bicycle and left it unlocked. The bicycle was stolen again.

What David B. Chan (1991) describes as "the China syndrome"—the vacillation between distaining and romanticizing—is closely related to the projection of the American self, which was either overly self-assuring or disillusioned with its own ideals in different time periods (Harding, 1991). However, such a centering of the self over the other, in whatever form it appears, has been challenged in the past several decades by postcolonial, feminist, and post-structural critiques, among other discourses. The reversal efforts to center the other over the self, for instance, the China-centered approach, have also been challenged by postmodern approaches. I believe that the unsettling dynamic interaction *between* the self and the other holds the key to new possibilities.

The centering of the self over the other happened not only in scholarship; it was also reflected in cross-cultural educational practices. China–US educational engagement was initiated by the Western missionary hoping to remake China from a pagan culture into a Christian culture. For instance, the Yale–China association (Chapman & Plumb, 2001) has existed for more than a century and made major contributions to building bridges between two countries and two cultures by sending Yale graduates to China for one or two years to work at schools, colleges, and churches. Its initial purpose—to bring the Christian gospel to China—was clearly missionary. Only in the 1970s did the association change its mission statement to make it secular rather than religious. For the past several decades, the association has evolved into an educational enterprise of a more mutual engagement between China and the USA.

David's study of China happened in the 1980s and the 1990s, when the field had already shifted from Western-centered approaches to those more respectful of China's own perspectives, and his experience of teaching in China was also situated in the context of more mutuality than earlier. From his stories, we can clearly tell his respect for another culture, even though he became aware of the stereotypical images each had towards the other, including the Chinese's prejudiced view of his own country. In the early 1980s, however, not many Americans shared this teenager's enthusiasm for living in a foreign country. During those years, the reports of Americans' experiences in China were much more negative than positive (Chan, 1991; Harding, 1991). Ahead of his time, David was more impressed by the Chinese people's endurance and hard work in a difficult life situation than anything else.

The state violence of 1989 that David witnessed personally reinforced the image of a totalitarian China for many Westerners after their initial hope that China was changing in the direction of becoming a liberal democracy. While Marie-Claire Bergere (1990 [2002]) points out that the 1989 event should not be analyzed in the framework of students' pursuit of Western liberal democracy, David was adamant about students' pro-democracy stand, and his position has been supported by others (Cunningham, 2009; Han, 1990; Yu & Harrison, 1990). After the bloody crackdown, the question of "Why not democracy in China?" consumed him. The fact that he personally experienced the event unfolding from those exciting "democratic salons" to the tragedy of the government's brutal suppression contributed to the intensity of his frustration and later his personal drive to understand the so-called "China problem."

With his further studies and work, David gradually stepped back from the event and, further, questioned his own assumptions in the very question he had asked. He was later influenced by Michel Foucault's work (although David perceived Foucault's analysis as historically problematic), which does not pursue a grand vision but examines specific forms that enact various forms of violence. The shift of his attention to a historical understanding of the state mechanisms of power intersecting with social and cultural forces outside of the state not only led him to more in-depth and broader scholarly inquiry but also pulled him out of the particular framework of Western democracy. He realized that there was no easy answer and no easy fix to the problem at hand. In his scholarship, he also paid particular attention to areas of Chinese history that traditionally had been neglected in order to shed light on blind spots for new and nuanced understandings. As he was eager for new experiences in his life, he was paving pathways to new awareness in his scholarship as well.

The issues that Cohen (1984 [2010]) raises about the dilemma of the relationships between insider and outsider, or between the self and the other, were reflected in David's stories. First as an outsider, David nevertheless experienced Chinese students' loss deeply and his own inner landscape was shattered due to his witnessing others' tragedy. He responded by becoming a mediator who negotiated spaces for international exchanges, and in such a role, the clear-cut boundary between the self and the other blurred. A mediator is neither fully an outsider nor an insider but stays at the intersections, overseeing multiple worlds. Moreover, Cohen's (1984 [2010]) concerns with addressing transnational human dimensions without objectifying China into the essential other were reflected in David's pedagogy, which positioned China as a member of a shared world community. To a certain degree, cross-cultural educators are situated in an ambiguous position as they deal with multiple cultures simultaneously in both contents and methods of teaching or other dimensions of their educational work. As a negotiator at the border, the educator has a unique opportunity to embody cross-cultural and intercultural relationships and model the process of understanding the other and the self anew, as David did. I turn to educational issues in the next section.

Organic Healing, Nonviolent Relationships, and a Pedagogy of Mutual Engagement

After all these years, David did not want to go back to the city in central China where he had witnessed the student movement and the government's violent crackdown, as he imagined that it would be quite disorienting. To heal right at the site of the wound is not what Chinese medicine prefers, either. Healing can be organic, as are Chinese traditional herbal and acupuncture practices, which are influenced by principles of *I Ching* and *Tao Te Ching*. Body and mind are considered an interactive whole, and symptoms of illness are treated through balancing the whole body rather than the specific site. For example, when I had a headache, my acupuncture doctor preferred not to put needles into the area of my head where I felt pain, but to put needles into my neck, legs, feet, and hands. Putting the needles into the area of hurt may have more immediate effects, but treating the whole body has a long-term effect to relieve symptoms more completely. This approach is compatible with William E. Doll, Jr.'s (2011) "systemic" viewpoint based upon Bateson's ecological approach in which each person is systemic and the relationship between the person and the environment, including society and the cosmos, is also systemic.

It seems to me that David's sustained engagements with China had been healing the wound without the need for him to set foot in the original site of the trauma. As Li (2002) phrases it so well, the Chinese view of balance is "a balance between the individual and the whole web, a balance between the polarities in the web, a balance between the polarities inside the individual, a balance between the polarities in the web and those inside the individual" (p. 22). In such an approach to tension and balance, restoring harmony is related to achieving the balance within, between and across the individual and the web. A sense of interconnectedness is essential to enabling organic healing to transform difficult emotions and establish nonviolent relationships not only with others, but also with one's own memory.

How a Vision of Nonviolence Emerged

I clearly remember how shocking it was for me to first hear David's story about the 1989 tragedy. I could not believe that I was hearing it from an American, only a few years older than me, who shared the same trauma with me, even though our experiential standpoints were different. It was a personal and national trauma for me—even as I write about it now more than two decades later, it is still deeply emotional. Traveling between the city where Song (see Chapter 3) lived and the city where David lived, both cities where I had strong personal relationships, listening to both participants' life stories, the particular moment when David elaborated on the event and its impact on him brought me a crystal clear vision of nonviolence, which had been already emerging for several years in my teaching (Wang, 2010a).

The timing of my interview with David was also close to my first interview with Teresa (see Chapter 4), who told me how her parents had passed away one by one and how she had felt a spiritual connection with them at the moment of their leaving this world. Teresa's moving account made me face the issue of death and life, reliving my fear in those critical moments when "life or death" seemed so near (including a one-week sit-in on the Tiananmen Square in 1989). Making peace with life in the midst of death and with death in the midst of life (Pinar, 1992) is "an interminable process" (Kristeva, 1996). Furthermore, both interviews were conducted after Song (see Chapter 3) narrated the violence of the Cultural Revolution in various forms. If violence is based upon the mechanism of dualistic domination—through the psychosocial dynamic of repression and projection (Taylor, 2009)—to control the other, and, further, the self, then nonviolence is based upon a sense of interconnectedness in which both the self and the other are a part of a cosmic cycle of life, death, and rebirth. The defining moments of my interaction with all three participant's stories led me to connect with the lost voice of my own—nonviolence—but it was David's story that set the stage for my renewed quest for nonviolence education.

The year 1989 marked a turning point in my life: I became a nonbeliever over night. After returning to my own campus from Beijing in late May, I slept at least 30 hours without waking up, according to my friend, as if I could not wake up to face the disillusion with what I had learned for 21 years. Growing up in red China, I had never quite lived up to the revolutionary standard, because there was a built-in element of violence in Chinese revolutions (and other revolutions throughout the world), including the Cultural Revolution in the 1960s and 1970s. I never could understand, as a young girl reading all those revolutionary novels, why a person's class background should determinate whether one was accepted or rejected by a community, and I was sympathetic to those who were cast as enemies, so I was constantly on the wrong side of the fence. But my education and socialization justified revolutionary means to serve a so-called noble cause, and my history textbooks glorified all the violent rebellions of peasants to overthrow corrupted dynasties. To a great degree, violence was more normalized than nonviolence in the official stories.

By contrast, my mother's living example of caring as the basis for social justice instilled in me a strong sense of integrity based upon relationships, and the best part of Chinese traditions, through my studies and lived experiences, cultivated my compassion for others however others were portrayed. Caring for others was an important aspect of my upbringing and I did not like to see people fight among one another as a young girl, not even for the revolutionary ideal. Gradually, however, my own gut feeling about nonviolence—not doing harm to another human being—gave way to intense studies, since academic competition subsumed my concerns with the relational aspect of life. Belonging to a generation coming of age after the Cultural Revolution in a relatively peaceful time, I had not witnessed the past horror and had a limited understanding of Chinese politics. I more or less believed that the purpose for government was to serve the people. The killing of students by our own government tore me apart, and I was shocked into disillusion with the Chinese socialist ideal more completely than ever before (although I understood later that socialism was not necessarily the only cause).

My story did not end with the state's violence and abuse of power. It was much more complicated. I remember the dark night on the square at the end of May before I decided to go back to my university on the free train service that the government provided to disperse students back to their own provinces. I had not gone to Beijing to rebel, but I wanted to see with my own eyes what was actually happening after martial law was declared. I had not believed that military action would be used against students, but it became very clear that the army was closing in. One afternoon, a young man told me that he wanted to awaken the Chinese people with his blood and he was going to stay to the end. While admiring his courage, I did not feel encouraged. China has always had a protest culture, and a Confucian tradition of giving up one's life for a noble cause. But what have these traditions of sacrifice and cyclic uprisings throughout Chinese history led to? During that night, smelling the terrible polluted air, looking at the mess around me, and hearing a gun shot from the direction of the student leaders' center, I did not feel any uplifting spirit, but felt as if I were in one of the peasant uprising armies that I had read about countless times in Chinese history. As inspiring as it was in the beginning days after my arrival in Beijing, by then I felt that the city (and the nation) was at the edge of chaos, and the collective memory of the violence unleashed by the mass movement quietly whispered in my ears. The confusion, complexity, and intensity of that week were beyond my psychical and physical endurance. I left Beijing.

After I woke up from my long sleep, nobody wanted to hear my questions—not my peers, nor my professors, nor my family. "Thought reform" was immediately imposed on university students. One of my classmates, a student leader, was expelled from our university. I was lucky not to be the target of cleansing but I did not have a chance to deal with my own loss, fear, and disillusion—and my unconscious guilt for leaving (other students to die)—until more than a decade later when I started to teach in the USA (Wang, 2004, p. 160).

After disillusion, it was natural to look for something different. It was the difference between Chinese society and American society, rather than the transcultural universality that Cohen (1984 [2010]) argued for, that initially attracted me to the USA. The promise of individual freedom lured me to the other shore. However, my experiences in the USA, while enlightening and liberating in many aspects, have not yet offered a satisfactory answer. The American ideal of democracy, perhaps still one of the best models we can find that provides a certain degree of freedom and liberty, does not deliver on its promise. Although I bought into it for the first few years of my studies in the USA, I have seen how democracy has been used repeatedly to justify violence in local, national, and international settings, especially in a post-September 11 society and the No Child Left Behind era. While it is tempting to say that the use of democracy, rather than its principle, has been the issue, I would argue that democracy does not have an internal mechanism against violence, and that is why it can be (mis)used to justify violence.[4]

Ted T. Aoki (1993 [2005]) traces the notion of the individual or individual rights at the heart of democracy (p. 285). Cautiously, not critiquing all forms of individualism, Aoki asks us to move more deeply into it towards the edge of the language to see its limitations. A separate sense of the individual or self-centered individualism, whether in the sense of a person or a community, cannot guard against violence towards others, especially when others are perceived as obstacles to individual or group self-interest. Then, is there another language that can capture what I as a child felt so deeply in my heart for the humane relationships that human beings are capable of? Nonviolence does not justify any violence and does not perceive the "enemy" other as an evil that needs to be eliminated. It has an internal mechanism for compassionate relationships and against violence. As David's story struck a chord in me, I was finally able to hear the voice of nonviolence. My further studies of nonviolence in its existing theories and practices from multiple dimensions have affirmed the necessity and possibility of nonviolence education.

Pedagogy of Mutual Engagement

At the heart of cross-cultural engagement is the issue of self/other relationships, and as a revelatory result of this study and my own cross-cultural journey, I have come to realize that nonviolence holds a key to the issue. Although nonviolence is not a notion that David uses, clearly for him, the self/other relationship is a relationship of mutual learning, a learning that is not based upon positioning the other as strange, nor prejudicing the other according to one's own framework, but is based upon the notion of a bigger world of which we are all part even though we can be radically different. In all the work he has done, David felt that he has learned so much from the process. He was also good at creating positive experiences from difficult situations whether he was in China or in the American South, both of which posed cultural challenges. He welcomed all the challenges as learning opportunities. When he referred to his time in the South, he admitted that it required a lot of adjustment, but "I learned so much. Every situation was a great opportunity in another way—if you think about it." This ability to learn from a different situation and further transform the situation to create new conditions for realizing his own vision is intimately related to his early cosmopolitan upbringing and continuing cross-cultural engagement throughout his life.

In teaching, David was fully aware how the self could be positioned as separate from the other and he consciously taught against it. His autobiographical passion for "learning *from* the other," rather than "learning *about* the other" (Todd, 2003) was reflected well in his pedagogy. In not objectifying China into an alien, exotic culture for students to know *about,* he enacts relational dynamics in the classroom that challenge students to engage the other and learn *from* the other. David's pedagogy of mutual engagement and mutual learning was not only reflected in his classroom teaching, but was also demonstrated well in his deep commitment to bringing American and Chinese students together face to face to experience a life of "interbeing" (Hahn, 1989 [2009]) for an extended period of time. Such an experience of cross-cultural daily encounters—rather than like a tourist who only glimpses the exotic site of another culture—is irreplaceable in intercultural education. But experience itself did not necessarily work magic, and students had to spend time working on these encounters and experiences in order to make sense and find meanings.

David acknowledged that such learning was a process and that his own cross-cultural learning did not happen very quickly, so he had a lot of patience with his students. It seems to me that cross-cultural learning can be slower than learning a general subject topic, and teachers who teach students another language or/and another culture (or teachers who teach foreign students) need "pedagogical thoughtfulness" (Aoki, 2005) to accompany students during the process. Ted T. Aoki (1992 [2005]) tells us, "Authentic teaching is watchfulness, a mindful watching overflowing from the good in the situation that the good teacher sees. In this sense, good teachers are more than they do; they are the teaching" (p. 196). David, who embodied his own cross-cultural personhood in the classroom, was the teaching.

A sense of interconnectedness in cross-cultural encounters is also accompanied by a sense of strangeness, disruption, and drama. David's teenage encounters, as difficult and dramatic as they were, set his relationship with China into a position of mutual learning. But he was thrown off the ground in total shock when he witnessed what happened to the students in 1989. Those moments produced ruptures, discontinuity, disjuncture, and "non-sense" (Kristeva, 2000) that he had to work through in years to come. But even during that time, he was adamant that educational exchange between the two countries should not be stopped by such a political event. Many years of effort to understand Chinese history and to engage in educational exchanges with China had gradually helped him to piece ruptures back into the whole. As Fowler (2005) insists, "staying with difficulty" is the key to opening up new possibilities. David had stayed with and worked on difficulty through different angles over the years in a process of reaching new understandings. Such a staying, however, does not necessarily mean remaining in the original site of difficulty, but working with difficulty through multiple and multidimensional movements that lead to breakthroughs.

A nonviolent relationship with the self and a nonviolent relationship with the other, in David's case, go hand in hand, and in working with non-sense, he treated strangeness, disruptions, and ruptures as opportunities for growth so as to learn from differences. I was interested in understanding more about David's approach to cultural differences. Did he think that in order not to exoticize the other, shared humanness (as Cohen argued for and as David practiced in teaching) was more important than differences in seeing everyone or every culture as part of the world? What did he think about the relationship between universality and difference? Since he did not answer my follow-up questions, I am not clear about his responses. However, one thing that I have learned from his stories is that he did not approach difference as something negative to push away, but neither did he overvalue differences, as he insisted on an approach of the self to the other not in opposition but in relationality. This approach echoes Peter Hershock's (2009) call for shifting away from the pursuit of being "different from" one another to the interconnectedness of being "different for" a community.

Such a sense of human connectedness, however, did not prevent David from experiencing ruptures, and he had to work hard to unravel the knots produced by his experiences in China. I would argue that ruptures are also necessary for weaving a web; just as *Tao Te Ching* (Chapter 11) says, an empty space enables the existence and usefulness of the vessel. Organic relationality includes the role of disjuncture and the network includes various configurations of both connections and disconnections. In my own cross-cultural pathways, I have privileged the role of difference—as I mentioned above—and in pursuing what is different, the unrealized potentiality within me has emerged for a fuller self. Contradiction, rupture, or disjuncture is a familiar scene in my inner landscape, and I have continually worked on these cross-cultural and intrapsychic fragmentations to produce more connections. This nonviolent work with oneself—whether through shared similarity or difference or both—is especially important for educators because the nature of our profession is relational, and pedagogical relationships are directly influenced by our relationship with the self.

Nonviolent pedagogical relationships can mean different things in different contexts, including, for example, patiently supporting students as they work with difficulty over an extended period of time, creating conditions for students to make sense of cross-cultural and intercultural relationships face to face, hand in hand, "eye to eye" (jagodzinski, 2008), interrupting existing patterns of thinking and living that reinforce dualistic consciousness (Bai & Cohen, 2008), deconstructing any form of violence, or reflecting the unknown in students back to themselves so that they get in touch with their own potentiality (Kristeva, 1996). While I will discuss more in the last chapter about what nonviolence means for education, David's pedagogy of mutual engagement offers important lessons for building nonviolent and organic relationships across differences.

Notes

1. The term "trauma" was first used by me when I listened to David's story. As he narrated what he experienced in 1989, I could not help but comment: "It was a trauma," to which David immediately agreed: "Yes, it was a trauma."
2. Chinese language reform in the 1950s and in the 1960s changed the written form of the Chinese language to simplify it while making the best effort to preserve the spirit of the traditional Chinese ideograph. Now what is used in mainland China is the simplified written Chinese, different from the complicated form of written Chinese used in Taiwan and Hong Kong.
3. In cross-cultural moves and intercultural education, we need to acknowledge the diversity within each language and each culture, rather than imposing one uniform system. More often than not, the standardization of language is artificial, imposed by a central system, and in David's case, although his southern accent did not conform to the standard, he had obtained it from his lived experiences. In this sense, his dialect was more authentic than the standard pronunciation.
4. Certainly here my critique of democracy forms an interesting contrast with David's question of "why not democracy in China," which implies the inherent goodness of democracy. While David believed a democratic government should have replaced state violence—at least at that time—I believe that although democracy is better than autocracy, it is not adequate to counteract violence, as it does not necessarily have an internal mechanism against violence. I am not clear whether David would agree with me on the power of nonviolence since I did not have a chance to discuss it with him, although I think his moral center denounces violence in various forms.

2
BEYOND THE CATEGORY

Cross-Cultural Imaginations

When I was in graduate school in China, I had a professor in educational theory who advocated the importance of reading classical works in the world literature of education. He read all that literature himself, relying on translation, but his interpretations were most in-depth and faithful to the original works. His readings of John Dewey's work, for instance, went far beyond many Chinese (and American) scholars' simplistic positioning of Dewey as child-centered. He did not have firsthand experience with American culture, but the quality of his engagement with American thought was exceptional.

When I started this study, I thought of him and his teachings, and wondered about what happened when a scholar's engagement with another thought did not have an experiential basis. My participant Fen, who knew English but not to the degree of using it comfortably as a working language, also engaged Western theories mostly through translated texts, and she did not have any substantial experience of living or studying in any Western country. Here I use the term "West" to indicate Fen's broad engagement with Western thought, rather than specifically American thought. When I first found her on the Internet, I was impressed by her publications, which demonstrated her expertise in Western discourses including cultural studies and postmodernism, but I did not know that she was in a situation similar to that of my former professor in relying on translations to get access to publications in English.

I was able to conduct only two interviews in the fall of 2009 with Fen due to her busy schedule and a week-long national holiday when she traveled. She also gave me some of her writings, including an essay about her teaching and a reading list for one of her courses. She did not respond to my follow-up questions, so I asked to schedule another interview with her in the summer of 2011 when I went back to China.[1] She was surprised that I still had not finished my book—she must be a quick thinker and writer—and agreed to let me interview her again. I wish I could have heard more stories of her life, but interestingly, even though her undergraduate major was Chinese literature and she worked as a part-time journalist for three years in the 1990s, she did not tell detailed stories but presented impressionistic views. We discussed her perspectives more than her life stories.

Because of her background and her storytelling style, in this chapter I focus more on Fen's intellectual engagement in the historical contexts of Chinese engagement with the West. I first provide Fen's autobiographical sketch reconstructed from interviews; second, I discuss her preference for not separating Eastern and Western thought; and third, I analyze the historical contexts of Chinese engagement with Western thought, particularly in the fields of philosophy and literary theory, from the turn of the 20th century to the recent scholarly debates. Then I return to Fen's pathways as a female leader on the site of contradictions and ambiguity. Finally, I discuss the implications of Fen's story for education and nonviolence.

An Autobiographical Sketch

Born in a small town in the northeast part of China in 1965, I was the oldest child in my family. My father was a worker and my mother also worked part time to help with family expenses, but she was mainly a housewife. I have a younger brother and a sister. As a child, I liked to play but had to do housework; for instance, I cooked meals for the whole family. When I could steal a moment, however, I would sneak outside to play on the slippery ice[2] and then run back in time to finish the work. When I was eight years old, I dropped out of school for a year to take care of my sister. My sister was three years old; when she cried, I held her to comfort her. Imagine an eight-year-old taking care of a three-year-old!

Studying at school was smooth for me. I always had good scores although I did not work very hard. I could easily memorize what the teacher said in classes to get good scores in exams. Primary school was not demanding for me, and I went to the best secondary school in the town. It was some distance from my home, so I rode a bicycle every day to go to school. Later I was the only student from my class who went to college. I was also the only one in my family who went to college.

My father died right before I went to college—one month before I took the national entrance exam for college—and he died young, only 40 years old. I was shocked: It was like a dream! His death was caused by a medical accident. My performance on the exam was negatively influenced. I was closer to my mother and did not have a lot of interaction with my father, who was serious and strict with me, but losing him in that way was difficult. It was especially painful for my mother. I felt a lot of sympathy for her. My mother passed away when she was only 45 years old, and I believe that it was due to both sadness and hard work. My mother had been working so hard for our family. I can hardly compare to her in this aspect.

I studied Chinese literature as an undergraduate student. My first encounter with Western thought started in college when I read many foreign novels, such as English, French, and Russian novels translated into Chinese. I cannot remember them now, but novels such as *The Red and the Black, Anna Karenina,* or works written by Honoré de Balzac. But the most important thing in college was that I fell in love: It changed my life. I am now still living in the city where I attended college: my husband and his family live here. After my graduation, I wanted to stay in the university where I had studied in order to be with my fiancée, which meant that I needed an advanced degree. I went to another university to pursue a master's degree and majored in modern and contemporary Chinese literature. I wrote a thesis on a modern Chinese novelist and compared Eastern and Western cultures as reflected in his novels. So literature was my entrance to the Western world.

When I began work as a university professor, I was not fully invested in the academic life and felt that the university was like an ivory tower, out of touch with social reality. So I became a part-time journalist and worked for three years while teaching at the university. Doing interviews with both well-known and ordinary people, I had experiences with people from all walks of life. Those experiences of being a news reporter immensely expanded my horizon and deepened my understanding of life. It was a good exercise. As a teacher, we see people as equals. When I had a chance to talk with people ranging from the lowest to the highest social status, I approached everybody in a calm and equal way. I also had a chance to know what was really happening in society. I liked to be among events and people and to be part of what was currently going on in life.

After deciding not to pursue a career in journalism, partly because my parents-in-law did not approve of it, I continued to teach at the university. At that time in the late 1980s and early 1990s, young people were more interested in the outside world than in an ivory tower. But one of my former professors and then a colleague had a calming effect on me. His style, personality, and value system, which did not follow the popular stream of that time, impacted my own life pathway. I also realized through doing journalism that the business mentality that was rising to the peak in China was problematic. My conversations with this mentor friend about various aspects of life pacified the impatience and turbulence in me and helped me make peace with living an academic life.

I decided to pursue a Ph.D.. Since my family did not want me to study in another province, I had to stay with the university, which did not have a Ph.D. program in literature. Actually, I had not been really interested in Chinese literature before I went to college, but I ended up with it as my major. For a doctoral program, which major should I choose? Friends suggested that I study philosophy. Well, I needed to see whether I was interested in it, so I took a class on Western philosophy. The theories introduced in the class, such as Schopenhauer's theory, made deep impressions on me, and I loved abstract thinking, so I decided to major in philosophy. My own thinking style is more abstract than specific, and my scholarly lines follow theoretical understanding. I loved poetic writings in philosophy and I was poetic when I was young, but later I was drawn more into theoretical inquiry.

During my doctoral program, I encountered cultural studies that had a close relationship with Western Marxism, one of the research traditions in the part of China where I lived. My major professor was a well-known scholar in the area. So I combined my literature background and cultural studies for my dissertation. After my graduation, aesthetics was becoming a specialization at my university. Because of my dual background in literature and philosophy, I became the leading person in that area. I have continued reading Western philosophy, including feminism and postmodern theories, and I have used different theoretical lenses to analyze Chinese literature and popular culture, but I don't feel any exclusive affiliation with one particular school of thought. As Chinese say, "There is one key to one lock," so I improvised my theorizing according to each situation.

Later, I became an Associate Dean for my college. Becoming an administrator while still teaching and undertaking multiple tasks matched my personality, and although it was not initiated by me, I welcomed such a change. I am the kind of person who does not like to stay with one thing, so doing something more than teaching is good for me. As an associate dean, I was mainly responsible for the academic aspect of the administration, including research and grants. I learned a lot and then later I was asked to take on the dean's position for another college in the university.

Being a dean has been a different experience from being an associate dean. But it is a good exercise. This college is relatively new and was not in good shape when I came in. The college has multiple departments with almost 100 faculty members, so I have had to do a lot of mediating work. I have found out, though, that if I treat everybody equally, it is not too difficult to get things back on track. Another trick is that since I am not in their specialty, there is a healthy distance between me and those under my supervision, which gives me more room to play. Furthermore, I have been successful in helping faculty to promote their research, engage in team work, and get a lot of grants from the university, so professors are grateful for my strategies to highlight their scholarly abilities. I also argued for a different system of evaluation to show their artistic strength at the university, and the university evaluation criteria were changed as a result of my advocacy. I have been able to use the dean's position to make a positive change in the university academic culture, and I feel good about it.

After the twists and turns of my career choices, I have actually begun to appreciate an academic life. For more than 10 years I have rented a study room in the library to have a space of my own. In the beginning, I had to discipline myself to concentrate on my studies, especially when I was a doctoral student. But gradually this study room has brought me a sense of peace and become a solitary space for my intellectual explorations and a haven for me to get away from the noise of an administrator's work. Every day I must find time from my administrative and teaching schedule to go to this room to recharge myself.

I see my own role of being an administrator as making a broader contribution to society, beyond being a professor or a scholar. I don't want to be a lone scholar who does not participate in the current social change. But I really don't plan to follow the career ladder of administration since I don't have any interest in power games, and I won't change my straightforward personality to appease higher-level officials. I simply need something more than teaching to feel that I am an active participant. I did not actively pursue a career as an administrator but only followed what naturally came to me. I am, of course, also aware that when one goes onto a certain path, the path itself leads you to places where you did not plan to go. So in a sense, I am open to future directions.

Can East and West Be Separated?

From the above sketch, we can see that Fen's understanding of Western thought was initiated first through her reading of foreign novels and later through studies of modern Chinese literature. Modern Chinese literature as a field originated in the May Fourth era in the late 1910s when traditional Chinese culture was under serious critique and new literature along with new culture was advocated (Lin, 2005; Wang, 2009). Many Chinese intellectuals, including philosophers and literary talents during that time, studied abroad and returned home to rebuild China. Autobiographies and biographies of Chinese thinkers (see Feng, 1984 [2004]; Luo, 2006; Zhou, 1984) show each individual's different responses regarding how to integrate Chinese and Western cultures in order to deal with internal turbulence and external threat. As a result, descriptions of Western culture and comparisons of Chinese and Western cultures were well reflected in the modern literary work. Modern Chinese literary criticism also borrowed Western theories, since scholars not only observed contemporary Western society but also studied Western intellectual traditions across time and place. Thus the field of modern Chinese literature is complicated, going across China and the West, continuity and rupture, and tradition and modernity. Without setting foot on foreign soil, Fen had to confront Western intellectual traditions. In her master's thesis, she contextualized one modern literary figure's work in the intellectual, social, and political situations of his generation who encountered the Western culture. She discussed this novelist's shifting viewpoints on China and the West. Her doctoral study in philosophy further enriched her intellectual foundation for laboring in this complex field.

For Fen (2009), "There is no sharp distinction between Western and Eastern thought, because ideas and thoughts go across national borders." When I asked about contemporary Chinese literary criticism theories, she admitted that many scholars still used Western theories to analyze Chinese literary texts, and explained,

> Using Western literary theory to analyze Chinese literature is a common practice in Chinese universities. In fact many modern Chinese writings in

the early 20th century were influenced by Western thought. So I don't feel much problem with using such a theoretical lens.

Her position challenged my cross-cultural assumptions in this study. However, if modern Chinese literature was already a hybrid product, then I need to situate her approach in the history of modern Chinese literature.

Cui (2008) traces modern literary criticism in China back to the May Fourth era, which established various theories based upon critiquing Chinese traditions and learning from Western theories. Later, the politicalization of literary criticism reduced the diversity of early theories into an exclusive focus on Marxism with the 1949 revolution (Lee, 2002). Since the Cultural Revolution (1966–1976), the recent decades of developing literary criticism have been distinctively marked by drawing upon Western theories again, including sociological critique, psychoanalytic theory, historical critique, reader-response theory, postcolonial critique, feminist critique, cultural studies, hermeneutical critique, and deconstructive critique, in addition to the mainstream Marxist analysis. When Fen was in graduate school, many Western literary theories were particularly vibrant and influential in China. Her research in feminist theories, cultural studies, and postmodern discourses were at the cutting edge of her time.

In a broad context, reclaiming native traditions in a postcolonial and global society has been ambiguous. South African scholar Crain Soudien proposes the notion of "modern-indigenity" (quoted in Pinar, 2010, p. 223) when responding to my question about what indigenous resources South African educators can draw upon to contest the history of colonization. He argues that four centuries of colonization have made it difficult to have any "pure" indigenous tradition that is free from the influence of colonizers' approaches. Different from South Africa, China went through half-colonization, with some designated port cities open to the colonizers; and a distinctive sense of Chinese identity has remained throughout the turbulence of the last century. But the past century unsettled the notion of Chinese tradition and Chinese identity. As Xu (2005) asks, what can be counted as characteristics of native Chinese culture? Should we name Confucianism, Taoism, Chinese Buddhism, or Chinese Marxism? I also would like to add: What about other hybrid traditions resulting from China–West encounters?

Fen's assertion of knowledge beyond the category of East/West also came from a certain sense of the universal in which knowledge is knowledge, truth is truth, and literature is literature. As Ge (2006) points out, while criticizing the universal is becoming another master-narrative today, the Chinese intellectuals of the May Fourth generation searched for universal truth as a way for society to advance out of internal and external difficulty. The legacy of that time might have influenced Fen's perspective. Moreover, after the Cultural Revolution, to challenge the political and ideological control of literature, Chinese literary scholars called for asserting literature's independent status. Several of Fen's publications explore literature's essential and transcendental functions.

Such a call to assert literature's essence actually forms a paradoxical relationship with Western discourses: On one hand, it resonates with the Western Enlightenment philosophy that emphasizes objectivity and universal truth; on the other hand, it is at odds with Western postmodern theory that reveals the political nature of objective rationality and questions metanarratives that assume neutrality. The legacy of the quest for modernity is still unfinished in China while Western society has been stepping into a postmodern condition. The inherent conflicts of different Western paradigms coexisting in the Chinese intellectual field add another layer of question: What counts as the West? In general, Chinese intellectuals in the 21st century are faced with conflicting directions in their engagement with Western thought, as modernity, premodern, and postmodern conditions coexist in China. For Fen, although she was influenced by cultural studies and postmodern theories concerned with the issue of difference (albeit in different ways), she did not consider the differences between Eastern and Western thought significant in her work. Fen's disregard of category was also consistent with her writing style. Fen did not claim her affiliation with any particular scholarly tradition, and when she analyzed literary work or popular cultural products, she drew upon diverse theories and theorists to make her arguments.

Furthermore, Fen's refusal to enter into the East/West discourse made me aware that my discursive imagination of Western thought was implicitly linked to liberal Western philosophy to the exclusion of Marxism. But the Marxism that triumphed in China was already a hybrid product of Chinese and Western thought. Marxism was not native to China, and Chinese Marxism was one response, among other alternatives, to the challenge of building modern China. If Fen did not feel any sharp difference between Eastern and Western thought, her scholarship in Western Marxism and cultural studies might have contributed to a certain sense of continuity. Even though Fen also studied postmodern approaches, her entrance into postmodernism was through cultural studies that originated in (and went beyond) Western Marxism.

Another participant in my study, Song (see Chapter 3), studied empiricist liberal Western political philosophy and theory, in sharp contrast with Marxism; and it was this very contrast that initially attracted his attention. So the differences within Western thought (or within Chinese thought) can be as sharp as the differences between Chinese and Western thought. In Fen's case, a stronger sense of continuity between modern Chinese literary theory and Western theory, rather than rupture or differences, characterizes her scholarship. Refusing the category of East/West did not prevent Fen from comparing particular aspects of Chinese or Western traditions, but her refusal of the category has stayed with me for the rest of my study as a critical reminder to attend to my own assumptions.

To understand Fen's intellectual lineage better, we need to go back to the May Fourth era of the last century. Situating contemporary Chinese scholars' pursuits in intellectual history is beyond the scope of this chapter, so I offer only a brief discussion here. But understanding the beginning of the last century is important for re-examining the beginning of this century, and such a contextualization is also useful for us to understand other participants' stories, particularly Song's story.

Intellectual Engagement in Context

For Chinese intellectuals, the dramas of China–West conflicts were a major preoccupation during the 20th century, especially during the first half of the century.[3] It was a period when clashes of culture, politics, thought, and religion raised important questions about Western learning and Chinese learning, tradition and progress, and universal truth and national salvation.

Historically, Western thought was introduced into China with the Western missionary efforts in the early 17th century (Huang, 2007). Through translation and dialogues with Chinese scholars, missionaries brought not only Christian philosophy but also natural science as well as Greek philosophy to the Chinese intellectual elite, some of whom welcomed the new knowledge. However, the exchange stopped at the end of the 17th century. Then a new "exchange" was imposed by the Opium Wars in the mid-19th century when the Western colonial powers defeated and invaded China. Chinese intellectuals, still carrying on the "scholar-official" tradition, confronted "Chinese backwardness" in the context of Western imperialistic and colonialist encroachment.

Different approaches emerged during this period: An initial response was a self-strengthening movement that advocated learning from Western technology but holding on to the traditional social and political system; a reform movement followed, in which the transformation of the social and political system was perceived as necessary for moving forward; then revolutionary efforts adopted a more radical approach to initiate a totalistic break with the past to establish new systems. These approaches did not necessarily emerge sequentially and mostly coexisted and comingled, but at the governmental level they were put into practice sequentially. Both the self-strengthening movement and the reform movement under the Qing Dynasty failed, and the Republic of China was established in 1911. Later, in 1949, the Chinese communist revolution declared victory.

Because of Fen's specialty, I discuss the fields of philosophy and literature that were intimately related in the New Culture Movement of the 1910s and 1920s. Chinese scholars generally agree that the birth of modern Chinese philosophy and of modern Chinese literature was related to introducing, translating, and interacting with Western philosophy and literature, along with transforming Chinese traditions (Hu & Yang, 2008; Liu, 2002; Wang & Chen, 2009). At the same time, it is important to point out that although the external Western influence intensified such a change in the Chinese intellectual field, the Chinese internal mechanism of change had already operated for centuries. Echoing Cohen's (1984 [2010]) argument, we cannot reduce the complexity of the Chinese situation merely to its responses to the West (Cui, 2008). For instance, the changes within Chinese literature were already underway and vernacular literature existed in previous dynasties. As Lee (2002) points out, HU Shi[4] (1891–1962) saw literary revolution as a renewal of the effort initiated in the Song Dynasty (960–1279).

The New Culture Movement era marked a time of unprecedented influence by Western thought. The variety of Western philosophy introduced into China includes different time periods (such as ancient Greco-Roman thought, Christian theology, and Enlightenment philosophy), different traditions (such as British empiricism, American pragmatism, and analytic philosophy), diverse philosophers (such as Plato, Aristotle, Spencer, Kant, Hegel, Nietzsche, Schopenhauer, Bergson, Russell, and Dewey), and conflicting political orientations (such as liberalism, anarchism, and socialism). Such a complex mixture of Western philosophies from different historical contexts flooding into China simultaneously produced a kaleidoscopic and chaotic view of the intellectual landscape. It required time and space to sort things out and reach a mature level of integration. Unfortunately, the subsequent war with Japan in the 1930s and the civil war in the 1940s, followed by Communist China's exclusive official ideology of Marxism prematurely disrupted the various lines of inquiry.

The introduction of Western philosophy and literary theory in the beginning of the 20th century was influenced by the Chinese intellectuals' own concerns and lenses (Cui, 2008). When Western theories entered Chinese debates, Western discourses had already been changed. Li (2010) further suggests that the translated Western literary texts had both "heterogeneousity and nativeness" (p. 4). In this sense, China's encounter with the West was mediated. Although many agreed that it was imperative to "change from within" for national salvation, what kinds of change and how to achieve such a goal were extensively debated.

Different Schools of Thought in Philosophy

In general, modern Chinese philosophy includes three major schools of thought: reformers' thought, or what Furth (2002) and Schwartz (2002) term Neo-traditionalism; liberal thought; and Marxism. Even though such a category reduces the complexity and variety of hundreds of schools of thought during that time, for the purpose of this chapter, I build my analysis along this line.

Conservatives did not want to change, while Neo-traditionalists wanted to change but did not want to abandon the whole of Chinese traditions. Originating from the works of KANG Youwei, TAN Sitong, and LIANG Qichao, these reformers adopted the Western evolutionary theory, specifically Social Darwinism, and made an effort to integrate the Chinese tradition of *Datong* (great peace) and the notion of progress for China to enter modernity (Furth, 2002; Huang, 2007; Schwartz; 2002). Liang also argued for the formation of a "new citizen" who was progress-oriented and independent of political authority. Such a concern for transforming personhood to meet the needs of a new era has persisted and been re-articulated throughout the 20th century.

Neo-traditionalist approach, although critiquing tradition, did not reject all of the cultural heritage, and although calling for change, did not support revolutionary change. The effort to integrate Western learning and Chinese learning developed in new directions after the 1911 Revolution and the 1919 May Fourth movement. For example, LIANG Qichao, LIANG Shuming, and FENG Youlan drew upon different traditions from both Western and Chinese philosophy (Schwartz, 2002). This approach has continued into the contemporary era in Hong Kong, Taiwan, and among oversea Chinese scholars, although it was discontinued in mainland China after 1949 (until its revival in recent decades).

Both Liberalism and Marxism were important to the New Culture Movement. The overthrow of the Qing dynasty in 1911 did not lead to democracy but to frequently changing warlord governments, so the need for cultural transformation was deeply felt. Soon, the publication in 1915 of the magazine *New Youth*, with its radical direction of challenging the Chinese tradition as a whole, indicated the beginning of the New Culture Movement. Its editor, CHEN Duxiu (1879–1942) initially collaborated with HU Shi to start the Literary Revolution. After 1919, however, Hu and Chen went on to different pathways as representatives of Liberal and Marxist thought, respectively.

Hu advocated science, democracy, individual freedom, and literary revolution and argued for the total reconstruction of Chinese culture. Hu's notion of science, influenced by John Dewey, was an experimentalist approach of applying tentative hypotheses to problematic situations, and his notion of democracy was to apply scientific methods to studying cultural problems cooperatively for social progress (Schwartz, 2002). As a liberal, Hu's advocacy for civil rights and intellectual freedom (free from politics) did not change throughout his lifetime no matter who was in political power. Liberal thought was largely excluded after 1949.

Chen approached scientific reason as instrumental to changing Chinese people's thinking and used Social Darwinism to challenge traditional values. Influenced by French thought, Chen's notion of democracy was related to revolutionary transformation that called upon social action and political activism, which characterized the May Fourth movement. While Hu was concerned with thought and culture, Chen and his colleagues directed *New Youth* towards Marxism, which considered economic relationships as the basis for cultural change. In the 1920s and 1930s, Marxism, centering on class struggle and mass mobilization, quickly developed in China and became the official ideology after 1949.

The May Fourth Student Movement: A Turning Point

If many Chinese intellectuals were greatly impressed by the liberal West before the 1920s, they became disillusioned later, and the May Fourth student movement was a turning point. On May 4, 1919, students went into the streets in Beijing to protest the decision at the Paris Peace Conference that allowed Japan to retain the entitlements of Germany in Shandong Province, a result of secret agreements between Japan and several Western countries during the war, with the Chinese warlord government's complicity. The movement not only marked a new height of nationalism against foreign imperialism but also marked a fuller break with Chinese tradition. As Furth (2002) points out, reformers' approaches to Western imperialism were "more self-critical than anti-Western" (p. 37), but the May Fourth movement led to a different position, critiquing the liberal democracies of the West and calling for a more complete transformation of traditional culture. Marxism seemed to promise an alternative approach, and the first major Chinese Marxist theorist, LI Dazhao, claimed that "Marxism was the true carrier of the Western scientific and democratic heritage" (quoted in Furth, 2002, p. 95).

Similar to the situation in the sixth century bc in ancient China when the diversity of schools of thought blossomed before being subsumed into the institutionalization of Confucianism (Wang, 2004), there were many different approaches regarding China-West engagements during the May Fourth period, but their complexity was often reduced to the meta-narrative of their giving birth to revolutionary Communist thought when Marxism replaced Confucianism after 1949. However, the May Fourth movement has left diverse and conflicting intellectual traditions, despite the classical view that the May Fourth Movement gave birth to "a political activism of patriotic awakening, and socialist commitment" (Yeh, 2006, p. 294), a view prevalent in both Chinese and Western readings of the event. Such a reading reifies the victor's storyline and a particular historical choice while suppressing multiple historical possibilities.

As an important cradle for the May Fourth movement, Beijing University was under Chancellor Cai Yuanpei's leadership at the time. Scholars from various schools of thought were invited to teach at the university, and students had opportunities to study with professors ranging from the most conservative to the most radical. Influenced by German philosophy and the pre-industrialization German university model, Cai emphasized academic freedom and "the independent development of the university as a center of a new culture, which was a synthesis of both Chinese and Western knowledge" (Lin, 2005, p. 49). Students were allowed maximum freedom to choose what they wanted to learn and how they could learn, and three student newspapers were published, from Left, neutral, and Right orientations, respectively (Feng, 1984 [2004]). With the variety of thought present both within faculty and students, efforts to mediate between Chinese and Western thought led to new intellectual and cultural movements. Such a tradition of intellectual freedom was not allowed under Chinese Marxism after 1949, even though both Beijing University and the May Fourth Movement were officially celebrated.

The existing political authority's re-appropriation of the May Fourth Movement's historical significance (Yeh, 2006) and Beijing University' symbolic meaning (Weston, 2006) function to celebrate socialism as the historically inevitable route to a modern China. However, the central messages of the May Fourth Movement regarding questioning the existing political authority (internal and external), pursuing individual and intellectual freedom, and promoting humanistic thinking and democratic spirit have been marginalized. It is this suppressed aspect of the May Fourth legacy that needs attentive listening, and it is this aspect that David and other scholars refer to when they compare June Fourth in 1989 with May Fourth in 1919.

Literary Revolution, New Literature, and Fen's Literary Reading

The Language Reform and New Literature Movement was part of the May Fourth era. HU Shi and CHEN Duxiu advocated the vernacular language, using the expressions and vocabulary of the everyday speech of ordinary Chinese as a way of transforming culture because classical writing was only accessible to scholars. The literary revolution was officially launched by *New Youth* in 1917, but by the early 1920s the Ministry of Education had already prescribed the use of the vernacular in writing at school (Furth, 2002), so its sweeping effect was evident. New literature promoted transforming literary content and style along with language reform according to the needs of the cultural transformation.

New literature—or May Fourth literature—shared the rebellion against rigid traditional writing that reinforced Confucian morality and family filial norm, advocating free expressions of thought and feelings. It had a strong individualistic orientation, breaking away from the constraints of the family. Women's emancipation through romantic love was often portrayed along this line of pursuing individual freedom. But there were frequent debates too. Several debates related to the polemics of literary creativity versus revolutionary orientations regarding the artistic or political functions of literature happened between different camps in the 1920s and 1930s.

In Fen's scholarship, she discusses literary figures or products belonging to the New Literature era, and her choice of authors does not necessarily come from the mainstream. She also reads the major literary figures using her own lens, rather than following the official line. One major leader she wrote about was LU Xun.[5] Although Lu aligned with the Left in the last decade of his life and was re-appropriated by the Communist Party after 1949, his party-line position had been ambiguous, although his literary accomplishments were recognized by all sides. Lu is well known for his sharp, thorough, and relentless critique of traditional Chinese culture. Some Western readers (see Lee, 2002; Furth, 2002) have presented Lu's worldviews as fundamentally pessimistic in contrast to the Chinese official celebration of his revolutionary spirit.

Fen argues that Lu's tragic reading of Chinese culture did not lead him to pessimism or nihilism, but that the pursuit of transcendence and the true meanings of life is always the subtext of Lu's novels. Fen does not read Lu's novels and essays through the official lens of revolutionary literature, either, but is most interested in his commitment to the ontology of personhood. She believes that Lu's ultimate concern with humanity and with the essence of literature transcends the political, instrumental nature of the new literature during his time. For Fen, even though the notion of a new citizen had already been brought forth during the reformer era, it was Lu's novels that took off the masks over individual existence to reveal authentic personhood. Although he sharply criticizes human passivity, stupidity, hypocrisy, self-deception, and blind obedience in China, such a critique intends to inspire the transcendence of the existing human condition. Fen credits Lu for bringing literature back to its essential task. While she uses the Marxist theory of human alienation to read Lu's work, she also borrows the lenses of other Western philosophers such as Nietzsche and Heidegger.

To a great degree, debates about how to negotiate between Chinese and Western intellectual thought are still ongoing. During those decades of the closed door to the liberal West after 1949, the West was changing, and postmodern perspectives have become influential since the 1980s. The irony of facing the unfinished task of Chinese modernity—Leo Ou-Fan Lee (2002) makes it clear that the May Fourth movement was hardly heading towards Western modernity—while entering a postmodern globalized society adds layers of complexity. In the 1990s, there were debates about what the May Fourth Movement meant for contemporary China, ranging from the most critical to the most sympathetic responses (Wang & Chen, 2009). While the introduction of Western theories both at the turn of the 20th century and in the 1980s hardly left much space for matured, sophisticated, and seasoned analysis for possible integration, the hope is that the Chinese intellectual field now is in a better position for digesting and negotiating differences. Fen (2009) asserted that the intellectual freedom in China was much better now, and she felt at ease to speak or write about her independent ideas.

Now we have seen that three important schools of modern Chinese philosophy were all indebted to Western thought and that the field of modern Chinese literature was influenced by the West. In this sense, Fen's position of not separating East and West is historically grounded. I admit, though, there are times when I wonder whether her administrative position as the dean of a college in a comprehensive university put some limits on her viewpoints—despite her assertion of freedom. In not carving out a distinctive line, she does not have to deal with the complicated, highly politically charged issue of China-West debates because Chinese politics put a certain limitation on what she can or cannot say. However, I also think that Fen's refusal to categorize is a consistent line in both her scholarship and life, as I will turn to her life experiences next.

A Female Leader's Pathway: A Site of Ambiguity

The path to becoming a strong female leader could not have been easy for Fen, particularly in an area of China where traditional gendered expectations have been strong. But in her own narrations, she never dwelled on any particular difficulty, but saw every opportunity as a "good exercise." She also emphasized that she followed the flow to become an administrator. But she was clear about one thing:

She could not feel fulfilled with doing just one thing such as teaching, so administration simply became another avenue to exercise her talents. Fen's approach went beyond the dualism between being active and being passive, and she was receptive to what life opened up to her and took every opportunity as a chance for personal growth. She pushed the limits to play out her creative potential.

With multiple passions for life, Fen had a keen interest in social participation, as her part-time journalist experiences indicate. This broad interest in society and culture contributed to her taking up leadership positions at the university. Fen (2011) stated, "It is better to have both [academics and administration]. Only having one is boring." Janet Miller (2005) describes her mother's capacity for handling multiple tasks and holding both relationality and independence at the same time. For Miller, women's subjectivity is fluid and can stretch to meet multiple demands. Fen excelled in stretching out for the multiple.

I noticed that she was good at multitasking. During our interviews (she chose to talk with me walking along the university track field, which was a meeting place for students and faculty during the evening time), she could steal time to talk with others on the cell phone when I was switching the recorder's batteries, or stopped on the way to talk with others, or permitted others to interrupt our conversation. None of the distractions seemed to bother her at all. When she took care of various things at the same time, she did so with a graceful flow. While her scholarship crossed disciplinary boundaries, her administrative experiences also crossed different disciplines. She was currently a dean of a college outside of her specialty, but she perceived such a difference as an advantage since her faculty could play out their own potential without worrying about the dean's judgment. Similar to David, she saw positive aspects in various situations and could make the best out of these situations.

Part of my interest lies in understanding the relationship between life and thought. In Chapter 1, we can easily see that David's experiences in China contributed to his cross-cultural intellectual engagements, but Fen denied any direct relationships between her life experiences and scholarship. When I asked her if her experiences of growing up in a small town, or her life as a woman, had contributed to her scholarly interest in cultural studies, her answer was a straightforward "no." She believed that the interdisciplinary nature of cultural studies in its connection to both literature and philosophy appealed to her.

When I referred to her childhood experiences, she said:

> When I was young, I went along with life just in order to live. Not like now, we want to teach children to be like this or that, pursuing a certain kind of life, and positioning within a certain value orientation. I only followed life naturally. Of course, since it was not easy during my childhood, after I grew up, I was not picky and can endure pain. So I can face everything and can deal with difficulties. . . . And since I have had so many experiences, I can see things in a broad way rather than a narrow way.

Fen attributed the strength of her personality and the breadth of her worldview, but not her scholarship, to her childhood life conditions. The relationship between life and thought is certainly never linear or direct, but Fen's insistence on a non-relationship surprised me. I had little understanding of the link between my scholarship and my life while I was in China. Only after I came to the USA for my doctoral studies did I begin to see the missing link and realize how my previous scholarly interests were grounded in my concerns in life. Such a discovery had a healing effect for me because it brought intellectual alienation back to the circle of life.

Certainly I don't assume that such a discovery can be applied in Fen's case since conscious understanding of the link—if there is any link—between life and thought does not happen to everyone, and I don't assume that such an awareness is necessarily beneficial. In addition, Fen's critiques of cultural studies also played a role in her refusal to link cultural studies with her life. The categories used in cultural studies such as class, race, and gender were like cookie cutters for her, and she did not believe anybody's life could be categorized so. Just as a gap existed between life and thought, contradictions and ambiguity were woven throughout Fen's stories. From a post-structural lens, however, contradictions, gaps, and ambiguity reveal deeper layers of reality more than continuity and transparency (Miller, 2005; Smythe, 2012). In the following analysis, I focus on different aspects of such an ambiguity.

Traditional Versus Radical

More than once Fen commented that she was a traditional woman, and she (2009) also mentioned her mother's influence: "My mother was a strong woman who worked very hard to give us all the opportunities that she could give to me and my siblings. She had a strong influence on me, including her commitment to family." While her mother did not have a stable job outside of the home, Fen was working as a college professor and an administrator who was simultaneously committed to both family and career:

> I am a traditional woman even though I have an open personality. Family is very important to me. I have always tried to balance my pursuit of career and my family's needs. Now although I am a dean, my family actually supports me since they not only know that I need to do something besides teaching to release my energy, but they also know that I will try my best to balance between family and work. They are not particularly worried that my work will make me neglect taking care of family. I have a good relationship with my parents-in-law.

Her balancing act had won her family's support of her work. A daughter-in-law's position in a traditional Chinese family is most difficult (Wang, 2008), so it was quite an achievement for Fen to have a good relationship with her parents-in-law. Such a balance required a certain sacrifice since her parents-in-law intervened in her career and university choice for her Ph.D. program. But Fen did not express any regret; she simply approached her choices as her own after considering all concerns.

The line between traditional and radical was drawn during the May Fourth movement to indicate people's orientation to either traditional (Chinese) culture or modern (Western) culture. Fen's self-image had a gendered layer since traditional Chinese women were expected to be committed to family, and part of the May Fourth radicalism was the attack upon the traditional family structure. As a scholar well versed in the May Fourth philosophy and new literature, Fen advocated the pursuit of individual freedom and the transcendental concerns of literature, but she perceived herself as traditional in her life. However, as a woman philosopher who wrote extensively and a successful leader who pushed the boundary to transform the university culture, she was hardly traditional. While she was committed to family, she was also committed to social engagement. Fen seemed to imply that being radical meant breaking fully away with the Chinese family tradition. But I found her commitment to both family and public work as a strength, more meaningful than a rebellious posture of making a full break. It is easier to break than to negotiate, but negotiation benefits the healthy human (and ecological) network in the long run (Wang, 2010b).

The contrast between the traditional and the radical was also about the contrast between China and the West. Fen (2011) claimed that she was not into "that radical stuff in the West" such as radical lesbian feminism. But here is another interesting twist: Fen (2009) also claimed that contemporary Chinese women were more progressive than Western women because of their economic independence. She argued that Chinese women were fully engaged in the work force and took on all kinds of professions, and that fewer of them were housewives than Western women. While many studies show that economic independence does not necessarily lead to women's equality, Fen stated that the economic basis determined ideologies, in typical Marxist language. Citing LU Xun's (LU Hsun) (1923 [2007]) article "What Happens after Nora Leaves home?" Fen argued that if Nora had had economic independence, she might have survived in society; if not, she would have had to return home or die of hunger.

Different from Fen's approach, Julia Kristeva (1996), a French thinker, does not believe that women's staying at home, when needed, is necessarily detrimental. She argues for a flexible arrangement in which women can be free to choose to stay at home for a certain period of time—particularly for being a mother—and then find a job after they leave home. Such flexibility is a mark of social progress for Kristeva. But for Fen (2011), economic independence is the basis for social participation, because through public work women can "get in touch with society and they can play certain roles in society." Fen also believes that Chinese women have strong personalities, just like her mother, who could overcome numerous hardships and obstacles.

Fen's studies of Western feminist theories have been extensive, ranging from the classical writings of *The Second Sex* to third-world, postcolonial, and poststructural feminism. In counteracting the assumption of Western women as being more liberal and progressive than Chinese women (Mann, 2000; Teng, 1996), Fen reversed the categories of traditional and progressive women between the East and the West. Was this reversal her intention to challenge the West-centered feminist assumptions, particularly interacting with overseas women scholars? Was it because her own life gave her a sense of confidence as a woman? Fen did not comment on my further questions related to emotional, intellectual, and sexual dimensions of gender equality in China. While I agree with her on the strength of Chinese women (Wang, 2008)—but not in a comparative sense of being stronger than Western women—what appeared as the mismatch between the multiplicity and richness of Fen's studies of Western feminism and her one-dimensional judgment puzzled me.

Another gendered layer of Fen's self-perception as traditional was that she did not think she had any ambition to climb up the career ladder to the top. She believed that as a woman, it was okay not to go all the way up. Such a description seemed to suggest that despite her teaching and studies in feminism, she still accepted the limitations of being a woman in leadership. But she perceived it not so much from the external constraints as from her internal choice. She also repeatedly referred to the benefit of such a choice as being able to do what she would like to do, so her preference for individual freedom was as explicit as her acceptance of gendered limits.

Fen's gendered tales are messy and ambiguous. In these tales, being traditional and being radical are a complicated affair: They are simultaneously intertwined, contradictory, different, and oppositional, and the variety of her shifting positions is beyond categorical description. The tension between, or the mixture of, the traditional and the radical can be productive when it can cultivate a humble, broad, and tolerant attitude as Fen credited to herself, but the gaps, contradictions, and ambivalence revealed in Fen's stories remain provocative for us in rethinking gender, culture, and personhood in the context of cross-cultural education.

Carefree Personality and Disciplined Negotiator

While positioning herself as traditional, Fen described her personality as "open," "carefree," "energetic," "frank," or "natural," and believed that such a style was beneficial for working with men:

> My personal style makes it easy for me to be an administrator among men and I work with men well. I am a frank person and can be playful with men when working with them, and they respect me. I think I am more like a man, so it is easier to work with them.

I experienced her personality from the very first meeting when another professor introduced us to each other. Fen told me right away that she was not a bookworm like me and that she was not an intellectual. When we walked out of the restaurant, she also commented on the way I dressed and told me how to change it according to the current fashion. But before she offered such advice, she said, "I see you as an insider," so she quickly included me into her boundary of friends versus strangers. Surprised, well, actually a bit taken back, by her frankness, I felt more at ease to a certain degree, since I imagined that interviewing her would not be difficult. Perhaps her colleagues might have had reactions similar to mine, so she was able to open up conversations in her college.

Fen's self-perception as "more like a man" is particularly interesting. Despite all her theoretical discussions about feminism, gender, and subjectivity, she attributed her leadership success to a personality compatible with masculinity. Such an alignment, however, was not without questioning the traditional gender norm:

> I am like an "I don't care" type of person, not paying much attention to details. Some women are very careful to present themselves in their every gesture and every smile. I am never like that. I am more natural. Since I come from a small town [rather than a city], my family education did not much emphasize Confucian feminine rituals or acting like a lady. I would like to do whatever I want to do, so it might look like I don't demonstrate good cultivation. But I like to be myself, and I don't like to be constrained.

Here Fen referred to her nature again, but she also mentioned her upbringing in a small town. She reversed the tendency to see women in the city as "better" than women in small towns (or the rural area)—similar to the way she reversed the categories of traditional/progressive between Chinese and Western women. She claimed that, different from the shaping of a city girl, her family education in the small town was less ritualized and more naturalistic, and thus was less constrained by gendered norms. Interestingly, the image of a rural woman (and man) is usually associated with backwardness in the Chinese tradition in the May Fourth literature with which Fen was familiar, yet she turned upside down this hierarchical category to claim that women from lower status are more carefree.

In China, there are three levels of administration: urban, small town, and rural/countryside levels. Historically, it was true that certain gendered practices started at the urban level and were extended to the small town and then to the countryside. For instance, the inhuman practice of footbinding started with the court dancers, then went to the gentry's families, and finally reached rural areas. For a certain period of time, footbinding was the "privilege" of gentry women (Wang, 2004). Fen turned the disadvantaged position of the small town compared to the city into a positive site for developing her personal qualities. Yet her privileging of the small town Chinese woman went together with her centering of a masculine personality for leadership work.

With a carefree orientation, Fen (2009) also recognized that being an administrator put constraints on her interactions with others and that her personal preferences must be negotiated: "I used to do things my way. But then I could not do so anymore. I must take everybody's thoughts and feelings into consideration." With a greater sense of responsibility, Fen was a disciplined negotiator to mediate among different groups and different people, and she was able to lead the previously divisive college out of trouble. Not to play the political game of power struggles, she preferred democratic discussions and encouraged everybody to bring issues to the table. With the increasing solidarity and transparency within the leadership team that she worked hard to achieve, Fen believed that the climate of the college had changed in a better direction. Fen also negotiated with the university to create a greater space for her faculty. She felt that as a leader, she could contribute to the university and society in a way that a professor could not.

As associate dean and then dean, Fen still taught classes in her original department. So her work went across different departments in multiple dimensions of teaching, scholarship, and administration. To negotiate all the tasks, she pursued her own space away from the administrative office, and a rented study room in the university library became her haven. She had rented this room while she was in her doctoral program, and admitted that in the beginning she had to discipline herself to study. At that time, it was fashionable for young people with great aspirations to go into business—the commercialization of higher education was at its peak—and it was a difficult time for academics. But she gradually made peace with being a professor and enjoyed the freedom provided by her professorship. After she became an administrator, she went to this room everyday to read, write, and think alone. In a sense, this room provided her a space to be carefree in the midst of institutional and interpersonal constraints. The beginning of our second interview took place in this room. It was a small, simple room with books, a computer, photos, and small handcrafts. We had to leave soon, but during this brief stay I could sense what this room meant to Fen.

Although a carefree personality seems to contradict what is required for a disciplined negotiator, Fen embodied both in complementary ways. The conflicts did exist, yet a carefree style made negotiation successful, and discipline helped to bring out her creative potential. The combination helped Fen to play with boundary and carve out her own leadership pathway.

Yuanfen (Chance/Fate) Versus Choice

Fen stated that she followed what life opened to her rather than actively pursuing a particular pathway. Commenting on one of her life decisions, she (2011) said: "It was not a fully conscious choice decided by me. It was *yuanfen*." This Chinese term is not easy to translate into English (Xie, 2002; Ma & Wu, 2011); translated in general, it means luck, chance, or fate that brings things or people together, although in Western culture, chance and fate seem to be opposite as the first is circumstantial and the second is predetermined.

Neither fully active nor fully passive, the Chinese notion of *yuanfen* does not assume individual autonomy but acknowledges the power of life situations that cannot be fully controlled by any individual person, although human effort still plays an important role. As Ma and Wu (2011) point out, *yuan* and *fen* are two words that, when combined, indicate the realization of a certain potential, but when separated—there is *yuan* but there is no *fen*—it indicates the failure to actualize a potential connection. Beyond the (modern Western) dualism between passivity and activity, Fen attributed her life pathways to following what is unfolded by chance, circumstances, or even constraints.

In Fen's narrations, her undergraduate specialization was not her own choice but due to circumstances; she went to graduate school because she needed to stay in the city where her fiancée lived; she gave up the job of a journalist partly because her parents-in-law disapproved; she became an administrator because she was invited. In these stories, she was not an active pursuer, but she did not push away opportunities when they were presented to her. One of Fen's experiences at college (2011) is telling:

> I was already chair of the class at the elementary school. And I had a good trail of leadership experiences at school and was selected as the model student in the district. When I went to college, I automatically became the chair of the class again.

So the so-called "natural flow" of becoming a leader was based upon many years of leadership experiences throughout Fen's life trajectory. While Fen chose not to focus on her conscious pursuit, her accomplishments could hardly have appeared without her inserting subjective positioning and directedness. She continues,

> But it was forced upon me as well. I was scared when I first went to college. I was 18 years old and moved from a small town to a big city. I did not want to be in charge of the class. I went to the students' advisor and told him that I did not want to do it since I did not know how to do it. He said: "You have not done it yet, so how do you know that you cannot do it? Just try it."

She tried it, and this assignment played well with her talents and skills; in other words, *yuan* and *fen* came together nicely. This spirit of "trying it" had stayed with her in her further endeavors. The notion of *yuanfen* is similar to the notion of fate in the Chinese context, and Ji (2006) believes that they can be used interchangeably. Similar to the notion of *yuanfen*, fate (*mingyun*) as a two-word Chinese term also has two faces: On one side it is something given, beyond human control; on the other side, it is actualized by human effort. Ji (2006) advocates the simultaneity of "making human effort and following the mandate of heaven" (p. 64).

Fen's following the natural flow is combined with her efforts to actualize potentiality in accordance with the fluctuation of time, place, and situation. In Chen's (2010) term, "fate as a web of causal and normative constraints that is developed by human thought, choice, and action" (p. 68) is *both* made *and* in the making through our life experiences. "The Janus face of fate: predestination and human endeavor; embodiment and freedom; 'made' and 'in making' " (Chen, 2010, p. 74) suggests that fate-made and fate-making go together in order to achieve the full potential of what is possible. The constraints of family obligations and situational circumstances led Fen in particular directions, but her decisions to choose a particular pathway came from her preferences, which were the results of informed understandings.

For instance, Fen accepted the location for her doctoral studies in order to take care of her family, but she took classes in philosophy before she decided to major in philosophy. As Chen (2010) suggests, letting things flow in their natural course does not mean doing nothing but means making effort to facilitate the flow to bring fate and human responsibility together. Fen did not fight with constraints but she still played an active role in shaping her own fate, finding a room of her own in various situations. Her situatedness in such a constructed and constructing interplay (Foucault, 1982) between the self and the world was not seamless but complicated, as she left a crack here and there in downplaying her own agency, leaving me to affirm her subjectivity through unspoken storylines.

In the Chinese worldview, fate is an important concept (Wei, 2010). As both Raphals (2003) and Chen (2010) point out, the Chinese notion of fate is often mistakenly reduced to fatalism because of its acceptance of constraints on humanity. However, in Lisa Raphals' (2003) study of the semantic history of fate, fortune, chance, and luck in Chinese and Greek philosophy—loosely considered as the contrast between the East and the West—she concluded that "pre-Buddhist Chinese accounts combine acceptance of fate with strong anti-fatalism and well-developed notions of strategy or maneuvering room within its decrees," (p. 561) while a significant fatalist element existed in the Greek accounts of fate. Regarding human choice, she points out:

> Greek metaphors of spinning and binding tended to express human powerlessness. Chinese accounts take the understanding of the harmony with fate (according to very different formulas) as a defining characteristic of the sage. Chinese accounts focus on the figure of the sage as someone who "understands" fate. (p. 561)

The Chinese notion of fate is situated in a difficult balance between understanding fate and finding a path in harmony with fate, and choice lies in this search for harmony. Educated in both modern Western philosophy and Chinese Marxism, Fen still tended to refer to fate or *yuanfen* to interpret her own life. Fate or choice is not an either/or issue.

Transcendence and Immanence

In Fen's scholarship, she was concerned with ontology and metaphysical layers of meanings, and she particularly credited LU Xun for his transcendental pursuit. She also criticized three schools of traditional Chinese thought—Confucianism, Taoism, and Buddhism—for their lack of ultimate concern for and suppression of individuality. While not wanting to distinguish between East and West, Fen nevertheless acknowledged that Western thought was more concerned with essence, metaphysics, and transcendence. According to Hall and Ames (1987), immanence rather than transcendence is a feature of Confucian thought.

Not only in Fen's analysis of modern literature, which was oriented by breaking away from the confinement of immanence, but also in her critiques of contemporary literature and popular culture, she approached literature as poetic understandings to demonstrate human aspirations for freedom and transcendence. She recognized the positive role of popular culture in challenging authority, liberating embodied experiences, and releasing individual creativity. But she also critiqued the lack of ultimate concerns and the emptiness of meanings in many contemporary literary texts, including the work of woman writers, and insisted that the essential task of literature in its transcendent function must not give in to the secularization and electronization of literature and culture.

Fen's lens was changing, however. When I interviewed Fen in 2009, I could feel the overall upward direction of movement in her outlook. But when I interviewed her again in 2011, a subtle change appeared in her tone. She (2011) realized that Chinese philosophy in its concerns with secular happiness is humanistic, and "if one is always concerned with ultimate questioning, it can be painful." Here the humanism she was referring to was Chinese humanism, which centers on personal cultivation as the basis for individual happiness and social harmony, not the humanism of the Western Enlightenment, which emphasizes the autonomy and agency of the human subject. Fen felt that she had become more secular than before:

> As I grow older, when I read novels that describe the enjoyment of childhood, it feels so endearing. Previously I could not read through such storylines: It was too trivial. But now as I read it, I am smiling and laughing. It evokes resonance in me. I think it is because that as we are aging, we are no longer as radical as when we were young. We can look at, experience, and evaluate things from multiple angles.

Just as Fen attributed her leadership success to her personality, Fen attributed this change to the natural process of aging, rather than to her life experiences. Certainly different life stages may present us with different tasks, and Carl Jung believes that the process of individuation—the integration of conscious and unconscious in the individual psyche—is the task of middle age (Mayes, 2005).

To a certain degree, Fen's change also implies a process of integrating differences within herself. However, I find it difficult to perceive such a change only as a natural result of aging. Aging itself does not necessarily lead to more awareness or openness to the multiple; it can be, for instance, accompanied by more stubbornness and rigidity.

While I felt a certain shift in Fen's outlook, she was not aware of it:

> If you had not talked with me, I would not have realized it. Dealing with administrative affairs every day, I would not jump outside to look at what I have been thinking. But such a change means that I have become more tolerant of people and can take a broader view to see through things.

Here Fen welcomed her internal change as positive. Interestingly, as a scholar with prolific writings, she did not seem to have a reflective understanding of how her own inner world had been influenced by the external world. This unreflective approach is paradoxical considering her studies of feminist theories, which assert the social and cultural construction of gender. In her account, her interest in ideas and theories—and her fondness for abstract thinking—did not necessarily connect with her as a person or her life experiences. So implicitly she conveyed a sense of disconnection between nature and culture, internal and external, life and thought, rather than co-construction, in her storytelling. To what degree were these missing links present in their absence? To what degree did these gaps reflect Fen's resistance to categorizing her life? She seemed to be comfortable with such gaps and did not feel the need to explain them away.

Since the time difference between my first and third interview was relatively short, I had not seen such a shift from transcendental concerns to immanent interests in her publications yet. It will be interesting to see whether she will interpret literary texts differently.

"Am I an Intellectual?"

As Zha (2012) points out, the notions of the intellectual in China and in the West are different. The unity of knowledge and action and the tradition of "sageness within and kingliness without" in Confucianism has shaped the central role of "scholar-official" in political and social life in China. The Western sense of academic freedom in supporting intellectuals' scholarly independence and their pursuit of objective knowledge in separation from societal utilitarian or political demand does not exist in Chinese Confucianism. While I agree with Zha's call for establishing a separation between the sage and the king in China, I also think the West has had a tradition of the "public intellectual" who directly participates in social and political transformation of the public realm. As I argue in Chapter 1, David played the role of public intellectual through his work in cross-cultural educational exchanges. However, different from Confucian scholar-officials, who practiced the Confucian moral philosophy of governing, Western public intellectuals do not serve government's interests but assert their independence in contributing to political change.

Aware of the role of the Western intellectual as critic, Fen (2011) commented, "In the West, intellectuals are in oppositional positions: They want to be woodpeckers." Familiar with the redefinition of the intellectual in cultural studies and postcolonial and postmodern approaches, Fen understood that the Chinese intellectual's role of building the nation and managing public affairs was different from the Western intellectual's independent status. She did not identify herself with either tradition: "I don't think about what I do or should do as an intellectual or as a resistant intellectual." She further identified herself as a teacher: "I simply think I am just a teacher. It is all right to teach well and do research well." In claiming herself to be a teacher, an ordinary self-identity—not even a professor—she contested the elitist tendency in both Chinese and Western intellectual traditions.

Not comfortable with the Western confrontational mode, Fen did not like the scholastic Chinese tradition, either. She associated an intellectual with a bookworm: "I am not a bookworm; I love to play." For her, an intellectual is serious, not playful. Her passion for multiple aspects of life went beyond the confinement of a study room. Fen (2009) also felt the limitations of her particular scholarly style: "I don't think I am the type of scholar who goes deeply into one particular area. I have jumped over all different areas so I have not gone into enough depth in any one particular direction." Part of it was due to circumstances that made her switch majors multiple times, but part of it was, I believe, due to her various intellectual interests. Her teaching and scholarship involved multiple areas including philosophy, literature, aesthetics, cultural studies, and film and media studies. Not many scholars can step into all these areas at the same time, so even if depth is sacrificed a bit, breadth is her unique strength.

Another unique style of Fen's scholarship is her ability to weave different theories for advancing her own perspectives. In reading her articles, I found that she did not adopt one particular framework to interpret a literary text or a popular culture phenomenon. She had her own line of inquiry and she drew upon diverse philosophical and literary theories as she developed her arguments. In this way, her Western learning and Chinese learning were organically integrated in her analysis, rather than a Western theory being applied to a certain Chinese situation. She threaded through various theories with her independent thought. I asked her whether she had any interest in developing a literary theory of her own since her own thought stood out in her writings. She said that she had not gone to the level of consciously defining her own style and that she did not have an ambition to go in that direction.

However, in the sense of participating in social change and transforming the university culture, Fen did identify her role as a scholar and took pride in what she was able to accomplish as an intellectual leader. She believed that leading others as an intellectual, rather than an official, had the advantage of using persuasive power through scholarship, rather than the authoritarian power of bureaucracy. Her leadership style was not confrontational but collaborative, inspirational, and scholarly. She did not identify with the intellectual's task as contesting and challenging, but approached it as participating, intervening, and implicitly transforming. Fen (2011) commented: "Confrontation does not work. Nobody welcomes others who want to fight. But tacitly we can make changes in life and even change peoples' perspectives so that we can achieve something together. We all have a tendency to become good." Such a belief in tacit change and transformation is compatible with the Chinese tradition of leadership relying on the change of heart (Wang, 2007). Such an approach also echoes Michael Nagler's (2004) arguments about nonviolence, which does not blame any person or any group for wrongdoing but evokes the goodness inherent in everybody in order to shift relational dynamics towards constructive directions. Fen quickly added that she was not afraid of fighting if necessary, but to get something through fighting is not appealing.

While Chinese intellectuals' historical ties with politics and their lack of autonomy have been questioned both in the West and in China (Davies, 2001; Yue, 2001; Zha, 2012), Fen believed that precisely because of these constraints, Chinese intellectuals' negotiation was particularly painstaking and faced more challenges than that of Western intellectuals who already had a relatively independent status. Whether or not she spoke out of her own personal experiences, she was certainly facing the challenge of negotiating between her scholarly and administrative identities.

As a female leader, Fen's pathway was woven through the site of ambiguity. Sometimes in direct contradictions, sometimes in complementary tensionality, sometimes in disconnections, sometimes in juxtaposition, different modes of tensions emerged in the sounds of Fen's footsteps. Whether harmony in difference (Wang, 2004) or noisy in cacophony, the gaps between Fen's life experiences and her cross-cultural thought illuminated the complexity of personhood. Her individual life history was situated in Chinese intellectual and cultural history, which in the last century was also full of dilemmas and contradictions. If we look through the cracks, we can cultivate new possibilities.

Educating Beyond the Category

What I have learned the most from Fen is her refusal to categorize within and across her scholarship, leadership, and teaching. She had an uneasy intellectual relationship with cultural studies due to its identity focus; she did not want to put her scholarship into any neat box; her leadership addressed the needs of situations beyond the barriers among different stakeholders; and her teaching followed students' own interests within the general parameters of coursework, as we will see below. Reversing the category of social or international hierarchy to assert the strength of the underprivileged, she also refused to define her intellectual interests by her life experiences of growing up in an underprivileged situation. Challenging categorical thinking, she went across disciplinary boundaries in her work.

I did not have a chance to observe Fen's teaching, partly because of scheduling issues, and partly because of her reluctance for me to do so. In the Chinese context, freely observing colleagues' teaching is not common, and it can put the instructor in an uncomfortable position. Her administrative position added another layer of discomfort. I suggested observation and asked her to invite me when possible, but she did not. But we discussed her teaching in interviews and she gave me some materials related to her teaching.

There was a shift in her teaching orientation from the beginning to now. Fen (2009) said, "I did not really learn about how to teach in my graduate program so my teaching methods were more rigid initially, but I have learned to use more student-centered strategies to encourage students' independent learning." It is not unusual that university professors do not learn curriculum and pedagogical theories in their doctoral program, except in the colleges of education in the USA or normal universities in China. Song also made a similar comment about not knowing how to teach at the beginning of his college teaching (see Chapter 3). So at the beginning of their teaching careers, professors often don't have much to rely on except their own experiences of learning at college. Although Fen did not discuss her own professors' teaching styles, I think lecturing was the norm at that time. Fen developed student-centered strategies as a result of her own preference for learning through experiences, her observation of how students responded to her teaching, and her learning from Western constructivism theory.

Fen wrote about her teaching and used an example in one of her recent classes on modern and contemporary Chinese women's literature. She started with a survey to understand students' backgrounds and interests. From the survey, many students expressed their fondness for a particular woman writer's work, so Fen used this writer's work as an exemplar of literary styles and meanings. Instead of lecturing about the writer and her work, she decided to let students run the show and asked student volunteers to teach a particular topic of their interest. Students chose a topic, read the related texts, found their own angle, did thorough research, and offered their own interpretations through presentations based upon all these thoughtful preparations.

When students presented their work, Fen was pleasantly surprised by both the content and the aesthetic quality of the presentations. Students covered a wide range of topics and used various lenses for analysis. Some used the existential feminism of Simone de Beauvoir to analyze storylines, some entered into the text through autobiographical reading, some used poetic presentation, and some examined some key words through linguistic—both Chinese and English—interpretation and translation. The aesthetic aspects of the presentations through music, stories, and creative design—many were computer-generated—were especially impressive. For Fen, reading and critiquing literary texts was an aesthetic activity marked by individuality. The individual experiencing of the text and the expressing of her or his understanding was important in Fen's teaching.

Growing up in a small town without much material comfort and becoming an administrator in a man's world, Fen must have experienced class and gendered disadvantages, but she refused to look at the world as if it could be easily categorized. In her pedagogy, she also taught against categories rather than reinforcing them. In teaching female writers' works, she did not use gender as the knot of analysis, but treated those works as literary works written by women. What she emphasized in teaching was to give students freedom to explore, to understand, and if a certain lens was useful, to use that lens. But there was no demand or even expectation from her for students to follow any particular path—feminist or not—since she did not want to confine her students, just as she did not want to confine herself, by any particular theory. This approach, however, did not mean neglecting teaching about specific theories and methods, as her students learned theories and methods of comparative literature, or discourse analysis, or gendered analysis for literary interpretation, along with their explorations.

Fen's approach of teaching against the category formed an interesting contrast to identity discourses in American higher education during the past several decades. In her unique carefree style, Fen did not categorize her own life through the lens of gender or class, even though she was influenced by and used the lenses of gender or class analysis when needed. She also understood the limitations placed upon women in leadership roles, yet she took limitations as a way of being freer to be herself. Advantage or disadvantage is fluid in her subjective positioning, so Fen did not trap herself into any particular identity, and there was no distinctive victor or victim storyline in her narrations. This fluidity made it easier for students from various backgrounds to relate to her teaching. Even though I did not have a chance to observe her teaching, it is not difficult to imagine that her students experienced a certain sense of freedom in her class. Fen explained that she was influenced by constructivism, which emphasizes the role of interaction, and I think that her personal spin on such an interaction brought a sense of flow to the class in which students could go beyond the scholastic tradition to play.

Play had been important to Fen since her childhood when her responsibility for her family did not prevent her from having fun whenever possible. She did not confine herself by serious stuff even after she became a dean. She enjoyed fashion and saw no need to adopt any dress norm for faculty even though other deans have implicit codes, and sometimes she dressed herself to lighten up the room when she entered. She was also excited to orchestrate the 10th anniversary celebration of her college in a big demonstration to showcase everybody's talents. She took pride in directing such a performance. Play was also part of her learning and teaching, as she played with ideas across disciplinary boundaries, and encouraged students to play with texts and with one another. Through play, curriculum becomes alive and education becomes meaningful (Aoki, 2005; Doll, 2012).

For Fen, education was a transcendent activity that led students to go beyond both themselves and their professors. In other words, wherever students started, they needed to move upward for more learning rather than staying within any particular boundary. It also meant that teachers must engage self-transcendence in an ongoing process. She argued that professors must be at the frontier of their own discipline so that they can lead students to the front lines. The process of professors' engaging in inquiry and research, if demonstrated in their teaching, can greatly encourage students' own inquiry and cultivate their respect for new discoveries. Thus she believed that a successful professor is also a great scholar. Without advanced scholarship, professors can only teach established knowledge and cannot challenge students to move ahead.

When Fen was a professor, scholarship was important for her to spark students' intellectual interests. Now as an administrator, Fen continues to read, write, and publish, and to advance herself intellectually. For her, teaching, scholarship, and leadership are interrelated, rather than separated, and all three areas need to advance together to be mutually beneficial. Although Fen did not have experience living in a Western country, her cross-cultural scholarly imaginations had carried her to the other side of the world to converse with Western texts. Perhaps she did not reach the depth of understanding that my former professor did, but the breadth of her understanding went beyond disciplinary limitations to broaden intellectual horizons. Beyond the category, Fen's teaching is not only for her students, but also for educators who are committed to cross-cultural and intercultural education.

Notes

1. When I directly quote from Fen, I use 2009 and 2011 to indicate the different times of interviews.
2. In Fen's hometown, it was very cold during the winter. When snow was frozen into ice on the surface, Fen could slide on it like skating but without wearing skates.
3. When discussing the Chinese situation at the turn of the 20th century and in the first half of the 20th century, I did not discuss the China–Japan relationship, although it played an important role. While Japan's domination and invasion were part of the external threat to China's survival, as a much more Westernized nation than China, Japan was perceived as building its power upon integrating the advantages of Western science and political systems. Many Chinese intellectuals went to Japan for advanced study and revolutionary activities. Because of the angle of this book, I only focus on China–West intellectual relationships.
4. In the literature published in English, especially in China Studies literature, the name order for well-known Chinese scholars is usually in Chinese sequence (family name first and then first name). I use that literature in this chapter. To avoid confusion for both Western readers and Chinese readers, I follow the Chinese name order when referring to Chinese scholars' full names but use capitalization to indicate Chinese family names to make it understandable for Western readers. However, when only the Chinese family name is mentioned, I use the regular format without capitalization of all letters.

5. For reasons of anonymity, I usually do not use the real names of theorists my participants studied. But since there are so many publications on LU Xun, I don't think mentioning his name will run any risk of revealing the author's identity. Particularly since I want to compare her interpretation with Western readings of the same author, it is necessary to mention the author's name.

3

FROM DRAMA TO PEACE

A Hermit in a Cosmopolitan City

Growing up and currently living in a cosmopolitan city in China, Song experienced the Cultural Revolution (1966–1976), the beginning of the open-door reform era in China, graduate studies in the USA, and also teaching at an American university. Like David, his major was also China Studies, but his journey was quite different from David's. The drama of his life in his formative years in China and his cross-cultural life experiences in the USA led him to disillusionment first with the Chinese ideology of his time and then with Western rationality and democracy. He was the only participant no longer invested in public engagement, as he withdrew into meditation after his return to China. While I was troubled by his withdrawal, I was deeply moved by his stories. I interviewed him five times, including one follow-up interview by phone. My hotel was a long distance from his home, so we shared meals after the interviews and continued our conversations informally. I visited him again during the winter of 2011, when he provided additional comments after reading the first draft of this chapter. The data generated from our interviews and conversations were most complicated, and I don't have enough space in this book to elaborate its full implications.

Song's journey evoked a resonance in me that was beyond my expectation. Before I started my interviews, my emotions were intense because my travels to various places where I had lived, studied, or worked had provoked strong responses that were difficult to digest. The intensity of my thoughts and emotions, ironically, was pacified by his dramatic stories. I not only laughed a great deal with him but also experienced moments of stillness that were integrative, restorative, and healing, moments in which I felt in tune with a deeper sense of interconnectedness, a sense essential for a vision of education through and for nonviolence.

The mutual engagement between Song and me leads to an experimental style of writing in the first part of this chapter. Letting narrative speak for itself through juxtaposition (Miller, 2005), I present Song's story in his own voice with my thematically related story inserted as a sideline on the right side of the page. Moreover, I use our dialogues to intersect with the double stories. These stories and dialogues are reconstructed from taped interviews, informal conversations, and my research journal. Here Song's story is central, told chronologically, but my narration is not formatted as continuous, although the reader can read it continuously as a whole, as it has its own internal, nonlinear temporality. For Miller and her collaborators, the strategy of juxtaposition is for inviting "inconsistencies, ambiguities, ambivalence" (Miller, 2005, p. 114) through excesses. To parallel Song's stories, my stories focus on different aspects of life. But I also use dialogues to highlight intersections in addition to ruptures in our cross-cultural approaches. Convergence and divergence in cross-cultural pathways are both illuminating. We share each other's awareness while mutually challenging each other's viewpoints, related to our intellectual, gendered, generational, and experiential differences. Both stories and dialogues can be read as a form of data analysis: When participant and researcher become mutual participants in an open-ended inquiry, storytelling and analysis happen simultaneously.

In the second part of the chapter, Song's cross-cultural pathways are situated in the cultural history of his time in China and the intellectual history of his field in the USA. Here, the "cross-cultural pathway" is interpreted in a broad sense because his experiences in rural China and the factories crossed the boundaries of his own intellectual identity, and those within-China intercultural experiences were intimately related to his experiences in crossing the national border into the USA. Finally, the implications of Song's cultivation of non-duality for nonviolence education are discussed.

Stories and Dialogues

Song's Stories

Chaotic Childhood

I was born in 1954. My family moved a lot due to instability after the 1949 Revolution. My father first worked as a high-level translator for the Communist Party and then as a university professor. When I was at school age, I was enrolled in an elementary school for diplomats' children. I liked my studies, but my passion was for playing table tennis. I wished to become a table tennis player, and I worked very hard in training. In the fourth grade, I was training at the district level.

However, the Cultural Revolution started and everything became chaotic.

> **Hongyu's stories**
>
> I do not remember much of my childhood. My memory is imprinted more by the movement of emotions, not much about events, details, or places. Those moments of eternity in emotional turbulence shift and change in my memory, and don't stay in the same original places. Sounds, smells, smiles, words, touches, and senses remain refreshing, but the external markers of the outside world leave little trace. I have a hard time locating those markers, not simply because places change. Memory of what happened may have changed, even to the degree of the unrecognizable, but emotions do not fade.

The training stopped. My heart was broken because at that time playing tennis was the most important thing in my life. Thus I was very unhappy with the Cultural Revolution for a personal reason. I did not understand what it was, but I hated it because stopping playing table tennis was a huge loss to me. "The Cultural Revolution is so ridiculous!" After I said this in the neighborhood, I was under attack by my peers. They imitated what they saw from adults and denounced me as a "counter-revolutionary" in a struggle meeting.[1] My parents intervened to stop the attack. It was the first time that I tasted what politics was.

For the three years from 1966 to 1969, all I did was to hang around on the street as schools were closed and teachers were under attack. Those well-educated children of diplomats, all of sudden, behaved like rogues on the street. The Red Guards from secondary schools were admired for their "bravery" in destroying things and attacking people. Everything was upside-down. Before the Cultural Revolution, children of officials were afraid of children of workers who liked to pick a fight and to threaten others with their physical strength. But when many officials were attacked and society became chaotic, those well-educated children rose to power among their peers. While their parents were under attack, they turned around to seek revenge on society madly by combining intelligence, violence, and social networking to fight against working-class children with cruelty and domination. I was astonished by how those previously well-mannered children became so violent over night.

> Mother likes to tell me that I did not retaliate against boys who bullied me in the neighborhood, but I do not remember. I do remember the wood logs in the backyard of my parents' home. When I was young, I sat on those logs in solitude to dream and make up storylines and affectionate endings for those characters in the novels broadcasted by the radio: my favorite pastime.

SONG: Everything comes from one.
HONGYU: Everything comes from zero.
SONG: We share one energy, which is *Tao,* like the ocean which holds nothing and everything.
HONGYU: Zero holds everything and nothing.

Schooling and Life in Rural China

My father soon became the target of attack, and he was sent to a rural area in a southern province. So my whole family moved there to attend the Cadre's Camp.[2] There were 200 people in one unit and all were professors. Life there became a form of education for me. The living conditions were terrible, with no electricity or in-house water or bathroom. The only food in the cafeteria was rotten vegetables. There was no entertainment. So I liked to go to the dormitory to hang around with adults who talked among one another. Under the miserable conditions, they still discussed scholarly, historical, political, social, and literary issues. I just listened to them without truly understanding what they were talking about. I learned chess there and could recite ancient Chinese poetry from listening to their recitations. Many of them were experts and well-known intellectuals in their specialty. For example, one person in the dormitory knew more than 10 languages and could translate all foreign radio broadcasts when he was allowed to listen to the radio upon receiving special permission. Sometimes those adults would try to drive me away: "Go away, little boy." I would go away for a while, but then came back to listen more. I learned a lot of things through this unintentional learning in the dormitory room.

> My first elementary school teacher said that I was not very smart although my mother disputed it and told me that I had in-depth understandings. Over time, I have learned to trust myself, trust my intuition that does not come from pursuing truth but from my struggles with feelings, all kinds of feelings, and from my persistence in following my heart despite the external conditions. This acceptance of my ordinariness and this faithfulness to my heart have saved me from fatal falls over the cliff during crises. So I have never quite held a grudge over my teacher's judgment. Today I am still committed to educating common souls with my own common soul.

The leaders of the Cadre's Camp decided to put all school-age children in a secondary school in a nearby town. We needed to walk more than two hours to reach the school. At that time the Town Secondary School was still open. Interestingly, in the city the Red Guards were anti-authority and rebellious, attacking teachers and all authorities, but in the small town, the Red Guards were pro-authority and supported school officials. At school we frequently went to labor in the field and did not study. We were not in any mood to study either.

A lot happened there, but here is one story of our naughty doings. Local children did not stay overnight at school, but the children of cadres all stayed at school. The food in the cafeteria was terrible. We were often hungry. An hour after the meal our stomachs began to protest, so we usually went to the town center to find food. There was only one restaurant, selling noodles, beer, and fried dumplings. We all loved eating dumplings but our money ran out quickly. We came in and out of the school, noticing that there was a lost-and-found box where dimes were collected. One night three or four of us were together, feeling hungry. Somebody said: "How about we take off the box and get all the money there to buy dumplings?" I did not dare to say "no," afraid that others would think that I was too timid. So we got the money from the box—it could not have been more than one or two yuans together—and put the box back in its original location. We were elated and went to the restaurant to enjoy a big meal. But quickly our deed was discovered and somehow they knew who did it. So the school organized a week of study group criticizing us, and the police in the town also came. The organizers yelled and shouted at us to confess our wrongdoings. We insisted on not confessing, even if it meant that we were going to be beaten to death. Then we knew that the next week they were going to organize a struggle meeting to denounce and interrogate us in public. So the guy who took off the box suggested that we run away. He and I went to a long-distance bus station in the town to buy the tickets. As I was preparing to buy the ticket, all of a sudden, my mother's face appeared in front of my eyes, and I decided not to run away: She would be worried to death if I did such a thing! When we came back, teachers and students there were looking for us all over the place. A leader of the Cadre's Camp also came and was relieved that we had come back. He urged the school leader to stop attacking us, and they canceled the meeting. We survived the storm.

> HONGYU: I am a terrible person. You told me all those sad stories but I burst into laughter.
> SONG: That is because I am not sad now but calm. As I am telling these stories, it almost feels like I am telling another person's stories, not mine. Now my heart is like still water and I am at peace with myself.
> HONGYU: That depends on what kind of water it is. If it is alive, it is good; if it is stagnant, it is not good.
> SONG: Water is water.
> HONGYU: That is right.

Things like this happened frequently. The fights between the children of the Cadre's Camp and the local children also continued. Finally, the school leaders decided that we were too much for the school to maintain order, so they expelled all students from the Cadre's Camp collectively—nearly 100 students. After a while, the leaders of the Cadre's Camp established a school for us. Those teachers were excellent, with great scholarship and wonderful teaching methods. They tried to teach us not only subjects but also learning methods. But we did not have much interest in studies in a chaotic time.

It was the first time for me to leave the city and go to the countryside. I had a firsthand experience of the poverty and misery of Chinese rural life. I stayed in the rural area for almost two years. Even though at the Town Secondary School I knew students from the local area, mostly I hung around with the cadres' children. Children of different backgrounds did not mingle that much.

Also during that time, I had a life-changing experience when my father gave me some money to travel by myself. I was sent to a lot of cities and places.

When I toured Mount Lu and witnessed the luxury on the top of the mountain, I realized the gap between those who were in power and the ordinary Chinese people. The contrast

> I did not feel poor as a child, even though we were poor, as the majority of Chinese were in the 1970s. I do remember one year during the Spring Festival when my mom was sad. She said that she could not give us anything special for the holiday, but she still managed to find a lantern for us to carry out. All we had as a family of seven was the minimum living conditions supported by my parents' hard work and my aunt's care. But I did not understand all that as a young child. With basic living necessities met since my childhood, I have never really been concerned with material conditions. Greed is not a problem for me, or so I believed. Until I realized that according to Buddhism, greed is not just an excessive desire for material things, but can also lie in excessive clinging to emotions.

between the rural life and city life was already sharp, and the contrast between those high officials' lives on the top of the mountain and ordinary people's lives was simply shocking. That was during my formative teenage years, and that impression has stayed deep in my heart.

Working at a Factory

When we came back to the city from the countryside, we supposedly graduated from the junior high school and waited for the authority's arrangement. At that time, only a few could go to a high school to study or go to a factory to work; the majority would go to the countryside again. It was one of those times when good luck mysteriously fell on me: I was sent to a factory. I stayed in that factory for five years, and gradually I felt that I had become one of the workers.

Workers at the factory all came from the neighborhood, and they were poor. They could not afford to eat fresh vegetables, and many of them went to the market to pay five cents or one dime for a pile of rotten vegetable leaves and then made pickles. They had to save their money for one or two years in order to buy a pair of pants. In the beginning, I did not get along with these workers, and their concerns with their children and daily life routine did not interest me. But gradually I could see their kind-heartedness and sincerity, and I began to like them, joked with them, and became their friend. I was mostly amazed by their ability to survive in the most difficult living conditions.

It was a precious time for me. I had been born into an intellectual family in the city, so I did not have much chance to come in direct contact with the lower level of the society. Even though I went to the countryside, I did not live with peasants. I was also too young at that time to experience a different life in a more in-depth way. But five years of working in a factory and living in a dormitory made me understand what it was like for those who lived at the bottom of the society, and I began to identify with them. Even though my background was quite different from theirs, I felt what they felt and lived what they lived, and I was sharply aware of the social and economic inequality. There was a shop located across the street on which the factory was located, so I could visibly see that the price of one item we produced daily at the shop was more than my monthly salary. My political consciousness grew strong, but most workers did not have such awareness, and some of them felt very grateful to have this job and worked really hard.

My critical attitudes sometimes would come out at unexpected moments. We usually had a mandatory political study meeting after work when everybody was already tired. During the meeting one day, some people were smoking, some people were weaving scarves or sweaters, and I was dozing off. The monitor of our unit said that there was a new trend in the class struggle because somebody was superstitious enough to mention God. Half unconsciously, I said, "Our constitution guarantees religious freedom."[3] As I spoke, I woke up and realized that I was challenging his authority. Then we quarreled back and forth several times, but I decided not to back down since I had already said it. The party secretary also came to demand that I admit my crime immediately for less punishment. I refused to admit any mistake, insisting that I did not say anything wrong. The secretary said that the next day he would call a whole factory meeting to denounce me. I replied: "I would say the same even if you gathered a struggle meeting to denounce me." After I went back to the dormitory, I was very depressed, not sure what would happen next.

> Feeling like jumping off a cliff, the world collapsed in front of my eyes, but I could not hit the ground as it forever retreated into an emptiness that wrapped around me as I continuously fell. Sometimes after the fall, there was total darkness. Other times, as I reached the soft hold of the bottom, another village appeared, with multiple pathways winding into the distance, covered by shady trees, embraced by the night light.

The next day, I put the constitution booklet into my pocket and went to work, anticipating a big day. To my surprise and relief, however, the party secretary decided to cancel the meeting—later I found out that it came from a higher authority and was related to internal politics—and I was spared of what surely would have been a big show of an interrogation. I was elated and felt like a hero. In a year, I passed the college entrance exam when it was restored after the Cultural Revolution, and was celebrated at the factory as a hero.

> SONG: Sometimes we have to have the courage to jump off the cliff.
> HONGYU: Yes. And one might become enlightened after jumping off.
> SONG: It happened from time to time in my life. I jumped off yet nothing terrible happened afterwards, and what appeared as dangerous in the beginning was resolved in the end without any predictable reasons. If I had given up in the middle, it would have only been worse.

While doing the lowest level of work at the factory, I had a chance to mingle with the family of a high-level official. It was astonishing for me to see the contrast between those in power and the factory workers. It was a split life for me with the daytime at the factory and the nighttime in luxury with that family. Many high-level officials and celebrities visited the family. It was crystal clear to me that they never talked about what was officially put forward in the news for ordinary people to hear. What a hypocritical life! They were only concerned with power games and never paid attention to the interests of the people.

Voting Trial at College

I majored in English at college. It was a great challenge in the beginning as most of my classmates were much younger with a much better background in English skills. Among all my classmates, only one other student, Hong, was also a former factory worker. But my maturity and experiences helped. The most important experience in college, however, was an experiment in "democratic" voting when I was a senior.

At the beginning of the 1980s, the selection of delegates to the National People's Congress, for the first time, was open to local nominations. Students in Beijing University and Qinghua University jumped at the opportunity to be nominated, but nothing happened in my university. I complained about this with my friends—Hong and another student, Qiang, a military commander's son—and then forgot about it. At dawn the next day, however, Qiang came over to grab me from my bed and announced that he wanted to run for the candidacy. Since he was so determined, I did not have much choice but to support him, and Hong also joined us enthusiastically.

Following my suggestion, Qiang announced his candidacy in the cafeteria, which was a huge success. Then I gave Qiang advice and wrote big-character posters[4] for him to sign and post on the bulletin board in the cafeteria. We went from dormitory to dormitory, from department to department, and from library to classroom to

> The drama of my life has been interior even though the internal drama has always been related to what was happening in the outside world. The emotional drama that has brought me all the ups and downs cannot be spoken in a linear narrative plot, and has been rendered unspeakable especially before the public eye.

persuade students to vote for Qiang. He drew a lot of supporters. Then, I wrote a provocative article about the public property system in China, pointing out that the system was actually not public but was controlled by those who were in power. Without democracy, a collective property system cannot exist. Qiang and Hong were thrilled to post it, and it drew the attention of the police and the party secretary at the university. About that time, the suppression of student leaders' voting activities began, and some student leaders were arrested in Beijing. I was waiting for the worst since my article criticized the political system directly, but luckily, the three of us only got a warning from the party secretary as we insisted that we were only following the Communist Party's previous call for public participation. Of course Qiang was not chosen as the delegate even though he got most of the votes. That was my firsthand experience in participating in Chinese politics and understanding its hypocritical nature.

> SONG: I really admired Qiang. He was brave, smart, dynamic, and full of persuasive power. He was not afraid of going to prison.
> HONGYU: He also had a father he could rely on. As long as his father was still in power, he could get out.
> SONG: He had so many interesting experiences and knew a lot of things. Once we chatted about Dunhuang[5] and forgot the exam time. For those children of high-level officials, on one hand, they were spoiled; on the other hand, some were truly outstanding persons.

HONGYU: So you don't identify with coming from an official family?

SONG: I don't. My father was an intellectual official without political power. Power elites such as high-level officials or military generals are what I am referring to. I identify myself as a middle-class intellectual.

HONGYU: In China, we don't really have a middle class.

SONG: But I was truly in the middle. I felt close to my friends at the factory. They were kind to me, and I took care of them like a big brother. I was also very sympathetic and empathetic with their lot, so I could have close friendships with them, but I did not have much intellectual exchange with them.

I liked to hang around with the children of elites due to their rich experiences and broader perspectives. But I knew I was not one of them. I realized later that Qiang's bravery was not for pursuing any ideal but for challenging the current authority, which his family was opposed to. Hong and I were excited about the possibility of promoting a progressive and democratic ideal. But those from the higher-official families did not care about what was good for China and only cared about their families' locations on the map of political power. Very few truly cared about truth; the majority did not have much thought.

HONGYU: What do you mean by "having thought"?

SONG: To pursue truth and goodness. My ideal was a middle class ideal such as democracy, and was Western-oriented. As I reflect on these events in which I was involved, I realize that my strategy was neither soft nor hard, but to stay in the middle of the road. Half of it was compromise but I never fully gave in. I have kept such a style, even in the USA after I went there.

The Beginning of Cross-Cultural Encounters

After I graduated from the university, I requested to teach in a branch college. Soon after I started to teach, the college became a tourist college, and I taught tourist English. I did not know how to teach in the beginning, but I learned that teaching students how to learn was most important. At the time, being a tour guide was part of my job, and I could travel with tourist groups without teaching for the whole semester. I had a lot of opportunities to be a tour guide for American or European tourist groups. As an instructor, I also had the freedom to choose the best route, so I toured a lot of different places, including Xinjiang and Tibet. I learned a lot from encountering the outside world more broadly and authentically, more than from foreign instructors at college. Previously, I felt that Westerners were mysterious, but face-to-face interactions made everything close and real. It was a breakthrough for me. At the time, we worshipped the USA and thought everything in the USA was perfect.

After working for several years, I was offered an opportunity to go to the USA as part of the program of American Field Services, which arranged for Chinese students to stay with American host families in order to understand American culture. The Chinese Ministry of Education did not want to send school children, so it sent instructors instead. That was my entrance into the USA, and I ended up staying there to study and work for 20 years.

My first experience of the USA was in the South. I was assigned to an elite school where students had no curiosity about the outside world, so I did not do anything there, but my host family arranged for me to visit other schools where my lectures about Chinese society, culture, history, and humanistic geography were quite successful. I also had opportunities to attend lectures and interact with philosophers at a local university who were interested in Asian thought. I seldom experienced culture shock in the beginning of my life in the USA, unlike others who suffered from language barriers. Since my spoken English was good, I did not have problems in communication.

> Coming to the USA was not a rational, or at least not a means-to-an-end, deliberate decision for me. I did not know what I was searching for except that I somehow became emotionally invested in seeing a different way of life to fulfill the calling from the hidden emptiness/opening in my interior life, an opening that could not be nourished where I had been living.

Life in the USA as a Graduate Student

Later I was transferred to a cosmopolitan city in the Northeast. My new host was a China expert. I was so astonished by how much he knew about China and how systematic, detailed, and sophisticated his circle had been in studying China. The intellectual circle he brought me into was amazing. I wanted to learn from them. The route to becoming a graduate student was difficult, but I was able to overcome all the difficulties and became a master's level student in education first and then a Ph.D. student in political science at one of the best American universities. My doctoral advisor was a China expert. Studying political science, I felt like a fish swimming in water. After two years of studies, I was awarded the President's Fellowship—I did not even know about it, but I was offered it due to my achievement.

When I started my graduate studies, I stayed with an American family as a live-in person who helped with housework. The husband, Joe, and wife, Mary, were both experts in Asian studies. We got along so well that they considered me a part of their family. I stayed with them for 10 years until I found a job and moved to another state. They often invited friends to get together in their house, so I had a lot of opportunities to mingle with their guests. Living in American families was the best way to get to know a different culture. I was impressed by the couple's outstanding qualities. For example, they always planned ahead to arrange everything in advance, not like the Chinese, who liked to do things spontaneously. They followed a good life routine and they were trustworthy. Even though they had taught for so many years, they still prepared for every class.

Of course, they were among the successful intellectual elite and could not represent all Americans. What impressed me the most were their humane concerns with the world and their commitment to global welfare. When they got together with friends, they seriously discussed American and international affairs, talked about what was happening in Africa, or Afghanistan, and they knew much about India, Pakistan, and Sri Lanka. And they wanted to find solutions to all these issues. Joe was a pacifist and everything for him was about peace. Their cosmopolitan lens and their genuine concern for humanity were particularly touching to me.

> I did not feel culture shock in the beginning of my studies in the USA. I needed to learn a lot of new things, but language and culture did not present much obstacle to me as I had already become more or less familiar with both while in China. (It took me years to actually understand the impact of cultural differences on my life.) I also came with a strong sense of Chinese cultural identity, as China was (re)emerging as a powerful nation in the middle of the 1990s. My studies of American scholarship were not based upon the assumption that it was better, but upon my wish to learn something different. The belief in cultural equality was the starting point of my journey in the West. I did not suffer from Western rationalism, which usually prevailed in the social sciences, because I was immediately introduced to the deconstruction of Western philosophy and tradition by the Curriculum Theory Project at Louisiana State University. Sometimes I wonder what my life would have been if I had gone to a traditional program. My initial situatedness in an in-between space, rather than having to be assimilated into the mainstream of empiricism, however, has not made for an easy trip, as integrating differences has been a continuing intellectual and emotional challenge.

Joe and Mary were so kind to me and treated me, a stranger from another continent a great distance away, as if I were their son. Once I got sick in the subway and was sent to the hospital. Mary got the news but could not find me. She was so worried and could not do anything but wait for news. She spent hours cleaning the bronze table as a way of passing the time in her anxiety. When I finally came back, she jumped up and put her arms around me crying. The table was shining after her hours of cleaning! I was very moved by her affection.

SONG: As I am looking back on the 20 years of living in the USA, I feel that my life in China was much more eventful than my life in the USA, even though a lot happened there as well. Perhaps because I was Chinese, I got more involved in Chinese life. Perhaps I did not truly feel a part of American society and remained on the margin.

82 Nonviolence and Education

                  Is Chinese life more complicated, more emotional, more up and down, more unpredictable? Or is it because I am a Chinese? It is an important question.

HONGYU: Interesting. You apparently bonded with China as you grew up, and the period of your formative years as a child, teenager, and youth was the most turbulent time in China, so your psychological experiences were more dramatic. By contrast, the American society you entered was more stable, with mature systems.

SONG: Yes, but another reason could be that I was not an American. I remained an outsider in the USA. But in China, even a newly known friend may share his own difficulty with me. It feels like social relationships in China are more intimate, and persons intermingle with each other more freely and more deeply.

HONGYU: At the same time, the mutual invasion of each other's personal space can be stronger.

SONG: That is also true. That is why life in China was more eventful, because boundaries were thin. But I feel at home here. Watching what is going on in this neighborhood makes me feel connected. As a friend says, I am connected to the breath of the earth in China.

The topics of those classes in political science were what I was interested in: change, revolution, reform, peasant movements, industrialization, development, East Asian politics, American politics, and modernization in different countries. The university was a place where all ideas and thoughts came together to stimulate new thought. I was committed to scholarship and wanted to understand all these problems. At that time, I really admired American scholarship and found it more advanced than Chinese scholarship that does not emphasize systematic analysis. In my doctoral studies, I learned the procedures of conceptualization and how to conduct systematic, objective, rational analysis free from emotions and values. I was convinced that their scholarship was better than ours: accurate, reliable, and scientific. So, for that time period, I completely accepted their scholarly traditions and value systems. Those leading American scholars' cosmopolitan lens, world citizenship identity, sophisticated studies, and personal character were all too impressive and fascinating for me to take a critical stance.

When the 1989 students' movement happened, I was in graduate school. We got together every day and were excited, perhaps as excited as the students in Beijing. Since we were professionals in studying politics, we analyzed everything with mixed feelings. Although excited, we did not simply think that the government was bad and the students were innocent. The whole of China would be in total chaos if the movement got out of hand. The struggles within the Communist Party led to bloodshed. It struck me that it was not so useful to study politics because political events were very unpredictable. For instance, the direct cause of the shooting was that the truck carrying guns got into an accident. The various interests involved were too complicated to grasp. It made me realize the limitations of theory. Any important historical event has multiple dimensions, and is never simply black and white. I felt there was naïveté on all sides: Without any strategies or clearly defined goals, political leaders, intellectuals, professors, students, workers, and citizens simply carried on everything without knowing what the next step was.

> My life in the USA brought the memory of the Tiananmen tragedy back to me. During the first year of teaching multicultural education, when I had to struggle with the issue of identity and responsibility in relation to historical trauma, the memory of this traumatic experience in my life returned. Not only because it was a life-or-death event, but also because what happened afterwards in the official cover-up and cleansing of dissenters, plus the students' internal disputes, my voices were silenced. And since I was not the one who was physically injured or the one who became a target of party cleansing, I swallowed the pain without recognizing at that time what a huge loss I suffered. In silence, difficult emotions of sadness, anger, and guilt were also repressed, but they lingered in me, putting invisible walls and barriers in my cross-cultural pathways.

That was probably the beginning of my doubts about concept and theory building because rational analysis could not capture the complexity of political life. I studied the relationship between the Communist Party and the military in China to understand Chinese politics. The one-party regime's exclusive monopoly on violence was negotiated with the army. It took me years to finish writing my dissertation, however, as the strong motivation behind my studies had begun to fade. I spent a year in the University Services Center[6] in Hong Kong, and the intensity of my studies in a small community of China scholars helped me to finish my writing.

HONGYU: I agree with you that American culture has a strong aggressive aspect, and as you state several times, it only wants *yang*, not *yin*. But a lot of passive aggression exists in Chinese culture—in addition to active state violence—which is as damaging as active aggression.
SONG: That's right. Chinese aggression is a chronic torture.
HONGYU: No matter whether it is active violence or passive violence, both are harmful to both the self and the other. If education can soften or dissolve different forms of violence and cultivate nonviolence, more possibilities in humanity can be opened up.
SONG: That is an ideal at the deeper existential level, more important than the system of democracy. Political science deals mainly with systems and policies.

Working in the USA

The first year after graduation, I did not find a job, but I did teach a class at the university. That was my first time to formally teach in the USA, and it was at a prestigious university. So I was very nervous and spent a lot of time fully preparing for the class. I wrote down the lecture notes and then condensed them into outlines. I organized everything along a central theme and laid out a good structure: Those notes were the quintessence of what I had learned. I prepared everything and could recite all the notes. The content of my lectures was excellent although the teaching methods were not very creative. In the class, I lectured for an hour and a half and left half an hour for questions and answers. Students in the class were graduate students, motivated to learn as much as I was motivated to teach. I was pleased that students loved the class and enjoyed its intellectual challenges.

After that year's teaching experience, I found a tenure-track position in a Midwest university. I taught all the courses related to East Asia and a required undergraduate course on American Government. Sometimes I had 300–400 students in that undergraduate class. Imagine how I taught that class! I also taught a class on the history of Western political philosophy—nobody else wanted to teach it. During 10 years of working in that university, I became more and more critical of American thought, systems, and culture. Several aspects contributed to this change.

First, I could not fit into the local culture and the university. My colleagues and I did not share much common ground, and they quickly found out that I was different from them. The intellectual engagement I enjoyed during my doctoral studies with professors, scholars, and classmates no longer existed. Folks around me were not interested in scholarship, and the social activities surrounding football and rodeos did not interest me at all. When I tried to find some space for myself, I was always blocked off from pursuing a different path.

I was teaching East Asian politics but students did not have any curiosity about what happened in those "uncivilized" countries. They were not only ignorant about the outside world, but they were also utterly uninterested in knowing about what they did not know. The American self-centeredness appeared clearly in front of my eyes. To a certain degree, the intellectual circle of my doctoral studies was not free from this self-centeredness either, because subconsciously or consciously, those intellectuals saw themselves as the masters

> My first few years of teaching at Oklahoma State University amounted to another culture shock, a delayed cultural shock that I did not experience when I first came to the USA. But many years of my own emotional work had cultivated my tenacity and endurance, so I could hold on to what was painful, and the inner opening to alternative views helped me to stand on the ground to create a home-place for an alien soul. Attending to students' own inner voices using my third ear has gradually brought me closer to myself, and cultivated a sense of play with differences, and a sense of flow sometimes appears in my teaching.

of the world, and their concern for other countries masked the desire to model the world upon the American system. But their self-centeredness was much more subtle and implicit.

SONG: Why did God create the universe? I have been thinking about this for a long time, and I have found only one answer: play. Look at young children: All they want to do is to play. There is a seed in everyone to play.

HONGYU: Have you introduced this sense of play into your teaching?

SONG: Not really. There were occasions when I told stories and students were curious.

HONGYU: The scholarship you studied in the USA was empirical and did not allow for a sense of play. That was probably part of the reason that you became disillusioned with it.

SONG: The empirical, rational intellectual tradition is the mainstream of American scholarship. It is about thinking your way out, not about playing with the messiness. Playfulness is transcendent. Both teaching and writing should have an element of transcendence, a sense of spirituality. I did not cultivate enough patience for students to carve out a space of playfulness.

Second, I was appalled by the Bush administration. I could not understand how Americans could vote for him not only once but twice. Americans say: Cheated once, shame on you; cheated twice, shame on me. Shame on Americans! There must be something wrong with the system of democracy to elect such a president. I trust the majority of Americans were anti-war, but Bush won over Gore to be re-elected. As I took a more critical stance, I tried to find negative materials for students to debate in class. Sometimes students were unhappy with my position and would give me trouble intentionally.

Third, I had gradually lost interest in political science and further questioned the meaning of scholarship in general. I used to be committed to pursuing truth. But all these theories and models were actually full of holes and did not really reflect reality. I'd had the best education an American graduate school could offer, and I had climbed to the top of the scholarly mountain. So what? When facing reality, could any of these theories help? The purpose of studies was to understand the principles of change and grasp the unfolding of events, but actually, theory did not make any difference, nor could it clarify what was going on. It was like a game. In 1989, I had this vague sense but was not tired of the game yet. After a few years of working in that university, I had more and more doubts about the meaning and significance of scholarship.

Gradually I came to understand that truth and concept were not the same. Truth was not an idea. I used to consider concept, ideology, and theory as the condensed form of idea. I believed that once refined and generalized, concepts could powerfully represent true reality. I would feel liberated to get access to truth. But I realized later that if one stayed at the mental level, one did not get anywhere close to truth. But there is truth. What is truth? Truth is beyond idea. Now as I practice meditation, when I close my eyes and my whole body becomes quiet, there is a life energy emerging from within my body: That is truth.

> Truth had never been my main concern. I came to the field of education due to a romantic notion of education as a profession of love and relationality, thanks to Russian educators' books sitting on my mother's book shelf. Mom was strongly opposed to my choice of teaching, and our compromise ended up with my majoring in education as a generalist and not majoring in any subject area at college. (Little did we know that it would become a major obstacle for me to find a job in American teacher education since everybody is supposed to have a subject area, including curriculum generalists.) In my studies and work in education, I have been truthful and faithful to my existential concerns about the role of education in cultivating personhood.

I discovered that modern Western philosophy and social science, including political science, mostly stayed at the superficial level: To think your way out, think your way out of trouble, think your way into truth, think your way to peace and justice. It is a hopeless enterprise to stay at the mental level. Conflicts can never be resolved: You have an idea, I have another idea, and an idea can be changed almost at will. You have a theory, but I can immediately propose a different theory: Which one is real? Which one is true? The concepts of right/wrong and good/evil lead to all kinds of war and violence. But life is beyond concept, beyond idea.

When I questioned academics, I also looked elsewhere for answers. Since Christianity was an important aspect of Western civilization, I attended many religious activities, including the high-level National Prayer Breakfast. But as I experienced it more, I found that mainstream Christianity also stayed at the mental level with built-in dualism: Good versus bad, right versus wrong, heaven versus hell. So it was actually similar to Western science in its emphasis on preserving *yang* and eliminating *yin*. Americans only want half of existence: Democracy versus authoritarianism, stability versus instability, and certainty versus uncertainty. One part is good and the other is bad, and they try to build systems to ensure the good part and eliminate the bad part, without realizing they are two sides of one coin.

I have found that there is a branch of mysticism in every religion that goes beyond the conceptual level. It is in Judaism, Christianity, Buddhism, and Islam. But the difference between Eastern religion and Western religion is that mysticism is more part of the mainstream of Eastern religion than in Western religion. There has been a long history of suppressing mystics in Christianity, for instance. The development of science and technology in the West followed the mental pathway of rationality and is compatible with the mainstream Christian religion. It can be quite destructive.

SONG: The real truth is One, the *Tao* that cannot be split, the *Tao* that is an eternal, unchanging force, including both *yin* and *yang,* including all aspects of life.
HONGYU: Why do you call it "one," not "zero"?
SONG: It does not matter what name we use to label it. For example, in Laozi and Zhuangzi's philosophy, it is sometimes termed "alone"; it is unique. *Tao* is one, and devoted to the middle way.
HONGYU: I don't like this "one" because autocracy is one, like the Chinese political system. "Zero" is more inclusive.
SONG: Yes, I understand what you mean. It is "zero," but that "zero" is not nothing. Everything is in it. If you like "zero," you can call it "zero," but its name is not important.

Fourth, I began to practice meditation. It was crucial to my efforts to go beyond the difficulty I had with the academic path. As I was losing interest in scholarship, I began to explore other things. Disappointed in Western thought, I came back to Eastern thought. I came across Tolle's (1999 [2004]) book *The Power of Now* on cassettes. It had an immediate influence on me: I was captivated by his calm yet powerful voice. I found a lot of books on similar topics and read whatever I could find. In the beginning, my meditation practice was sporadic, but experiencing the awakening of Kundalini[7] (without knowing its name when it happened), I became fully committed to yoga and meditation practices.

The first Kundalini awakening happened a couple of days after I felt a huge pain in my heart. When I was walking in the corridor to go to class, the pain hit me out of nowhere. I went to the medical center for examination, but everything turned out to be normal. I took a few days off to rest. Then one day in my room, as I sat for meditation, all of a sudden, energy came from the base of my spine right up to my head, and there

| I began to practice calligraphy (only for a while) and *Taijiquan* (periodically) after a few years of living in the USA. I never thought about practicing them in China. But the tension I had felt in my body in a third space urged me to pick up those practices well-known for restoring balance. The strokes of my brush and the movement of my body do bring a sense of flow that I would love to have in my life, even just momentarily. The intensity of my emotions gradually dissolves as my hand paints the black ink onto the white paper, or when I move to the rhythm of *Taiji.* After years of working in teacher education, I have been able to feel more at ease with tensions in teaching, leading to spontaneity and creativity in the classroom. I wish it would happen more often. The emotional knots, the old and the new, quietly began to loosen as more flow of life let go their stubborn hold. |

appeared a white light like lightening: The room where I was disappeared, my self disappeared, and I was just sitting there in total bliss. Although mysterious to me, I later found out that it happened to many other people with or without meditation practices. Apparently, I did not have any heart problem; perhaps the blocked energy was on its way out. As I regularly practiced meditation later, I felt that meditation gradually removed the dirt from my body and cleaned off the psychological traumas I had suffered for many years. I am curious to know what else is going to happen after more practice: There is a lot of talk about different miracles.

SONG: Meditation has changed my viewpoints about life. Now I feel that this energy is the original source of the universe, is what you call "zero." It is the root for a myriad of things in the universe; it is truth.

HONGYU: The root of a myriad of things cannot be truth.

SONG: So called "truth," or we can call it "life."

HONGYU: "Life" is better than "truth."

SONG: Your life and my life and everybody's life are from the same source. Like the ocean, every wave is part of the ocean. All languages and all poetry are all trying to capture this source. It is heart. It is consciousness. Before I was born, it was already there. I have traveled in a circle: China, USA, Ph.D., teaching, research. Now I no longer care about what I cared about before: Democracy, justice, development, modernization, and nationalism are no longer that important. The world is an interconnected community, humanity is shared, and we are all brothers and sisters, coming from the same energy.

HONGYU: But engagement with life is still important. Without engagement, one cannot reach deeper interconnectedness. Like Mother Teresa, her energy was infused in her engagement with worldly affairs.

SONG: There is no dualistic opposite between engagement and nonattachment. They are mutually exchangeable: Nonattachment at the extreme becomes engagement and engagement at the extreme leads to nonattachment. They are intertwined.

I decided to go back to China, even though I could practice meditation in the USA. After I went through all the dramas in both countries, I still feel more connected to China, and coming back to China makes me feel whole. I am now teaching political science to both Chinese students and international students. I am not enthusiastic about teaching since my value system has changed. I still teach about why China fell behind in the 19th century, why China went through revolutions, what Mao's strategies were, why the Open Door policy was adopted later, and what problems the reform encountered. But I no longer believe in democracy, modernization, and capitalism; instead, I think that there are fatal problems within capitalism and that modernization has become a tool for imposing the Western model upon other countries such as China. Reform in the sense of pursuing instrumental reason is meaningless. If I could become a sort of spiritual teacher, it would be more interesting. But I cannot speak out clearly now even though I experience it deeply in my heart. I have to wait until I find the right language if I want to follow that path.

> The moment when I saw the image of the Great Wall moving in front of my eyes, I knew the national boundary no longer confined my loyalty. The cross-cultural bridge I have stepped on is no longer a bridge but an intercultural non-bridge passage (Aoki, 2005) in which I dwell with a free spirit. Though my cultural roots will remain deep and strong in my heart, the guilt and loss I had felt unconsciously in leaving China had softened, and the emotional knot that was fastened by the terrible trauma in 1989 finally loosened. I felt freer to walk on my own pathways incorporating the multiple, not constrained by pre-existing patterns.

What I have learned in my own cross-cultural journey is out of the mainstream without instrumental value, so I don't want to mislead the younger generation since they are at the stage of climbing up the mountain before seeing through the surface of life. Sometimes in teaching, I introduce a bit of my own perspective such as that modernization can become a curse. But I cannot go deeper, and on most occasions I stay with the usual path, which I no longer believe in. Teaching does not take much effort now, though, and students appreciate my classes.

Now I stay at the level of lucid dreaming: When one is dreaming, one knows that one is dreaming and the dream is not true. Life is like a dream; clarity is needed to see it through. There are two versions of the self: the small self and the big self. The small self is dreaming while the big self is watching the small self who is dreaming. Such an eternal watching leads to peace and happiness. Loss does not matter; gain does not matter; everything is honored. It does not mean not to engage, but the best is to engage the world in a transcendent manner with nonattachment.

Even though I still identify as a middle-class intellectual, identity is no longer important to me. I've lost the instrumental heart. My journey to the USA was meaningful because if I had not lived through it, I would not be able to see through the futility of reason. Now, the Chinese are most concerned with the material level of life. I think individual freedom and liberation are more possible in Western postmodern society. Westerners suffer more from instrumental rationality, so they resist it more. They also have more

> Water has a spirit, and I always like a place with water running through it. Where there is water, there is usually a mountain. Mountains and rivers are one of most important themes of traditional Chinese painting. My memories of places are usually tied to water. My youngest sister lives in a port city in China, and when I visited her for a month during my sabbatical leave in 2009, I climbed the mountain behind her apartment every day and breathed the fresh air from the ocean. In those difficult times in my life, water accompanied my pondering steps quietly and comfortingly. Water connects different landscapes. Water also speaks. I have learned to listen to water, attentively.

access to resources and information, so they may find more pathways through which to pursue spiritual transcendence.

Now as I look back on my life in that university town in the Midwest where I stayed for 10 years, I feel like it was a sacred place. Although it arrested my soul for a long time, once I worked through boredom, depression, and anger, I found peace and joy within the self. There was a lake near where I lived and I spent a lot of time walking along the lake. Water has a spirit, and it is connected with the life energy within me. The eternal truth emerges naturally when one can become truly quiet to experience peace, joy, and love. Now I am a hermit in a cosmopolitan city with the future open to what life energy will bring to me.

SONG: I have come full circle after walking the path of Western rationalism. In the beginning I worshipped it, and then I negated it, but it was a partial negation. I have also learned from it. The struggle in the West is orderly, following principles, and operates through different interest groups. Chinese *yin* and *yang* mingle together and change all the time according to contexts. The Chinese situation cannot be managed well because there is always a personal element in it. Western conceptualization attempts to achieve eternity through manipulating forms to create a world of peace, justice, and prosperity. But *Tao* is beyond forms.

HONGYU: The form—political science—through which you reach the formless *Tao* is still a useful tool that you have played with.

SONG: Yes, it was an important medium. *Tao Te Ching* says, "The *Tao* that can be spoken is not the constant *Tao*."[8] It cannot be spoken clearly. It is most clear when we are at the state of zero. Afterwards, it becomes chaotic when we try to speak about it. But then we have to speak about it, because it is a journey.

HONGYU: The insights are usually reached *after* one's pursuit of a particular pathway, even though afterwards the pathway is no longer important. But the West is not alone in pursuing instrumental reason. It existed in China, too, although not at the Western metaphysical level.

SONG: I don't like Confucian moral reason, either. Confucianism is located between Western philosophy and Eastern religion. Due to different levels of development, China currently is mainly pursuing physical or material forms, and the West is still predominantly pursuing mental forms, but the third level lies in energy that is beyond physical and mental forms. In Buddhism, any form

	is secondary. Science and technology cannot liberate humanity. But the third level does not negate forms per se. The issue is not to pursue any form in extreme.

HONGYU: Yes, the fierce challenges to Western rationalism also come from within the West.

SONG: East or West, instrumental reason cannot lead to the desired destination: Gain and loss go hand in hand. The true tragedy, according to WANG Guowei,[9] is not accidental damage or the hurt caused by others' malicious acts, but is the loss in the natural course of life. Nothing is permanent: first gain it, then lose it. Buddhism is interested in losing it after obtaining it; Taoism is interested in obtaining *Tao* through losing the self. If you could see through the true tragedy, life becomes a comedy.

HONGYU: How can it become a comedy?

SONG: Because we all come back to the ocean. Or we don't need to call it comedy, but everything goes back to the same source which gives birth to everything. The journey through life is still important, so coming back to the original is not the same as the original starting point. I feel very lucky that I have overcome the fear of death before I actually die.

Stories in Context

Putting into parallel Song's stories, our conversations, and my brief autobiographical narrations, I intend to leave readers room for pondering, questioning, and relating their own lived experience in a global society, so I resist bringing different elements back into a neat analytical discussion. One aspect worth mentioning, however, is that I purposefully highlight the contrast of my concerns with emotional life with Song's pursuit of truth. Although concerned that this arrangement may reinforce gendered stereotypes, I intend to show different pathways. But a category is usually arbitrary, since truth and feelings can be integrated. For example, Gandhi's notion of nonviolence as truth is an organic integration of knowledge, emotion, and action (Easwaran, 1972 [1997]). In this sense, truth and emotion can be woven into a meditative mindfulness that cultivates nonviolence. Furthermore, highlighting our different pathways also intends to show that excessive concern with either knowing or feeling needs to be emptied out in order to establish nonviolent relationships with both the self and the other.

In the following discussion, I situate Song's life stories in the cultural history of China and the intellectual history of political science in the USA. I focus on two important aspects that greatly impacted Song's cross-cultural life: the Cultural Revolution and Western rationalism.

The Violence of the Cultural Revolution and Its Impact

Jing Lin (1991) asserts that "it is impossible to understand today's China without understanding the Cultural Revolution" (p. 1), an assertion that rings particularly true for understanding Song's life history. It is beyond the scope of this chapter to discuss the complicated pictures of the Cultural Revolution in China, but since its impact on Song was so profound, I attempt to provide a sketch.

The Cultural Revolution was officially announced as the Great Proletarian Cultural Revolution in which the proletarian masses mobilized to overthrow both feudal/reactionary and bourgeois ideologies and to cleanse society and culture of any elements that did not align with the Communist ideal (Spence, 1990). The Cultural Revolution went through different stages: The first two years (1966–1968) were marked by youthful Red Guards' destructive activities against authorities and traditions, incited by Chairman Mao (for factors contributing to the Red Guards' path to violence, see Lin, 1991); the following few years were marked by the intervention of the People's Liberation Army to control the chaos created by the Red Guards; and the next stage was the consolidating period with political instability in the 1970s (between 1971 when Mao forced out the Army head and 1976 when Mao passed away). The enemy classes included landlords, rich peasants, bourgeois, counter-revolutionary or reactionary intellectuals, and other categories depending on the political situation at the time. But the enemy line was volatile since one's ally today could become an enemy tomorrow. The classification of revolutionaries versus counter-revolutionaries was also changeable, as many different authorities were under attack during different periods throughout the chaotic 10 years.

Categorical thinking, as Lin (1991) points out, became a source of the Red Guards' violence. What was peculiar about these 10 years, ironically, was that the hierarchy could be turned upside down quickly, so categorical rigidity and the constant collapse of categories coexisted in reality, leaving individual persons at the mercy of the collective mobilization. As Song's stories reveal, Red Guards' activities in the rural areas were in direct contrast with those in the city, and the domination of diplomats' children over working-class children was contrary to the official ideology. While class and revolutionary dualism intended to create a new order, it effectively created chaos. Contradictions were abundant in the "unique combination of anarchy and dictatorship, of strident popular rebellion and coercive state action" (Esherick, Pickowicz, & Walder, 2006, p. 18) under Mao's absolute authority. Uniformity of thinking and highly individualized ways of survival also coexisted. Song had survived small and big storms—what was included in this chapter was only a small part of what he went through—by improvising fluid responses in order to minimize the damage of violence.

The violence of the Cultural Revolution has been well documented, including the Red Guards' crimes against their elders and their internal fights leading to death, murder, and suicide (Lin, 1991; Mitter, 2004; Walder, 2009); the persecution and cleansing of dissenters involving the army's participation, which resulted in many more casualties than the Red Guards' attacks (Spence, 1990); Mao's deliberate manipulation of mass movements to serve his own interests (Fairbank, 1986; Spence, 1990); the destruction of national economic, social, and cultural infrastructures (MacFarquhar & Schoenhals, 2006); the destruction of Chinese traditions, religions, and customs; the violation of human dignity and trust (Li, 2002); the devastating forces released by the massive participation of rebel factional organizations and their struggles against one another (Esherick, Pickowicz, & Walder, 2006); and the uniformity of political, cultural, and personal life imposed on all Chinese people (Esherick, Pickowicz, & Walder, 2006). No list can exhaust the destructive impact of the Cultural Revolution.

Although I grew up after the Cultural Revolution, reading those accounts and novels—it was called "trauma literature" (Hong, 1999 [2007])—was a horrifying experience for me when I was a teenager. I think the biggest crime of the Cultural Revolution was to unleash the worst aspects of human cruelty and to expel the compassionate side of humanity to produce various forms of violence against human beings, including but not limited to physical, intellectual, social, emotional, cultural, and spiritual violence. Many Chinese, however, refused to give in to its nightmares and chose to keep the spirit of human connectedness alive, and many stories describe the prevailing of the human spirit in the darkness.

Song lived through the Cultural Revolution during his formative years and youth, and its impact on his life was irreversible. His school education and identity formation were violently interrupted, and the emotional and psychological traumas the Cultural Revolution inflicted on him cannot be overemphasized. But not all the impact was negative because he learned how to play with boundaries, accumulated inner strength to make sense out of non-sense (Kristeva, 2000), and transformed his sense of the self.

Song grew up on the street confused, scared, and unsettled. In elementary school, he had already tasted the threat of being attacked at a struggle meeting by his peers, simply because of one comment. Witnessing those teenagers (a bit older than he was) exercising violence upon others, watching the horrible aggression that the Red Guards unleashed in mass movements, later experiencing authority's abuse of power in villages and factories, Song's inner landscape was permanently marked by the horror of human violence. As his stories show, the dualism of the Cultural Revolution in its march to destroy enemy classes went against itself because the ever-changing power struggles led to blurred boundaries and interchangeable categories. Song experienced how messy life could be when the traditional moral dualism collapsed and the political dualism was accompanied by social anarchy.

Living through such a chaotic time under Mao's dictatorship, it is no wonder that Song embraced Western democracy at college in China, and it is not surprising that Western rationalism with its promise of truth and stability was appealing to him during his doctoral studies in the USA. The vivid memories of his encounters during the Cultural Revolution revealed the depth of its influence over his psyche in multidimensional and even conflicting ways, and I believe that its legacy also contributed to his later disenchantment with the mainstream Western intellectual leadership because he knew from his gut feeling that life could not be controlled neatly.

Since life situations during the Cultural Revolution were imposed on Song, he had to improvise through cracks to find space for himself in his negotiation with outside forces. He developed a particular way of resistance, a Taoist way, which did not return the attack with a direct counter-attack, but curved its power around to find more spaces for freedom. Song cultivated a strategy of curving movement that could not be easily crushed by authority, and he did not give in to authority. This strategy helped him escape from the harshest punishments for his "wrongdoings" in the countryside, at the factory, and later, after the Cultural Revolution, at college in China, yet it allowed him to express his own thoughts and feelings that were different from the mainstream of that time to assert his independence. He also used this strategy when he had difficulties in the USA after he crossed the border. His *Taiji* movements, persistent and resilient, helped him overcome all kinds of obstacles in cross-cultural settings. Surviving the Cultural Revolution, he had gained a strength that is unconventional, a strength that incorporates the endurance of softness (Wang, 2008), a strength that requires "improvisation" (Aoki, 2005; Li, 2002) to negotiate with and among the multiple. Song went to the USA carrying pain, endurance, and creativity as a survivor of the Cultural Revolution.

Born into an intellectual family who had to be "reformed," Song did not belong to the proletarian class. Intellectuals were an ambiguous category in the political dualism of the proletarian class against enemy classes, sometimes belonging to the "right" side if they followed the "right" party line, but often thrown into the enemy camp. Song crossed different social landscapes, including living in the rural areas as a teenager and then working in a factory for years while at the same time visiting a high-level official family. Reflecting on the diversity of social classes that he encountered, Song believed that the years of working at the factory had greatly influenced him and raised his political consciousness of social inequality and injustice. As painful as it was, Song considered his factory experience a meaningful way to understand others' lives. After encountering and experiencing different individual's lives, including those of intellectuals, peasants, workers, and elites, Song still identified himself as a middle-class intellectual, but he felt deeper connections with people from all different social backgrounds. Since his further journey in the USA and his embracing of meditative philosophy and practices, identity is no longer important to him: "Authentic self is no self." Now he sees everything and everybody as part of the web of life and affirms non-identity.

Disillusion with Western Rationalism

White (2009) credits Chinese and Chinese-American researchers, especially the cohort of Chinese students who entered tertiary education in 1977–78 after Chinese universities reopened, for vitalizing the American field of China Studies in political science, because they brought new perspectives and new lenses as insiders to broaden the field: The Chinese interconnected perspective on politics, philosophy, and culture is one of these contributions. Many of these students graduated in China in the beginning of the 1980s and went to American universities for their graduate studies. White commented that "their intellectual wattage was exceptional, as was their will to understand China's politics" (p. 230). Song was one of those students who carried his passion for seeking truth to the USA with a strong desire to understand Chinese politics and learn from American intellectuals, without much concern for external rewards.

Similar to those in the field of Chinese history in the USA, American scholars in political science have moved from using an exclusive Western lens to incorporating a more complicated lens to understand Chinese politics. Nina Halpern (1993) identified three paradigms in the postwar period: totalitarian, pluralist, and institutionalist. The Cold War mentality undoubtedly produced an antagonistic mode (White, 2009) in the 1950s and 1960s, which led to the dominant "totalitarian" paradigm "that assumed a basically unified leadership" (Halpern, 1993, p. 121) imposing policies from the central control to understand Chinese politics. The Cultural Revolution in China changed this lens and the field moved to a more "pluralist" paradigm, which identified the major competing groups to discover which actors or coalitions of actors were more powerful in determining policies. In the 1980s, structural concerns about "how institutions or structures—meaning enduring patterns of political authority, not simply formal institutions—shape political actors' interests, ideas, and resources" (p. 125) became important. What followed were studies of interactive local and central bargaining processes that cannot be predetermined by any single factor. These shifts reflect the larger changing field of American political science, but they are also related to the changes in American academics in a postcolonial and postmodern global society to unsettle Western-centered readings of other cultures.

Song's doctoral studies were situated in this changing intellectual landscape. He did not perceive Chinese politics through the totalitarian lens. For him, leadership was hardly unified, and Mao as the central figure did not have total control over the party or military leadership, which was why Mao had to initiate the Cultural Revolution in order to restore and solidify his power. Song did not believe that the Western framework of competing interest groups could explain Chinese politics well, and he saw Chinese society as highly situational and contextualized, influenced by personal and local negotiations with rules. Later, when he began to ponder the personal and social meanings of politics and political life, none of the existing paradigms could address his existential concerns.

At the beginning of his doctoral studies, Song was preoccupied with all kinds of questions about China and hoped to answer those questions—for instance why China was lagging behind—through learning from the West. All the issues discussed in the political science classes interested him greatly. He not only got the best education through graduate school but had firsthand experiences with the American intellectual elite. The Western pursuit of reason, truth, and democracy—the *yang* aspect of human life as Song phrased it in later years—provided the comfort he needed to make sense of the painful experiences he had gone through in China. However, as he reached the limit of the masculine power and climbed to the top of the scholarly mountain, *Tao* turned his attention around to the feminine flow of life and led him downward to dwell in a generative energy of stillness. The dynamic of *Tao* is initiated by the mutual embeddedness and changeability of opposite forces, symbolically expressed in *yin* (feminine, receptive cosmic energy) and *yang* (masculine, aggressive cosmic energy), which are both available to man and woman. When one opposite accumulates strength to an extreme degree, the direction of the dynamics will change so that the other force plays a more important role. Seeing through the "tough guise" (Jhally, 1999) of Western masculine rationalism, Song's cross-cultural pathways eventually led him to engage receptive energy and integrate opposite aspects of life. SHEN Heyong (2004), a pioneer in bridging Jungian analytic psychology and Chinese Taoism, links Taoist integration with Jungian individuation. Just as Carl Jung suggests individuation as the middle-life task (Mayes, 2005), Song has stepped onto such a path in his middle-life stage to empty out instrumental concerns and to turn inward for existential insights, integrations, and wisdom.

Furthermore, the dominance of the empirical research methodology in Western social science became increasingly problematic for Song. Similar to American educational science, "American political science has now privileged statistical over non-statistical research in all fields, regardless of the results in knowledge about politics. So China hands increasingly generate, find, and crunch numbers, hoping the data may be meaningful" (White, 2009, p. 245). Such an over-concern with empirical data in American political science contributed to Song's disillusion with the mainstream academic field. For him, those surveys did not produce meaning and certainly did not contribute to understanding what was really happening in the political world. At first he used empirical data, but then he realized that numbers could not represent human life in its complexity, richness, and unpredictability.

Importantly, it was his life experiences in the West that led him to return to Eastern philosophy and meditation practices. Initially his studies at the university and the intellectual circles of his host families opened a whole new world for him, and his intellectual advancement went hand in hand with his admiration of those intellectual elites and their way of life both in the family and in public. Their hospitality for others and cosmopolitan viewpoints provided a home-like atmosphere for Song. I wonder what Song's academic life would have been if he had gone to a conservative college town instead of a cosmopolitan university city in his first 10 years of studies, and to what degree that would have influenced his relationships with mainstream Western scholarship. In the second 10 years, he ended up working in a conservative college town where his life experiences were hardly inspiring or pleasant. Song did not feel he belonged in its cultural, political, and academic climate, and clear demonstrations of American self-centeredness from his students and colleagues made him question the foundation of American society and American scholarship. While in the final years of his studies, he had already begun to lose his strong passion for truth, his life experiences in that Midwest town greatly contributed to his disillusionment. Those walks along the lake near his university passed the spirit of water into his wandering steps and led him to the source of life beyond idea. He did not give up truth per se, however; instead, he now experiences truth in stillness.

As he began to read Eastern philosophies and religions, he also practiced meditation and yoga, although he did not follow any particular branch but followed his own insight in practices. The first Kundalini awakening marked a turning point in his spiritual journey, and in that sudden illuminating moment, his life was transformed. As he continued his practices, stillness spoke from within. Diving into stillness to embrace life energy, Song felt liberated from external and internal constraints to walk a path of his own, regardless of what happened in the outside world. Even though he could practice meditation anywhere, he decided to go back to China, as he felt more connected to his homeland.

Improvisation Against Violence, Non-duality, and Inner Peace

To a certain degree, both David and Song shared their efforts to understand the Chinese situation better, and both wrestled with the question of democracy. But the intersection of their pathways quickly diverged. Engagement was the key to David's search for answers, but nonattachment became Song's way back to his origin. I discussed in Chapter 2 different intellectual and political positions in Chinese intellectual history: conservative, reformist, and revolutionary. The conservative position held on to the status quo, the reformist position advocated change (either gradual, instrumental change or more substantial change), and the revolutionary position pursued overthrowing the existing power structure and reestablishing a new order. But I have not discussed the hermit tradition with which Song became identified. Critiquing the status quo, hermits withdraw from the political and social turbulence to pursue their own spiritual freedom, believing that neither reform nor revolution will work.

Historically, the hermit tradition has been long established in China and remains respected and respectful, with considerable influence over Chinese aesthetics and indirectly over politics (Hu, 2011; Shi, 2010; Wen, 2009). Artists, disillusioned politicians, and scholars who had talent but retreated from secular affairs have been among the hermits. Only intellectuals who were well-educated with in-depth knowledge, insight, and wisdom can be considered hermits. The historically intimate relationship between intellectual thought and politics (through the tradition of the intellectual-official) and between intellectual thought and aesthetics (through the bridge of Chinese language connecting Chinese thought, calligraphy, painting, and poetry) makes a sharp demarcation between intellect, art, and politics impossible, but the identity and identification of the intellectual lies at the heart of the hermit tradition. We have many tales of wise scholars living in the woods and mountains in ancient China, secluded from society, refusing to become officials even if invited by the king. In contemporary China, the turbulence of the 20th century and the speed of modernization and globalization have made it almost impossible to be a hermit, although the spirit of the tradition survives.

What is interesting about Song's stories is that he became a hermit in a cosmopolitan city, meditating in his own room away from the world while still enjoying the company of the busy street life when he steps outside of his home. Song did not make a full separation from society, still teaching regularly and enjoying the sounds of the city life, but he minimized social activities and does not participate in any university affairs except teaching. The spirit of his thought and action was free from external constraint, and he has achieved a great deal of inner peace, which made him a contemporary hermit without dwelling in the wildness of nature or in a secluded place. According to Cui (1992), Zhuangzi's ideal is to be a hermit who pursues spiritual freedom in secular life, rather than secluded from society. It is no coincidence that Song appreciated Zhuangzi's teachings more than Laozi's teachings.[10] He felt that an implicit instrumentalism still existed in *Tao Te Ching*, but not in *Zhuangzi*, whose transcendence was more complete. As Shi (2010) argues, the notion of the hermit in China has evolved from a political concept to a way of life. Song embodied such a way of life, and as much as he pursued freedom from secular concerns, Song's transformation was based upon his deeper understanding of the interconnected nature of life—including human life—and it was this sense of connecting with others that made it unnecessary for him to separate from society.

Looking at Song's life history, from the time when he rebelled against the "sacred" Cultural Revolution as a young schoolboy, Song remained critical of the conservative mainstream. Neither was he an advocate for revolution. Going through the Cultural Revolution, he witnessed the damage that could be done by massive movements manipulated by authority figures. He reacted to the 1989 tragedy a bit differently from David. The fear of another chaotic time exercised through "popular justice" (Foucault 1977; Miller, 1993) in an unconstrained mass rebellion must have been at work in his reactions. Song could not forget the crimes of the Red Guards who were students. They did not merely follow Mao's order blindly, but as Jonathan D. Spence (1990) points out, the unleashing of rage and violence against elders was related to multiple dissatisfactions among those different groups of youth (pp. 606–607). Two decades later, while excited about the possibility of a democracy-in-the-making with students' nonviolent protests and demonstrations in contrast to the youthful violence two decades earlier, Song also had his reservations. For him, the call for democracy was not substantiated by any clear goal or strategy, but people from different social groups simply participated in voicing their dissatisfactions. I did not experience the Cultural Revolution, but I appreciate his concerns, because when I was in Beijing in 1989, I felt everything could have collapsed in a moment.

When Song went to the USA, he was a reformist seeking more self-understanding—the individual self and the cultural self—and looking for ways to reform China to catch up with the West. From a reformist pathway, however, Song turned in another direction to become a hermit. For Song, the highest ideal was to engage life in a nonattached way, but right then he wanted to concentrate on meditation and see how far he could go. I was most intrigued by his capacity to create a hermit lifestyle within the noise of the Chinese academic world and to stay on that path despite its unpopularity. Although his administrators in China were not happy with his minimum public engagement, they gradually began to accept it, especially since no one else could teach international classes as well as he could. He gained a hermit reputation among his colleagues and occasionally they refer to his style positively as an exemplar of a different way of life.

I also struggled with his hermit position; even though there is a hermit within me, engagement is also important. Since I felt that he had so much to offer others, I could not help but challenge his nonattachment once in a while, suggesting: "What if you become a spiritual teacher?" On the other hand, Song challenged my dualistic thinking throughout our interactions. Such a mutual challenge can be seen clearly in the dialogues above. Duality is not only part of Western thinking; it can be inherent in all thinking. It is the nature of thinking to separate the knower and the known, at least to a certain degree. Non-duality (Loy, 1988) in Buddhist and Taoist approaches is hardly achieved and practiced by many Chinese either. Even though I appreciate Taoist and Buddhist principles, I still tend to split things into good or bad, but Song was at ease bringing the split back to the whole due to years of meditation practices. Disciplined cultivation of stillness of mind had given him a clarity that I did not have. To deconstruct dualism and achieve the insight that "subjects and objects only exist *interdependently*" (Vokey, 2008, p. 302; emphasis in the original), we cannot rely on thinking alone. Practices of meditative stillness seem to be necessary.

Song also demonstrated his nonattachment to ideas or concepts by following my own arguments and using the language of my own preference to express similar ideas. The dispute between one and zero is a good example. He no longer cared much about the name itself and did not insist on any particular term, but neither did he hesitate to interrupt my thinking when needed. To achieve inner peace requires the cultivation of a non-dualistic mind and an interconnected heart. Song was at peace with himself in residing in his native birth place—a place he did not remember but was reconnected with—and living a hermit life with a deeper yet non-clinging sense of connectedness with people and life in general.

In Song's case, inner peace came from living through and working through all kinds of drama, not only eventual dramas but also subjective dramas. One important lesson I have learned from Song's stories is the role of his noncooperation with and improvisation against violence, even when violence was at its peak during the Cultural Revolution. Noncooperation with violence was enacted on a local scale for Song, either individually or in small groups. The voting trial did involve a lot of students, however, so its influence extended to the whole university. In the story of stealing money from the lost-and-found box as a teenager, his concern with his mother's reactions stopped him from running away, and he would not give in to peer pressure. Making that choice, he was facing the possibility of being attacked in a struggle meeting by the whole school, but his concern about causing pain to the beloved one made him stay to confront possible violence. Such an inner compass supported him through the turbulence of his life. In the story of asserting the constitutional right to religious freedom as a factory worker, his own perspectives leaked out, but he would not give in to the authority who threatened to incite collective violence upon him. He insisted that he had done nothing wrong in saying that the Chinese constitution allowed religious freedom. In the story of the voting trial at college, he participated in, or led behind the scenes, political critiques of the existing system, and when the situation became worse, he and his friends insisted that they were only following the call of the party for reform to push the issue aside and avoid being arrested. In the latter two cases, Song followed the official line *to make it go against its own logic;* by revealing the inner contradictions within the party line, he negotiated a space to legitimize his noncooperation with violence.

In all these stories, Song prepared for the worst to happen, but interestingly, the worst in all three cases did not happen, and he was able to survive all the storms. Although he felt that he did not directly initiate efforts to go against authorities, I find his improvisation in following the flow and finding strategies to swim out of turbulent water without giving in to authorities illuminating. In dark times, direct confrontations with the terror of violence can lead to destruction (as many Chinese were killed or committed suicide), yet giving in to violence eliminates human conscience and independence. Negotiating with the situation, Song found ways of surviving difficulties according to what the situation required without giving up his own conscience. Song phrased it as the way of staying in the middle. This middle position of improvisation (Li, 2002) is not an easy position to maintain, as it dwells within the unpredictability and uncertainty of an unfolding event and it requires insightful readings of both involved parties and the situation. As I discussed earlier, this mode of resistance is different, engaging power relationships in specifically critical ways and exerting its influence through the ripple effect as people at his school, factory, and university were shown alternative possibilities for challenging injustice through noncooperation.

Song's noncooperation went together with his ability to improvise fluid movements out of trouble. He had to work through cracks or "interstitials" (Gazetas, 2003) of categorical thinking both in China and in the USA to carve out a space for his own thoughts and feelings. Ted T. Aoki (1990 [2005]), drawing upon jazz musicians' wisdom, approaches improvisation as "a way to create spaces to allow differences [in the lived world of teachers and students] to show through" (p. 368). This capacity to improvise is also intimately related to the process of musical instruments, music, and body becoming one "in a living wholeness" (p. 368). Song's improvisation allowed him to sustain his differences from dominant lines of thinking, yet he was also successful in revealing the contradictions within the official ideology to curve the force of its violence away. His ability to improvise according to the situation also helped his cross-cultural journey in the USA, which was more gradual than dramatic. His meditative practices of cultivating a non-dualistic unity within himself in the latter part of his life could not be separated from his life experiences of surviving violence and improvising cross-cultural pathways.

With the expansion of Chinese higher education, under the pressure of modernization and globalization, and in the high speed of both Internet and scholarly production, it is almost unimaginable that an overseas professor could return to China to live a hermit life, yet Song was able to accomplish such an impossibility with a certain degree of acceptance by his colleagues and administrators. I think this accomplishment was also a result of his improvised, nonviolent negotiations. Improvisation against violence, in Song's case, set the background for his getting in touch with the interconnected spirit of life to heal the splits caused by violence, and experiencing the liberating effects of non-duality through meditation led to a sense of calmness. With inner calmness, he could settle what was restless in the outside world.

Song's stories of non-duality, improvisation against violence, and inner peace have important implications for nonviolence education. An educator with such an inner peace also has the capacity to settle what is unsettling, not by transmitting knowledge but by weaving the tensionality of life into the whole to bring clarity and open alternatives. Such an ability to weave is dependent upon educators' capacity to see conflicting sides of the same issue and follow the two courses at the same time in an interconnected web of life. When situated in a broader context, what are initially perceived as conflicts become connected parts of the whole. Here Zhuangzi's story about the monkey and the monkey trainer is particularly illuminating:

> Once upon a time, there was a monkey keeper who was feeding little chestnuts to his charges. "I'll give you three in the morning, and four in the evening," he told them. All the monkeys were angry. "All right, then," said the keeper: "I will give you four in the morning, and three in the evening." All the monkeys were happy with this arrangement. Without adversely affecting either the name or the reality of the amount that he fed them, the keeper acted in accordance with the feelings of the monkeys. He too recognized the mutual dependence of "this" and "that." Consequently, the sage harmonizes the right and wrong of things and rests at the center of the celestial potter's wheel. (*Chuang Tzu* [Zhuangzi], Chapter 2, translated by Mair, 1994, p. 16–17)

This ability to follow two courses at the same time and choose either direction depending on the needs of the context provides a deep insight into the ways things are and goes beyond the confinement of either right or wrong. Song followed the wheel of life to reach the transcendence of dualism. Conflicting situations can be solved with a shift of the lens, a lens that sees through problems for a bigger picture to open different possibilities. This Taoist playfulness with paradoxes and contradictions emanates a sense of humor that relieves the fixation of any orthodoxy. Song was able to see through the intellectual violence—a term I used first and Song adopted—of Western instrumental reason to become playful. He was not only playful with ideas but also playful with the Chinese language after his cross-cultural journey (I will discuss his insights into language in Chapter 5). Education for, about, and through nonviolence needs to be playful rather than serious (see the final Chapter 0).

In the university where he completed his doctoral studies, the intellectual elites saw Song's teaching as successful because his passions and expertise meant much to his students, who were already motivated to learn. His teaching of students in that Midwest American university coincided with his disillusionment with scholarship, and his students had no interest in what he taught. The interaction between the instructor and the student was hardly appealing to either side. Song's teaching in China after he returned was greatly appreciated by students even though he was no longer interested in what he was teaching. His cross-cultural experiences made his teaching different from other Chinese professors, because his classes were much freer from Chinese ideology or any ideology, and his own lens made his independent thought refreshing for students. He also felt that now Chinese undergraduate students had many more independent thoughts of their own than in the earlier time. Since students were interested in and responded to his teaching, he became more energized in teaching. Even though the class size was not small—70 or 80 students—he enjoyed teaching, as he felt stimulated and inspired by the students. This situation was similar to his first teaching experience in the USA, although now he felt at ease with presenting materials. Even though his worldview was implicit in his teaching, intentionally or unintentionally, he had not systematically introduced it to his students.

I wrestled with the question of "so what" with Song's stories. Song felt that he had come full circle as a person, yet I still hoped that this circle was not full but open. Since being an educator was no longer essential to Song's life, how did I make sense of all of these experiences as an educator? Fortunately, I was able to bring my questions to Song when I visited him during the winter of 2011. His answers were thoughtful:

> I think there are different forms of education. Meditation, for instance, is a form of education. . . . For me, education is usually about rationalization, so there is a need for de-education. Education and de-education can co-exist at the same time. Education happens in my classroom but de-education happens outside of the classroom. For instance, there were five or six international students who were interested in meditation and asked me about it. I let them come as a group to my office and we discussed it together. Some of them had never practiced it before but got interested in it, including students from India.

I am interested in his notion of de-education, similar to the notion of "unlearning," which requires emptying out existing ideas and emotions in order to be open to new thought and new relationality. For Song, formal education is so tied to instrumental rationality that it takes nothing less than de-education to undo its damage. But if education and de-education can coexist, is it possible to have both elements in the classroom? Usually learning happens at school while unlearning happens at graduate school. What if we include both elements at all levels of education? (I term the combination of both education and de-education as de/education; see detailed discussions in the final Chapter 0.) If we can start with young children and sustain an integrated experience of body and mind in various forms throughout schooling and college education, what influence can nonviolence de/education have on both teacher and student? While the university is usually considered a site of new knowledge, it also needs to become a site for cultivating inner peace and outer peace, which often requires both professors and students to go through de-education and unlearn instrumental rationality in order to enable a non-dual approach to learning and life. Therefore it is important to take Song's stories not as a model to follow but as a challenge for rethinking education.

Notes

1. Criticizing and denouncing a person in a public meeting was one popular, brutal mode of public punishment of those who did not belong to the proletarian class in the Cultural Revolution. In such a meeting, the person under attack was subject to interrogation led by the Red Guards in front of the jeering audience. It often involved physical punishment which could lead to serious injuries. See Lin's (1991) definition (p. 4) for details.
2. The Cadre's Camp is a labor camp in the countryside where intellectuals were sent to work like farmers and were required to engage in thought transformation through labor and accepting farmers' reeducation. For a detailed explanation, see Guo, Song, and Zhou (2006). Usually it is translated as the Cadre's School, but I used the term "camp" here to avoid confusing it with the school that was set up for cadres' children, and "camp" is a better word to describe its labor-intensive condition.
3. Religious freedom, although included in the Chinese Constitution, did not exist in the Cultural Revolution, which labeled religion as a feudal superstition to be done away with. The Cultural Revolution was well known for destroying religious temples and terminating religious practices.
4. A "big-character poster" was a popular means of contestation in the Cultural Revolution. The posters were handwritten, wall-mounted posters using large-sized Chinese characters for a gathering crowd to read. Mao was one of the first who used it to attack his political enemies publically. See Guo, Song, and Zhou (2006).
5. Dunhuang is a cultural site in Gansu province, China. Historically it was a major stop on the ancient Silk Road, which carried silk products from China to other parts of the world. Dunhuang caves have a most extensive and exquisite collection of Buddhist paintings and sculptures in China.
6. The University Services Center in Hong Kong houses materials related to China and China Studies. Many students who major in China Studies go there to do research, and there is a community of scholars who gather there spontaneously. Both David and Song visited the Center during their studies.

7. A Kundalini awakening, as Song described, refers to the phenomenon of energy coming from the base of the spine to the top of the head. It is a profound mystical experience, usually emerging as a result of meditation and yoga practices, but it can happen spontaneously or be triggered by intense personal experiences.
8. From *Tao Te Ching*, Chapter 11.
9. Wang Guowei is a contemporary Chinese philosopher who speaks about three levels of tragedy. The first level is accident; for example, you are hit by a car. The second is damage caused by others who set things up to hurt you. At the third level, there is no accident and nobody else tries to hurt you, but life itself is a tragedy, as everybody becomes old and then dies.
10. There are debates about whether the founders of Taoism, Laozi and Zhuangzi (to a lesser degree), existed as real persons in history, but there is no dispute that the texts attributed to them, *Tao Te Ching*, and *Zhuangzi*, have profoundly influenced Chinese culture.

4

SERENDIPITY

We Teach What We Are

I found Teresa's contact information through the help of a friend at the university where she was teaching. Teresa immediately responded and accepted my invitation. She had taught in China in different universities from 2000 to 2004. Because of her parents' sickness and other family issues, Teresa went back to the USA, and did not returned China until 2009. She continued her teaching in China until the summer of 2012, when my study ended.

Teresa is a warm and enthusiastic person. Like Song, once she started talking, she did not seem to want to stop. During one of my interviews with her, I brought only one 90-minute tape because I was in a rush to meet her. As the tape was running out she was still in the middle of telling her fascinating stories, so I ran back to get another tape—luckily my hotel was only a few minutes from her apartment. I had three interviews with her and observed her teaching twice. But she periodically updated me with her new activities with students and in the community and emailed me new materials after our meetings. These materials include communications and flyers about service-learning projects, power point slides of various activities, students' written evaluations of her teachings, and Internet resources of youth organizations.

When I sent her my interview transcripts for her to check, I asked her to provide details for the missing parts, which I was not quite clear about. Particularly touching for me, she not only corrected the unclear parts but also extensively extended those stories. I could tell that it took her considerable time and energy to work on those transcripts. It felt like doing those interviews a second time. Her devotion to others and her commitment to service as a form of leadership can be seen clearly in her prolonged relationship with a researcher who was a total stranger in the beginning. While both David and Fen were administrators and leaders, Teresa was a pedagogical activist who engaged in community service and taught all her students—and colleagues—the significance of making a difference in society through participation.

In this chapter, I start with Teresa's autobiographical stories and then tell her tales of activism in China. I further discuss the concept of serendipity, service learning and peace education, and American activism traditions to situate her stories. Finally, I discuss the possibility of enacting a pedagogy of nonviolence using the double texts of Teresa's teaching and my own cross-cultural learning and teaching.

Serendipity: My Life Stories

Serendipity is a way of life to me. Long before I knew this word, serendipity had already worked its magic in my life.

I was born in 1944 in the Midwest in the USA. I was the oldest of six children, three boys, and three girls. We were quite close to one another and are good friends to this day. Growing up in a small rural area, with trees and gardens around our home, we all worked in the gardens to provide food for our family. As the oldest child, I took care of younger siblings and did babysitting jobs for neighbors. My mother had to find work outside the home because of my father's bout with cancer. In the 1950s that was unusual. I always did my best and went the extra mile in any job, so I got many babysitting requests, and I passed those jobs on to my siblings.

My mother was a natural teacher and read books to us almost every day. In the summer time, she would put a blanket on the lawn under the apple tree and gather all six of us together and read aloud to us. The little ones gradually fell asleep and napped while the older ones listened to the stories. My father also loved reading to us. He would sit on the floor in the hall between the open doors of our bedrooms and read aloud so that we could hear him when we were in bed for the night. As a family, we did a lot of fun and creative things, and we were active in church programs. We had an extended family since both my parents had lots of siblings. I enjoyed all those Christmas parties and visits with our big family.

When I was young, children and youth were given the opportunity to give a short talk at church, only a couple of minutes long. It was an excellent exercise for me and my siblings. Our mother helped us with preparing the talks, but my parents did not allow us to "read" the talk, so we were learning Gospel topics as well as the basic skills of organizing and presenting a talk at an early age. These skills were useful in my later life.

When I was 16 years old, in the 10th grade, a big serendipitous chance appeared in my life. I learned of a speech competition, where the state winner would receive an all-expense-paid trip to various important places in American history, including a one-week stay in New York City with an opportunity to study with other youths from all over the country at the United Nations. I was so excited because I had never traveled to those places, and I had not even traveled outside of my state.

The name of the speech was, "What the United Nations Means to Me" and I began the speech with an ancient Chinese proverb:

> If there is righteousness in the heart, there will be beauty in the character.
>
> If there is beauty in the character, there will be harmony in the home.
>
> If there is harmony in the home, there will be order in the nation.
>
> When there is order in the nation, there will be PEACE in the world.

That proverb introduced the message of my speech: Everyone is responsible for doing one's part toward winning *peace* in the world.

The first round of competition was held in my high school and two were selected to participate at the state level. I was chosen, along with a boy who was a year older than me with much more experience in public speaking. I felt very inadequate compared to him, and I told my mother that I did not want to go to the state competition. My mother encouraged me: Just do your best! Well, to make a long story short, I did go and did my best, AND I was chosen the winner!

The whole trip and experience at the United Nations was life changing, and the concept that world peace is *possible* burned deep into my heart. But the greatest learning came from traveling with and getting to know other youth from different states and various backgrounds. I learned that we were really all the same inside despite our differences. The teachings of my parents, that we are all children of God and that we should *love* and *care* for one another, were growing in my heart.

I became a teacher following a serendipitous path. During high school, I decided that I would become a nurse. I had been influenced by Jesus Christ's commandment to love and serve others and by the message of Dr. Albert Schweitzer, Nobel Peace Prize winner in the 1950s, who said: "The only ones among you who will be really happy are those who have sought and found how to serve." I felt that nursing was a career for me in which I could serve others. In an interview with a school counselor, she asked me: "Teresa, have you ever considered that a teacher serves people?" She then pointed out that my talents would make a better teacher than a nurse. This happened 50 years ago, but I still remember the excited feeling I had as I left her office, thinking: "Wow, would that be great!" I have enjoyed teaching for half a century now.

Open to new ideas when opportunities came to me, I often had surprising discoveries that led to more unexpected possibilities. An experience in high school was a good example. When I was a junior, I had a friend who was a senior, and I really looked up to this girl. She was a state officer in a student leadership organization, Future Homemakers of America (FHA), which was related to the home economics curriculum at school. It was just one of many vocational youth development clubs at school to help teens learn leadership, vocational, and citizenship skills. This girl invited me to join the FHA group. I told her that I was not even taking any home economics class that year, but she said that I took it in the ninth grade and so I was qualified. I went to the meeting with her, and guess what? I was elected by others to be the Vice President of the club, and would become President the next school year! This leadership role was totally unexpected, and I did not seek it, but the opportunity came to me. It was a great learning experience.

Little did I know at that time that I would major in home economics and consumer education in college, become a teacher and then an advisor to the FHA chapter at school, work with the FHA state organization, and then become a state advisor. Later, when I became a teacher educator, I served on an FHA Teacher Education Task Force, worked with teacher educators and teachers all over the country, and became a leader nationally, serving on the FHA National Board of Directors for several years. All these opportunities and challenges came to me in serendipitous ways. I did not seek them, but had the wisdom to accept and learn from each experience. My experiences in leadership development have benefited me in all other jobs, including now in China.

Meeting and falling in love with John was also serendipitous. I first dated his roommate for a while. In my first dance with him at a ball at college, I actually called him his roommate's name when I introduced him to my relatives. How embarrassing! But we enjoyed our time together. When I took him home, he fell in love with my family, as much as he was in love with me. John's mother passed away when he was a little boy, and he was not really close to his father. The intimacy of my family was endearing to him. Understanding how important my family was to me, he proposed to me at the family dinner table! I was so surprised because it was supposedly a private matter, and it was certainly unusual to do so in front of the whole family. I was expecting his proposal, but not the way he chose to do. It was a joyful surprise.

A surprising phone call brought me to China. I did not know much about China, except the Chinese saying I borrowed to write my speech in high school and some basic information about China in world history classes. I read several books by Pearl S. Buck about China, such as *The Good Earth,* and *East Wind: West Wind.* I also read *Wild Swans,* an autobiographical book about three generations of Chinese women in one family. But I certainly had never imagined living and teaching in China! A friend running a China Teachers program at a university phoned me with an invitation. Going to China to teach English? I replied: "I am not an English teacher." She said, "I know. But you are a good teacher, a native English speaker, and we'll train you." As she explained the program, I became excited and felt that it was something that I should do. I had never thought that I would be an English teacher, in addition to going to China, but the opportunity presented itself to me. How could I not take it?

John and I were on our way to China in 2000. And that marked an important point in my life. While in China, I first only taught English classes in the north, but as I was open to other opportunities, I began to teach different classes that matched my expertise. For example, in my second year of teaching in a university in the south, I saw a notice on the bulletin board seeking a professor to teach English to faculty. I volunteered and got that job, and now I have taught teaching methods to university faculty several times already. Over the years, I have not only used my experiences in youth leadership development to encourage students' commitment to service and activism through teaching, but I have also designed and taught new courses in leadership development and community service in other departments besides the foreign languages department. The relationship has been built over the years, and now I have kept coming back to the same university to teach. It has been an enriching experience for both me and my students. One phone call changed my life in an irreversible way.

As I stay alert to new possibilities, look for the best in whatever situation I am in, and make my best efforts, I continue to find something better than what was originally sought after. All these things in my life are connected, and I feel blessed to be able to follow the guidance of God to continue embracing new possibilities. What a great way to live through serendipity!

Activist Tales: "We Teach What We Are"

As service is key to Teresa's life, it is not a surprise that her teaching was also related to service, youth leadership, and community activities in whatever subject she happened to teach, both in the USA and in China. As we have seen above, she was involved in FHA, a youth development program that is related to home economics. She also worked for another program—4-H Club—and she used its organizational principles to engage Chinese students in service-learning and community projects.

4-H is a youth development, educational, and leadership program outside of the public schools (see its website: www.4-h.org/) in the USA. 4-H is similar to FHA in its focus on leadership and citizenship development for youth, but the difference is that 4-H is broader, and members can choose from a wide variety of projects—from computers to horses, sewing to drama, and cooking to medicine. Moreover, the organization is run by volunteer leaders, not public school teachers. The 4-H pledge is:

> I pledge my head to clearer thinking,
> my heart to greater loyalty,
> my hands to larger service,
> and my health to better living
> for my club, my community, my country, and my world.

A fundamental principle of 4-H is learning by doing. Through experientially oriented learning projects, youths develop their leadership, organizational, and citizenship skills. Teresa had worked for a university extension program that housed the state 4-H staff for 16 years before she came to China. Teresa believed in cooperation and teamwork to build a better community. And this spirit of service traveled with her to China.

Although Teresa taught only English initially, she was good at finding opportunities for service learning. The first year when she and John were in China, they involved students in a service project at an orphanage each Saturday morning. Serving those in need of attention was an important thread throughout Teresa's teaching in China. The second year, when they returned to China, they went to another university, where they initiated a service-learning project with students that has been ongoing for a decade already. The founding and development of this project itself followed a serendipitous path.

Before Christmas that year, Teresa organized a club using the 4-H model for undergraduate students she was teaching. Membership was optional and the club met during the noon hour when students learned leadership skills. Following the principle of learning by doing, she asked students to work with her to plan, organize, and implement a Christmas party. They located and decorated a room for the party, learned to sing some Christmas songs, and put a party program together. Since service was an important part of youth leadership and a Christmas tradition in her family, Teresa encouraged students to collect donations at the party to use for a service project. They did not know what to do specifically but wanted to help poor rural children to get a better education.

The university professors who were attending Teresa's teaching methods class also came to the party. Several of them took it upon themselves to find a school for this project. They connected with a special rural school for deaf students that needed volunteers' help. Students brainstormed to give this project a name: the "Light-Up Project" (a pseudonym). They traveled there to have a face-to-face, hands-on opportunity to serve the children of that school. This connection has been kept and university students have been going there for a whole day of activities with the children every semester (including the year when this chapter was written in 2012). Donations were used to buy some necessary facilities for the school and paid for some children's tuition or boarding costs. Over the years, volunteers have come from various sources including university students outside of Teresa's classes and some foreign professors. When Teresa returned to the USA in 2004, the project kept going. While in the USA, she continued supporting it through engaging activities among her family and friends. In 2006, they organized an event in which school children and Teresa's family members ran for donations on both sides of the ocean together. This tradition has become an annual event.

When Teresa returned to China in 2009, she directed the project together with others. She taught various classes including English classes, American history and society, teaching methods, leadership development, and community service. The impact of the Light-Up Project went beyond those school children, and each participant from the university and the university culture at large were influenced by it. Even the local government became more supportive of the school. As a part of her community-service class, she also organized a Volunteer Fair on the university campus to celebrate Global Youth Service Day, which provided opportunities for students to learn about various student-led service projects and volunteering opportunities. Teresa also reached out to make connections with people who worked for foundations in order to get support from the general public and, during the process, taught students how to seek out financial assistance from various resources.

In these projects, university students were learning how to volunteer and serve and make a difference in the world, lifelong skills that they could use for community building. Another student who took Teresa's leadership development class recently launched a project, inspired by the Light-Up Project, to help primary school students in a poor, rural community in northwest China. This new project built bridges between a southern university in the city and a northwestern school in a rural area, and it reached as far as the USA. Students' teaching evaluations and email communications demonstrated that the concept and activities of volunteer service had profoundly influenced their worldviews. In one email to Teresa, a student commented that his self-centered approach had changed: "This class [community service] not only gave me the opportunity to contact other people and learn how to cooperate with different individuals, but also told [sic] me the importance and meaning of serving people in need and making contributions to the society."

As an activist, Teresa also found many possible opportunities to promote cross-cultural exchanges both formally and informally in daily life. For example, she took several Chinese students to the USA to participate in a university's 4-H club training. She also believed that her family and friends benefited from her involvement in China. Her daughter visited them in China and was so fascinated with the work Teresa and John were doing there that she also applied to become an English teacher in China. Teresa's grandchildren participated in the service project from a distance. So Teresa approached her China experiences as beneficial for all who were involved. She also brought American activists or authors who were interested in writing or learning about the service-learning projects to campus to be connected with Chinese students and communities.

Sharing life with students, not merely teaching a subject, was important to Teresa's teaching. That was what she meant by "we teach what we are." What she is as a person intimately relates to what she teaches, and in return, students relate to her what they are in their learning and growth. As Takuya Kaneda (2008) points out, "It is more important for teachers to show *what they are* than it is to be concerned only with *what they teach*" (p. 190; emphasis in the original). Teresa embodied what she taught in what she was. She and John invited students to their apartment for gatherings, demonstrated their family traditions at Christmas including a Santa's visit (performed by John), and playing games. As they shared their lives, Chinese students and friends also invited them into Chinese family gatherings, and many long-lasting cross-cultural friendships were formed.

Stories in Context

From Teresa's stories, we can see the importance of serendipity for her life and of service learning for her pedagogical activism. Here I situate her life history in the notion of serendipity, service learning and community-based education, and American nonviolence activist traditions for a broad and in-depth understanding.

Serendipitous Life Pathway

"Serendipity is the theme of my life," Teresa told me as I opened our second interview. She also gave me a sheet that explained the concept of serendipity including its origin, history, and evolved meanings—she used this sheet to explain the word to her Chinese students. She was influenced by Richard M. Eyre's (2008) interpretation of serendipity; as soon as she came into contact with this concept, she felt a connection. Teresa described her marriage, her work, her travel, her teaching, and her cross-cultural adventures in China through the lens of serendipity.

In general, serendipity refers to unexpected, happy discoveries and good surprises in life. Eyre (2008) traces this term back to an 18th-century English author, Horace Walpole, who coined it according to a Persian fable called "The Three Princes of Serendip." The fable tells the story of three princes going out to find their fortunes. Although they did not find what they were seeking, they found something better. Fascinated by the fable, Walpole coined the term "serendipity" and defined it as *"a state of mind whereby a person, by good fortune and through awareness and sensitivity, frequently finds something better than that which he is seeking"* (quoted in Eyre, 2008, p. 2; emphasis in the original).

Following Walpole, Eyre emphasizes that serendipity is not a pure accident, but prefers the wise and the alert seeker who is open to what life spontaneously brings. Eyre advocates serendipity as a positive alternative to the control mentality that modern life often suffers from. He also further distinguishes spiritual serendipity from regular serendipity as a more advanced level in which *"we strive for awareness of God's blessings and of His will"* (p. 3; emphasis in the original). Spiritual awareness, sensitivity, and sagacity are essential for enjoying the gifts of serendipity, and taking detours and departing from preset plans when necessary can lead to surprising discoveries. In short, Eyre perceives serendipity as "a bridge between structure and spontaneity, between discipline and flexibility, between expected and unexpected, between plans and surprises, and between the forced and the fun" (p. 43).

Teresa embodied such a bridge in her life and in her teaching, so there is no wonder that she was enthusiastic about this concept. From the speech contest when she was 16 to her leadership positions at school and later at state and national levels and to her taking up an opportunity to teach in an unfamiliar, foreign country, her life was full of unexpected twists and turns. In accepting challenges she had been open to joyful surprises along the way. In following the flow, however, she had also been proactive and made best efforts in every encounter she had. From her youth when babysitting other children to the recent time when she painstakingly corrected interview transcripts, I can easily see that she went the extra mile for everything, but these efforts were part of her seeking, rather than controlling, and in her seeking, things came together at unexpected moments in ways beyond her plans.

Moreover, her early experiences as the oldest child in her big family to help with family responsibility also paved the way for her leadership preparedness. When she had the courage to take a challenge, like Fen, she was able to realize her leadership potential. When she taught the notion of serendipity in China, she discussed a sense of surprising discovery as a result of both preparedness and spontaneity and a sense of interconnectedness taking one on an unexpected journey. But she did not discuss her religious beliefs, at least not in the information sheet she gave to students, although her students knew she was a Christian. For Teresa, however, serendipity is spiritual and her faith in God is an important part of it.

In a broad context, the roles of serendipitous discovery in science (Johnson, 2010; Martin, 2007), literature (Sobol, 1999), business (Muller & Becker, 2012), and research (Freedman, 2001; Herzfeld, 2012; Luce-Kapler, 2009) have been studied. One unique contribution of serendipity to such diverse fields is its magical ability to find "novel connections" (Johnson, 2010, p. 108) among seemingly separate or irrelevant phenomena. Scientific, artistic, or even business creativity can be facilitated, not by competition, but by finding out surprising relationships. So the challenge becomes "how to create environments that foster these serendipitous connections" (p. 109), rather than trying to plan everything in advance and control the process towards a predetermined goal, as surprising outcomes are inherent in serendipity. At the same time, serendipity "happens to the prepared mind" (Luce-Kapler, 2009, p. 77) rather than by pure chance, and planning for the unexpected is the practice of poets who search for relationships between metaphors and ideas.

I think serendipity goes along with the notion of nonviolence because rather than imposing a preset objective, it is open to what emerges from the process. Serendipity and nonviolence also share a long-term beneficial outcome, as magic comes from a process of committed efforts. Opening to the other, the alternative, and the different is inherent in both. To the extent that both notions deconstruct the mechanism of control, serendipitous connections curve through nonviolent pathways to open up new landscapes.

A few studies in life stories or life histories of teachers (Kenyon, 2008; Spector, 2006; Sawyer, 1998), female leaders (Muskopf, 1998), and teacher educators (Wimmer, 2003), and self-portraits of university professors (e.g., Duszynski, 2008) indicate that serendipity played a role in their success. But few studies explore the relationship between serendipity and teaching (see Bjune [1995] for a high school teaching example). Perhaps because teaching at various levels is considered a purposeful activity, the built-in element of a surprising outcome in serendipity is seldom welcome. At the college level, however, there is more academic freedom;

at least professors usually can choose the texts they use in the classroom in comparison with school teachers who have little control over textbooks, so there is more space for teaching along serendipitous paths. I will return to the topic of serendipity and teaching later.

Service Learning and Community-Based Education

The 4-H Club youth development program has a history of more than 100 years. It was born in the 1900s when "economic prosperity generally characterized American agriculture, [but] there was a lack of opportunity for rural children that would propel them to a better quality of life" (Kress, 2006, p. 134). Creating opportunities for youth to learn about farming practices or new innovations in agriculture from land grant universities and apply them in their own communities, 4-H as an after-school program emphasized the development of head, hand, and heart, and the value of community life. Learning by doing and becoming lifelong learners are two hallmarks of 4-H programs. Today as many youth participants from suburban and urban areas as from rural areas learn about leadership skills, new technologies, and serving the local and global community. Teresa used the 4-H model to encourage Chinese students to engage in service learning. She integrated community service into English language teaching in the early years of her teaching in China, and later she designed new courses in leadership skills and service learning.

In a broad context, studies have shown that service learning contributes to peace education (Forcey & Harris, 1999; Weigert & Crews, 1999a) and various American universities have adopted service-learning approaches in their peace studies programs (e.g., Merrill, 1999; Roschelle, Turpin, & Elias, 1999; Scarritt & Lowe, 1999). The Chinese proverb that Teresa quoted in her speech contest is actually essential to the Confucian notion of cultivating inner peace in order to reach outer peace. Teresa's United Nations experiences imprinted the message of peace into her heart, and she believed that everybody had a share of the responsibility for making peace possible. Her commitment to serving the underprivileged student population in Chinese education through service learning was compatible with the notion of "positive peace" (Fitz-Gibbon, 2010; Reardon, 1988). The distinction between "negative peace" and "positive peace" was first defined by Johan Galtung (1964), who considers negative peace as the absence of war or violence and positive peace as the "integration of human society" (p. 2) through communication, collaboration, and conflict resolution. Here, Galtung's notion of positive peace is close to Michael Nagler's definition of nonviolence, as both highlight the human capacity for integration. This function of peace and nonviolence in community building is compatible with Teresa's service learning approach.

Michael Schratz and Rob Walker (1999) further argue that reflective practice lies at the heart of learning from lived experiences. Critically reflecting upon the experience and making meanings from various activities are crucial for learning to happen. They also talk about the complexity of students' participation in the outside world. One particularly interesting issue they bring up is how individual egos can get in the way in community organizations that are dedicated to peace and social justice. "The emotional warfare, naked ambition, and exploitation found in some volunteer agencies dedicated to radical change" (p. 42) can be shocking to students who do not expect to encounter them in such organizations. This realistic portrayal reminds us that there is some distance between commitment to peace and translating that commitment into daily practice and that individual practices of mindfulness are necessary for going beyond individual egos to pursue peace in our shared life. It also means that peace education is a lifelong process in which everyone needs to have an ongoing critical relationship with the self.

Teresa did not discuss the ethical complexity or ambiguity that was involved in community service. Although service-learning projects in China did not duplicate the American model of student placement into a community organization, I think the ethical issues that Schratz and Walker discuss arise in many social interactions and such a situation can become messy when students are directly involved in service projects. Since I did not participate in Teresa's service-learning projects while I was in China, I did not have a chance to observe the role of critical reflection on the part of students. What I have learned from teaching multicultural education classes to my American students is that it is relatively easy to offer help to others who are in need of help or to feel sympathy with others who are in unfortunate situations—in Jane Addams' phrase (1906 [2007]), to be "benevolent." But it is much more difficult to reflect on one's own privilege and how one's implication in a system of control might have contributed to others' suffering (Wang, 2008; Wang & Olson, 2009). I am not sure to what degree Teresa encouraged students to reflect critically on their own roles and to question the system.

American Nonviolence Activism: A Female Leader

In the tradition of American nonviolence activism, community-based education is an important component. Hull House, established at the turn of the 20th century, is a good example. Here I would like to detour through Jane Addams' intellectual and life history before returning to Teresa's stories. Influenced by Tolstoy's concept of nonviolence, feminist critiques of women's role in society, and visiting an influential settlement house in England, Addams cofounded and remained the major leader of Hull House, which was the center of a democratic, communal life (Hendry, 2012; Knight, 2005, 2010; Pinar, 2009). Hull House was in the middle of a poor neighborhood where immigrants lived. Addams and other female resident leaders at Hull House worked together with community members to transform the neighborhood into an energizing, nourishing, and vital community through offering classes to immigrant children and adults, engaging community activities, and providing services to those who needed help.

Through many years of dedicated work at Hull House and her immersion in the community, Addams was able to "perceive the connections between different kinds of oppression" (Knight, 2010, p. 96) including the links between social injustice in the domestic realm and warfare in the international realm. She (Addams, 1906 [2007]) rejected class and gendered oppression and the conquest of other nations but favored active and dynamic notions of peace as "the unfolding of worldwide processes making for the nurture of human life" (p. 131). The connection she made between peace and nurturance had a gendered implication. Addams was an educated woman with a strong sense of social mission, yet she was confined by the gendered expectation of her time. She had to work through her self-doubt and unlearn social norms before she became a visionary female leader in the Progressive Era. Hull House attracted many women who wanted to engage in public life and contribute to society.

Addams' commitment to nurturance and pacifism led her to go against war despite the public's patriotic support of war. Her leadership first at local, national, and then international peace movements was remarkable. During World War I, women got together across enemy camps to work for peace, and Jane Addams, as one of the worldwide leaders, met male politicians such as the American President Wilson to discuss diplomacy in wartime. The International Committee of Women for Permanent Peace, born in 1915, was later renamed the Women's International League for Peace and Freedom, with Jane Addams as its first president. Addams' work against militarism and for pacifism at the international level grew out of her experiences at Hull House and her life together with other female leaders who might or might not share her own perspectives. It was openness to differences—cultural, social, and intellectual—that Addams believed in and practiced as crucial to democracy. Addams engaged both constructive and oppositional aspects of nonviolence.

Jane Addam's insistence on learning from the immigrants at the bottom of society went hand in hand with her critique of hierarchical control in various forms. Her visionary leadership, a result of her lifetime commitment to and engagement with public life, was not necessarily linear but was curved. As Louise Knight (2005, 2010), her biographer, points out, it took years of living with the poor for Addams to relinquish the notion of "benevolence"—which implies the giver's superior position—in order to claim immigrants' vital role in regenerating democracy. The danger of holding a position of "benevolence" can be inherent in today's service learning if students only see their service as helping others without critically reflecting on themselves, but it takes time to understand more fully and deeply how the social fabric is woven together. It took Addams years to accept the worker union's strategy of the strike as a nonviolent response to oppression. While she never accepted the socialist principle of class conflict, she became an advocate for workers' rights.

Detours in an ongoing process were not always successful, even for Addams. For example, regarding racial issues, the communication between her and Ida B. Wells regarding lynching showed that she did not have the insights that Wells had into the racial dynamics of her time (Pinar, 2001; Hendry, 2012). Not questioning the excuse for lynching—Black man assaulting White woman—Addams' advocacy for women made her neglect to see the racism embedded within the rhetoric. Wells directly challenged Addams' position on this issue.

Jane Addams' life paths made me wonder to what degree Teresa's approach to her teaching in China changed over the years of living in China from 2000 to the present (with five years in the middle when she did not travel to China). To what degree did Teresa learn from Chinese culture to reexamine her own culture? If she found Pearl Buck's novels and *Wild Swans* as largely applicable to the contemporary Chinese situation, which I found inapplicable to my own life in China, was she seeing through her own lens or was she seeing Chinese reality? In her enthusiasm for service learning and her use of the principles of the American youth development organization to encourage Chinese students' volunteer work, was there an element of "benevolence"?

Serving society in China has a long-standing tradition (and I grew up with this message throughout my education); in this sense, the message of service is not new to China as Teresa seemed to believe. In a hierarchical society, however, it is usually up to the authorities to assign people work to do, rather than people initiating public projects they consider meaningful. Many Chinese youth, in their disillusion with the government, see any call from above for service as problematic, as only serving the government rather than serving the people. Ironically, in a society that is officially organized by socialist principles, individuals may learn to manipulate the collective system to serve personal interests. But when such a call for community service came from an American professor who was an outsider to Chinese politics and who had a real passion for contributing to society, the situation was different. As Teresa encouraged students' initiative to make a difference, she energized students' enthusiasm for *grassroots* efforts. Her unique contribution extended an existing tradition.

In my follow-up questions, I asked Teresa what aspects of Chinese culture she thought were positive qualities that could be blended with American culture to benefit both Chinese and Americans. She answered that she liked the natural way of life including traditional Chinese medicine and the daily exercise of walking and riding bicycles. She commented, "I would like to see both Chinese and Americans embrace the benefits of both 'natural, alternative methods' and 'Western scientific methods' of health care and well being." In a way, Teresa captured an important part of Chinese culture. In several years of living in China, she gained perceptive insights into a culture different from her own. Furthermore, she expressed a "both/and" preference that does not reject either side: (Chinese) natural methods *and* (American) scientific methods, even though these two approaches are different. She also found the Chinese values of family and respect for elders and teachers refreshing.

When I further asked her whether her experience in China made her rethink American culture and the American way of life, she said that it first reconfirmed her belief that "ALL men and women are brothers and sisters and should be treated with respect, love, and kindness." And she further commented: "I've become more aware of looking at an issue from both sides of the coin." She found it interesting to see how people of other countries thought about the USA and to see the "love-hate" relationship that occurred on both sides. But she found it ironic that although the Chinese official newspaper criticized American politics almost every day, many Chinese wanted to leave China and live in the USA. Furthermore, she stated,

> [My experience] has given me the opportunity to rethink many of the American government's actions not only in China but other countries as well, and at this time in the world, I would hope that we could adopt a more cooperative, global perspective with all countries.

Through her experiences of teaching and living in China she has acquired an additional lens through which to look at the world and to see "both sides of the coin." As she hoped for a more cooperative, global approach on the American side, she implicitly critiqued the current policy as less collaborative. Interestingly, one of the founders of peace studies, the Norwegian sociologist Johan Galtung (2009) made a distinction between the USA as a republic and as an empire. On one hand, the USA is admired worldwide for its republican qualities, such as its work ethic, productivity and creativity, freedom and liberty, and a pioneering spirit. On the other hand, the American military and political aggression abroad, the public ignorance of other cultures, and extreme materialism are resented worldwide.

While Galtung's arguments are highly controversial, this distinction is personally clarifying for me to understand my own ambivalent feelings. Since I came here in the mid-1990s, American foreign policy in its military violence has significantly contributed to my deep doubt about democracy. In today's American education, the push for tough masculine control prevails (Wang, 2008), and American educators have suffered from external-militarism-turned-inside-as-internal-aggression for the past several decades. In this sense the underlying mechanism for control and domination remains the same for both foreign and domestic realms. Yet I have also enjoyed much more academic freedom here than in my native country, and the American youthful energy, humor, optimism, and creative spirit have had my loyal admiration. In the classes I teach, I am often impressed by how much students are willing to unlearn and learn through discussions that challenge their long-cherished beliefs and assumptions. There seems to be a built-in openness in the American tradition that makes active learning possible.

A successful intercultural and cross-cultural experience invites not only engaging others productively but also looking at one's own culture critically. While such a critical approach did seem to emerge for Teresa as she acquired multiple perspectives as a result of cross-cultural engagement, how such multiplicity invites changing her own lens is unclear to me. Mostly I have seen her using an American approach to make a difference in China. I think Teresa warmly embraced

American values through her Christian belief and, as a part of this belief, she held a universal approach to humanity. Different from her, I was already critical of my own culture before I came to the USA, so critiques of my own culture have deepened as a result of my cross-cultural life, along with a more in-depth appreciation of its strength. The length of my stay in the USA has also sharpened both my appreciation and critique of American culture. Perhaps our different starting points make a difference in our approaches to the relationship between the self and the other.

Teresa's universal approach was also reflected in her views on gender as she affirmed that all men and women are children of God. For Jane Addams, difference was essential to democracy and should not be suppressed, including gendered difference, but Teresa never discussed such a difference. As Petra Munro Hendry (2012) points out, the image of God as mother or as both mother and father are not uncommon historically, but Teresa always referred to God as "heavenly Father." She felt fortunate that her husband and other family members supported her public work outside of the home since "most men in my religious culture[1] believed a woman should stay home and care for the children and the husband should work to provide the money for the family." She also believed that it was a good thing for John to get more involved with the children at home when she traveled for work. She had transcended the gendered boundary of her generation, although she did not question the maleness of God.

Teresa's mother not only taught her the universal love of God for all people but also modeled for her the value of women's public engagement. In the 1940s when racism was the norm, her mother was appalled by segregation and how Blacks were treated, and taught her and her siblings to affirm that everybody, Black or White, are children of God. Teresa believed that the message of Christ is love: "He sent his apostles to teach these concepts to the world, not with the sword, but in totally peaceful, nonviolent ways." She further commented that her mother's *total* belief in Christ's teachings put her mother ahead of her time. So in Teresa's Christian belief, love and nonviolence is a universal language for the world to unite different people, and affirming women's experiences and values comes from this universal outlook rather than from an approach that values gendered difference.

Toward a Pedagogy of Nonviolence

I have already discussed Teresa's activist approach in teaching, and here I focus more on what happened in Teresa's classroom. Several aspects of Teresa's teaching make important contributions to my formulating a pedagogy of nonviolence: first, integrating the five senses and integrating intellect and emotion through experiential learning; second, centering the role of relationships and community; and third, welcoming serendipity, surprise, and fun. I will also discuss Teresa's approach in the context of culturally relevant teaching. These discussions are based on my on-site observations, interviews, documents collected during and after the field trip, and our ongoing email conversations for three years. Particularly, I observed two classes Teresa taught: the first was a teaching methods class for young professors at the university, although many students came for the purpose of improving their spoken English; the second class was a writing class for freshman at a branch campus of the university, and I took the university bus with Teresa to travel there.

I use a double text again in this part, with italic texts flush on the right indicating my cross-cultural learning stories and flush on the left indicating my cross-cultural teaching stories, in order to parallel my own tales with Teresa's. Teaching cross-culturally for me has been doubled in another sense: first, my teaching of American students in the USA; second, my teaching in China after a decade of teaching in the USA. On the second occasion, when I was teaching in Guangzhou in December 2010, I intentionally adopted teaching strategies I used in the American classroom with Chinese students. So here the text of cross-cultural teaching is necessarily multilayered with multiple lenses, which makes juxtaposition an appropriate strategy to present multiple landscapes of teaching and learning simultaneously. In such juxtapositions, my stories sometimes echo Teresa's, sometimes complement hers, and other times contest hers.

Integrating Body and Mind

In teaching spoken English to Chinese students, Teresa gave students a hand-out to encourage them to speak *and* think in English. It emphasizes that learning to speak any language is a right-brain activity, including speaking Chinese, even though its writing component may require a left-brain activity. However, the Chinese educational system and teaching methods mainly promote left-brain development. I think that such a critique of Chinese education is largely accurate because Chinese schools focus on (especially logical-mathematical) intellectual development at the sacrifice of other dimensions, such as hands-on ability, aesthetic sensitivity, and social interactions. Teresa introduced Chinese students to learning through the five senses, not merely through their head, and designed right-brain activities. She adopted "learning by doing" in teaching, asking students to phone her to practice spoken English, teaching them poetry to exercise their minds in tuning in to rhythm and vivid imagery, letting them play games and do various activities in class, and showing movies to students who wanted to watch them after class. Promoting experiential learning, similar to what she did in the American classroom, marked Teresa's teaching style.

> *Coming fresh from China in the Fall semester of 1996 to begin my doctoral studies in Curriculum Theory, I attended my first class. Even today I still remember that class. My instructor asked students to create a metaphor of curriculum from the materials she provided to the class. I was totally at a loss while my classmates seemed to be at ease with creating visual representations from the abundance of*

> *various things and objects made available to them. I did manage to come up with something, although I felt awkward and out of place. I never did anything like that in China, whether as a schoolgirl or as a college student. That semester I also took a philosophy class with my doctoral advisor, which I did enjoy without much difficulty. He joked in a good spirit: "Then you've found the right advisor!" So philosophy saved my first semester. But over the years, exposure to different approaches in education has helped me to get in touch with the rhythms of language, and once in a while I am able to write philosophy with a poetic flow.*

In the freshman writing class I observed, Teresa asked students to create something out of aluminum foil she provided. She wrote down the six stages of the right brain activity: creating something out of aluminum foil; finding more resources; asking a peer to review the product; taking away whatever is not used; giving a title to the product and putting it on display; and taking a gallery walk to appreciate all the products. Teresa had to ask students to move on as they were slow to put the products on the table. When students were invited to walk through what they had just created, several used their cell phones to take photos. I could see amazement and implicit pride in their eyes, even though they had hardly imagined doing such an activity for a writing class. Then Teresa used this creative activity to illuminate a six-stage writing process: free writing, research, peer review, editing, naming, and feedback from others.

The activities Teresa did in the class, I suspect, would make any Chinese professor who tried to do the same appear out of touch with students, but she did so with a natural flow, and students, if surprised initially, were able to relate to her teaching well. In another teaching methods class, she started with a "show and tell" activity: students taught the class about a topic that they were familiar with or was in their own field of study. Several students came forward to use either PowerPoint presentations or their favorite objects to make a presentation in front of the class. During the presentation, Teresa corrected students' pronunciation, clarified sentences, related what was presented with what American students did in the USA, told family stories to explain a concept, and made connections between a student's hobbies and service projects that she was encouraging students to participate in.

"Show and tell" is a traditional teaching strategy in the American classroom, especially for elementary school children. jan jagodzinski (2008) discusses the problematic issues related to this activity, especially around "the gaze of the teacher." For Teresa, using this activity with her students was a way of modeling what could be done in the classroom, but the issues that jagodzinski discusses regarding how the student's subjectivity is at risk by the gaze of the other are absent in Teresa's teaching, as she embraced this method as an effective teaching strategy. While students might experience some discomfort under the gaze of the teacher and peers to participate in this activity, Teresa did not discuss such pedagogical issues with students. Especially since such an activity is not so compatible with cultural and pedagogical traditions in China, I believe that addressing those issues can help students to become more attuned to their future students' inner worlds.

I made up various activities for my American students to do in the classroom. Over the years, I've found several activities particularly helpful for students to present their ideas in different ways. I also introduced into the class short meditative exercises to demonstrate alternative ways of being, as American students are usually pressured to be on the go all the time and seldom have adequate chances to simply "be." But in my case, what students appreciated the most was not so much the activities that I organized, but rather particular ways that I connect students with difficult knowledge. My sensitivity to the emotional work that students must engage in to reach new grounds of understanding and awareness and my willingness to address those issues pedagogically—explicitly or implicitly—make students' learning more integrative and occasionally healing. Intellectually and emotionally challenging, most of my classes have had a way of working through the ups and downs, and at the end when we look back, we are astonished by how far we have traveled as a class. Teaching for more than a decade, there have been several occasions when pedagogical relationships collapsed, and I have learned and am still learning from them to find more sustainable ways to teach. Some students consider such classes life-changing, and such a change is a whole-being change with the potential to influence the public world since they are educators. To a great degree, such a change has long-term effects that I cannot see or predict. I am comfortable with making a difference in the world without seeing it myself. Life goes on in its own course.

My observation of the teaching methods class was in late November. The university classroom did not have heating facilities, so it was cold inside. In the middle of the class, Teresa stood up with a bag of snowballs and threw the balls to students: "Get up! Move! Let's have a snowball fight!" Students stood up to play, laughing, walking around, and warming up. Then she showed that the snowballs were made of quilt bedding, so they were soft, explaining that there were lots of ways of teaching young children using snowballs. Finally she asked: Rather than making students sit there all the time, what can we do to use such activities with children? It is interesting to note here that for Teresa, the integration of the five senses and of body and mind is through activities, while for Song, such integration is achieved by meditation and stillness (see Chapter 3). While both can be embodied, the specific aspects of the whole person activated by either action or stillness are not the same.

When stillness is not passive but active, when action is not unreflective but mindful, the flow of life energy can connect the person with the self and with the world. Inner peace and outer engagement with the world go hand in hand nonviolently (Lin, 2006; Wang, 2013a).

Relationality as the Heart of Pedagogy

Establishing relationships (between teacher and students, among students, and with team-teaching partners) was Teresa's strength in organizing experience-based learning. While social interactions among peers in a teacher-centered approach are usually lacking, Teresa made learning through partnership an essential part of her classes. She was a believer in cooperation and collaboration. She formally paired students for doing activities both in and outside of class. In Chinese students' teaching evaluations, a few commented that it was not very useful, but the majority found it productive and also beneficial for developing friendships. Teresa also gave exams—such as open-book exams of cross-word puzzles and word searches—that students completed in pairs. In her classes, students had a lot of opportunities for interaction.

Teacher-student relationships were cherished by both Teresa and her students. Teresa believed in mutual learning in cross-cultural contexts, and she intentionally organized activities that were not only pedagogical for students but that were also helpful for her in learning about Chinese culture. Her pedagogical relationship with students was not merely mediated through knowing but also feeling. I found that Teresa did not have much trouble sharing emotions, not only joy, which students appreciated very much, but also tearful moments. In one of the interviews, when she talked about the passing away of her father and then her mother, she choked on the words. While I wondered whether I had brought up an uncomfortable topic, she seemed to be all right with it. In the English composition class, when she was talking with students about service learning, she also paused for a moment and appeared emotional. But she was fine with sharing emotions and moved on comfortably. Such an acceptance of feelings, whether joy or sadness, was beneficial for creating a class atmosphere in which students could share their lives together. Through her modeling, students felt free to "not only share knowledge but also share feelings in the class," as one student commented.

> *During my doctoral studies, one of the things that impressed me the most was the ease and willingness and capacity of my professors to build a learning community in and out of class. One of my professors always opened the class by sharing news, and then asked us to name one thing each of us had learned at the end of the class. Another professor routinely asked all the students to share their responses to the weekly readings in class and no one was left*

> out. Another professor always had lunch with students after
> the seminar to carry on discussions during meals. We did a
> lot of small group work in class, and professors encouraged
> us students to have our own discussion group or writing
> group. And we had parties every semester! Complicated,
> intriguing, and creative intellectual work happened in such a
> mutually challenging and nurturing community. "Only in a
> profound relationship does deep learning occur" (Giordano,
> 2010, p. 9). I felt fortunate to be part of a community of
> profound relationships and individual growth.

Teresa was a passionate person, but her enthusiasm was not imposed on students, as she asked students' opinions first before making decisions. Students not only learned from her the content of the subject and the importance of service, but several of them also were motivated to become agents for cross-cultural communication. As one of her students said after taking the class on American history and American culture, "I understand the importance of communication between two different cultures, and I want to be an ambassador of culture communication too, just like you."

When Teresa first taught in China, her husband John was also teaching an English class in another classroom. So they arranged to team teach the two classes, switching half way through the class, and it worked well. Teresa's and John's teaching styles were quite different, as I observed part of John's teaching when I visited Teresa's English composition class. John was more formal and direct in his teaching, pointing out the issues in students' writings when it was his turn to discuss writing homework. Their styles were complementary to each other, and students found it beneficial.

Relationships are not just interpersonal but can be between students and what they learn. William E. Doll, Jr. (2008 [2012]) believes that developing "a network of connected and interconnected thoughts" (p. 30) is important for establishing a dynamic community in which the interplay between the personal and the social leads to new ideas. Drawing upon chaos and complexity theory, Doll (1999 [2012]) also sees both learning and teaching as the nonlinear weaving of a matrix in which understandings and awareness emerge from myriad layers of interactions. Teresa was good at building a learning network in which interpersonal relationships in class and the learning environment outside of class promoted active learning. She chose readings or American films based upon true stories so that students could learn about American daily life. Teresa also went the extra mile to interact with students outside of class, such as taking students to lunch after class, showing American movies every Friday afternoon, opening her apartment to gatherings, or introducing different aspects of American culture by doing things together. Along the way, serendipitous learning opportunities emerged. Students greatly appreciated her efforts to create a language and cultural environment that enabled them to experience learning.

Teaching in the USA, one of my worries was that students would not feel related to me as an instructor. Over the years, however, I have learned to approach the issue of pedagogical relationships in a different light, as I have seen that students can learn the best through relating—in contested ways—to texts and among one another under my guidance. Teaching effectively from an invisible position, I have learned to direct students' attention to learning, discussion, and conversing with the text, rather than with me as a teacher. That is a pedagogical position that jan jagodzinski (2002) advocates. I have also realized that in creating the best pedagogical conditions, I have followed the principle of Taoist wuwei,^{2} in the sense of enabling students to learn without an authority center. Such a principle belongs to the best philosophical and cultural traditions in China, and it has worked well in my pedagogical approaches in the American context.

Serendipity and Pedagogy of Play

Serendipity, play, and surprise were part of Teresa's teaching. In the freshman composition class, for instance, she brought a heater to the classroom. Pointing to the heater, she imagined it as a fire around which everybody in the class could get together to read, which made students laugh. In the two classes I observed, there was a sense of flow, and Teresa was at ease in following whatever students presented to blend language learning with their life interests. James B. Macdonald (1995) believes that language learning should be combined with everyday life. Teresa's ability to follow what was available in the teaching situation to open up new opportunities for students' learning was amazing to watch. Some of the activities that she brought to the class were unexpected, but many of the students enjoyed them and credited Teresa for bringing fun and pleasant surprises to their learning.

Teresa experienced serendipity as spiritual—as Eyre (2008) articulates—and spirituality is central to her life. Prayerfully living her life, Teresa always found something positive from whatever situation she was in and accepted unexpected challenges that new opportunities unfolded for her. She also understood that her seeking might not lead to her goal immediately, but fluid and curved pathways eventually led her to achieve it in unpredictable ways. With such trust and confidence in the unexpected, her teaching was flexible, fluid, and followed what the pedagogical situation called for rather than sticking to a predetermined procedure. Bradford Hall (2009) also takes up the concept of serendipity as a form of spirituality that "allows the spirit to go 'wither it goeth' " (p. 39) in his teaching at college. He emphasizes that serendipity is not a technique but a mentality of "openness that resists static conceptions of knowledge and pedagogy" (p. 39). With an element of unexpected emotional understanding, serendipity brings cognition, feelings, and spirit together to generate wisdom and joy. Although sounding paradoxical, Hall discusses planning for serendipity in the classroom through incorporating activities "that are not exactly what they seem" (p. 38) to create opportunities for students to experience unexpected feelings and thoughts.

Spirituality is also closely related to aesthetic experiences, and much of Eyre's (2008) formulation of serendipity is in the form of poetry. Ted T. Aoki (1990 [2005]) borrows the notion of improvisation from music performance to inform what we do as educators. The musician speaks of "how in improvising he and his fellow musicians respond not only to each other, but also to whatever calls upon them in that situational moment, and that, for him, no two situational moments, like life lived, are exactly alike" (p. 368). This ability to be attuned to both the situation and interpersonal relationships is a shared capacity for serendipity and improvisation. In serendipity and improvisation, both teachers and students are immersed in whole-being experiences to respond creatively to the lived moment. Thus Aoki suggests the term "curriculum improvisation" rather than "curriculum implementation" for animating educators' imagination and creativity. Furthermore, Aoki (2005) approaches tensionality as potentially creative and sees difference as a positive site for embodying the lived world of teachers and students. The living wholeness and surprising discoveries unfolded in improvisation and serendipity flow toward a lived space of nonviolence which embraces both difference and interconnectedness.

In my own schooling in China, spontaneity and improvisation were largely discouraged, even though they still happened once in a while. In graduate school both in China and in the USA, however, the expectation became different, as if creativity can naturally happen when one progresses into advanced studies. But the story I am telling here is about the serendipity of my dissertation study. When I was writing one of the qualifying exam questions, I used Dwayne Huebner's notion of the stranger. Then one day I happened to see the book, Strangers to Ourselves, *written by Julia Kristeva (1991), on a friend's reading desk when I stayed in her house. I naturally picked it up. The simple curiosity I had about the book led to my ongoing in-depth study of Kristeva's theory, even though I was not a fan of classical psychoanalysis. Over the years, Kristeva's theory has profoundly influenced my work and helped me to put pieces of myself together. In my dissertation, I negotiated a conversation—an impossible one—between and among Foucault, Confucius, and Kristeva. My return to Confucianism was also unexpected for me and I resisted it initially, yet I was compelled to go back to rediscover my roots with a fresh eye. Both unexpected turns led me to surprising connections "in a third space" (Wang, 2004). My doctoral advising committee contributed a great deal to my curved adventure. I began my doctoral studies without clearly knowing what I was looking for, but by the time I graduated, the basket of my study was full of serendipitous gifts.*

In an interesting study of serendipity in professor–student interactions and students' learning, Peter J. Giordano (2010) explores the phenomenon of a seemingly random, specific comment of a professor, contrary to a student's previous assumptions, leading to a transformative moment in the student's life without the professor's awareness. The student usually does not have an immediate awareness at the moment but then a shift in perspective happens, which leads to a dramatic change in the long run, usually in a positive way. While a professor cannot plan for such a serendipitous moment, she or he can learn how to become in tune with the rhythm of pedagogical relationships to make it possible. In such a case, the positive effect usually happens in the long run since "the *immediate* effect is one of disruption" (p. 19; emphasis in the original). In the short run, the student usually feels confused or disturbed before a shift in perspective can happen.

I was teaching Carl Jung's theory of the collective unconscious in a doctoral seminar. In the middle of the semester we were discussing how women tend to repress their anger, and a male student—a school administrator—interrupted to tell his own stories of coming to terms with anger. While acknowledging his perspective, I also pointed out the gendered aspect of emotional expression. During the break, I noticed and casually pointed to the administrator's badge that he still put on: "you still wear it in class." He was startled a bit by the observation, but I quickly forgot my comment. At the end of the semester, when I read students' final papers, I was surprised to learn that a casual comment on my part opened a door to new awareness on his part. He discussed how he began to realize that he took on the persona of an administrator yet his career success—following his father's expectations—was at the expense of his own passion for the arts. With the new awareness, he was contemplating welcoming an unexpected visitor in his imagining of the future. I have not seen or heard from that student since the class, and I have no idea what that moment meant for him; neither do I know whether he has learned how to integrate the other side of himself more fully into his life. Although it was unexpected, the conditions in the class including the book we read together, Jung and Education *(Mayes, 2005), and the* Currere *project[3] he had been doing for the whole semester, had laid out a foundation for his new self-understanding. Even the casual comment I made was informed by pedagogical intuition, since from the class discussions I had already seen the effects of his authority position. During that particular class, we were discussing the notions of persona and shadow in Jung's theory.*

Giordano's study clarifies several critical elements of serendipity: First it takes effort on the part of the student to reach a new level after a critical moment happens. In my story above, for instance, the connection the student made between a casual, joking comment and his life history would have been less likely to happen if he had not been engaging in a semester-long *currere* project *and* making efforts to understand Jungian theory. Thus, a serendipitous gift is not freely given but is earned. Second it takes time to realize the potentiality of a critical moment. In Giordano's narratives, it usually took years for a student to reach the new awareness after working with the mismatch between the professor's comment and the student's own self-perception through more experiencing and reflecting. Usually, the instructors are unaware of what is going on with the student internally unless they are informed years later. Third, although the serendipitous effect cannot be planned in advance, pedagogical awareness can be cultivated to facilitate such a process. Giordano reminds professors of the need for being mindful of the effects of our words on students, and particularly suggests that we should be more generous with "specific and *well-deserved* compliments" (p. 23; emphasis in the original). I would add that gentle yet evoking questions may also work magic, as in my student's case. Fourth, a critical moment may not be emotionally positive initially because what started such a moment on the part of the student is usually emotional dissonance that eventually leads to better self-understanding. Thus, serendipity in its own ups and downs opens a space for a pedagogy of nonviolence that calls out the potentiality in the student, who is challenged to find a more fulfilling pathway.

The Relevance of Culturally Relevant Pedagogy

I was interested in understanding whether Teresa did anything special to adjust to Chinese students' learning styles. Culturally relevant teaching theory (e.g., Gay, 2010; Ladson-Billings, 1995) in the USA suggests that teachers adapt their teaching to students from different cultural contexts. On the bus from the university's main campus to a branch campus where Teresa taught English writing to freshman, she showed me a folder with students' photos and their self-introduction writings and told me several students' stories. She knew her students well. By that time, I had already observed her teaching methods class, which used an experience-based teaching approach and positioned students as active learners. So I asked her if the methods she used in teaching Chinese students were similar to those she used in teaching American students. She affirmed that she did not change her methods: "letting the students take leadership in class, providing a lot of hands-on experiences, and using cooperative, group projects with discussion and creative, problem solving opportunities" remained the same in her teaching both in the USA and in China.

Then I asked her if it was difficult to open up conversations with Chinese students since they were not familiar with such an approach. Teresa said that she had not encountered any problem, although she had heard that a Chinese professor's students complained when he used this method, and that a student of her own also got into trouble by imitating her teaching style. But she did not find it difficult to do so with Chinese students, and she did not feel the need to change her approach since it worked well. However, she did several things to ease the transition. First, at the very beginning of the class, she set participation in discussion as her expectation for students and followed through with such an expectation, so students knew what to expect from her, even though it was different from what they were familiar with. Second, she combined various forms of discussion. The whole class discussion could be intimidating in the beginning, so she used learning partner discussions first. And then to enlarge the circle of discussion, she asked students to turn around to their classmates sitting in the row behind them to do a small group discussion. Third, she showed a genuine interest in students' own thought. When students understood that the instructor's interest was genuine, they would open up.

Certainly the professor's subjective positioning can play a role, as two Chinese professors failed in their experiments with discussion-oriented methods. Teresa, as an American professor, was expected by students to teach differently, and American teaching methods were readily accepted. On the other hand, acceptance of her methods also means that if a well-designed teaching strategy intends to evoke intellectual open-mindedness *and* compassion for relating to others, with the instructor's consistent expectations and persistent efforts, students can gradually learn how to respond open-mindedly and compassionately, even if they are not familiar with discussion-oriented methods initially.

In my observations of her classes, I paid close attention to students' facial expressions to observe their reactions. I saw excitement, surprise, *and* confusion. For those who smiled in strange ways, I knew they were trying to understand why such a thing was happening in a graduate level class, but there was an element of being amused in their confusion. Whatever emotions they had, however, students *responded emotionally* to the lesson, and even for those who initially looked confused, their puzzled looks were combined with smiles, and it seemed to me that they would be more likely to open up later rather than close down. In cross-cultural teaching, as I have learned from Teresa, the instructors do not need to feel hesitant to present the best strategies of their own culture because they may capture the imagination of students from another culture even if the two cultures are different. The strength of American ways of teaching—if there is such a thing—were played out well by Teresa. The key is certainly not about neglecting the local culture of students, as Teresa asked students to share their lives and made efforts to learn about Chinese culture. But Teresa did not assume that she must follow Chinese models of education to teach Chinese students. In my own teaching stories, I incorporated Taoist principles—unintentionally or intentionally—in teaching American students, who are not familiar with Taoism but benefit from such an approach. The issue of "relevance" is less about the assumption of any cultural entity (Edgerton, 1996; Moon, 2011) and more about what is the best in each heritage and how to match its best potential with the pedagogical situation at hand to both connect and stretch students' horizons. In such an effort, mediating between differences through modifying details—as Teresa did—can be helpful.

As a cautionary note to my questioning of the assumptions of culturally relevant pedagogy, the classes I observed were language classes (or perceived as classes for improving spoken English) and Chinese students were generally motivated to learn English before they entered the classes. Teresa commented, "They were so easy to love and teach because they were so open and wanting to learn." In the multicultural situation in American education, however, minority students' own interests and needs are often neglected due to structural and cultural racism, which leads to the disconnection between and among students, teachers, and teaching. For some minority students, there is an element of resisting the mainstream knowledge, which does not respect their own cultures (Kohl, 1993). In other words, some students already *refuse* to learn before they enter the classroom. In dealing with active resistance, multicultural teaching has to undo the historical legacy of racism to establish trusting pedagogical relationships. But in that sense, cultural relevance is much more than matching students' cultural backgrounds and teachers' teaching strategies; it is about unlearning racism.

It is also interesting to notice the general approach of sending American instructors overseas to teach English. As Jon Smythe (2012) points out, Peace Corps volunteers hardly had any pedagogical or linguistic training when they went oversea to teach English in Africa or Asia. They became English teachers simply because they were native English speakers. The invitation Teresa received from the China Teachers Program operated along a similar line, although Teresa was a teacher (in a different subject matter), which put her in a better situation pedagogically. She did not have expertise in teaching American culture and history either, but she was invited to teach it. From students' comments about this class, I can see that Teresa taught the mainstream American values that for decades had been under critical examinations by many American historians and sociologists. Not specializing in history or sociology, Teresa taught the class because of her American background and her reputation as a great teacher. Teresa's own optimism and uplifting spirit and her American values were reflected in that class more than the critical teaching of a historian or a sociologist. Chinese students responded to her teaching with their enthusiastic embrace of the mainstream American values uncritically, which is unsettling for me as an educator who asks my American students to question their own assumptions entrenched in the mainstream values in order to become reflective and mindful educators.

However, Chinese students' warm reception of her teaching, and the fact that she was invited back to teach multiple times, showed Teresa's unique contributions to Chinese students' learning. Her differences from Chinese professors contributed a great deal to her popularity, and in this sense, it was not cultural relevance but cultural difference that played a positive pedagogical role.

In December of 2010 in Guangzhou, China, I was teaching a short, two-week class on contemporary curriculum issues to Chinese graduate students. At the beginning of the class, during our first meeting, I realized that somehow the order of the pdf files I had sent to students in advance was messed up, so my pre-planned class activities did not seem to fit. I became a bit anxious. But quickly I came up with something flexible, and asked students to work with their table mates to look at whichever article they had read, find an interesting quotation from the text, and then share with the class what it means and their own thoughts about it. This is a simple exercise that I actually often use when I teach graduate students in the USA, especially in the initial sessions of classes. I do so with several purposes: First, class discussion needs to engage texts, rather than just speaking from one's own head; second, it is the engagement with the text—the sense that a student can make out of the text—that is important; third, students can present double lenses of meanings to the class; and fourth, every student has a chance to speak in the class. Feminist teaching has long acknowledged the necessity of letting every student's voice be heard in class.

But I had no ideas how Chinese students would respond to the exercise. My experiments in teaching Chinese students in an open format were to see whether they could engage in meaningful learning under guidance even though they had been accustomed to lectures. I never believed that Chinese students could not be taught in a discussion-oriented manner because debates and discussions were important to the Shuyuan *(academy) tradition as part of ancient Chinese education (Hayhoe, 2001). To my great relief and pleasure, students picked out interesting quotes and discussed their own thoughts in an in-depth way. They asked thoughtful questions, made connections to the text meaningfully, and expressed their own perspectives. Even though the majority of those students were young, master's level students, the quality of their thinking was quite impressive.*

In cross-cultural settings, the beginning point for Teresa was not difference; universal love was her foundation for connecting to a different culture. While acknowledging that Christianity could be used by Christians or churches to divide rather than unite people, she believed that her faith gave her the ease and confidence to venture to the other side of the world, without too many worries.

Similar to David, her adventure in China enhanced her self-confidence, but different from David, such an enhancement was not accompanied by any major change.

Teresa had had some cross-cultural experiences before she went to China, such as hosting exchange students at home and visiting other countries with her children. She also had a lot of experiences in Hawai'i, which is multicultural and international. But living and teaching in China was a big event in her life, although I am not sure to what degree her general outlook has been changed by her cross-cultural journey. Unlike David and Song, whose experiences contributed to dramatic changes in their intellectual and cultural outlook, Teresa's experiences in China might have mainly strengthened her existing worldview.

How to address differences is part of my own pedagogy, although I enact such pedagogy through an interconnected lens (Wang, 2004; Wang & Olson, 2009). While I do question whether the notion of the universal may lead to suppression of human difference, I also understand that for Teresa, and also for some leaders in nonviolence activism such as Gandhi (1927, 1929[1993]), commonality or universality rather than difference should be foregrounded as the basis of nonviolence. On the other hand, post-structural thinkers such as Levinas and Derrida emphasize the importance of the otherness of the other, which cannot be assimilated into the self, as the basis for forming an ethical, nonviolent relationship between self and other (Todd, 2003; Bernstein, 1991). I think that whatever starting point we adopt, the tensionality and interplay between the universal and the particular or between the self and the other must be lived creatively to bring out a dynamic wholeness that does not suppress or fragment differences. Differences cannot be erased because as Aoki (1987 [2005]) poetically puts it, it is in experiencing difference and tension that we feel alive. But differences should not lead to alienation or fragmentation that breaks the fabric of our shared life. Not doing violence to the whole and not doing violence to the part, a pedagogy of nonviolence is a dance of interplay.

Notes

1. Teresa's church is The Church of Jesus Christ of Latter-day Saints. From its name, readers may understand that Teresa's faith belongs to a particular religious branch of Christianity. In my conversations with Teresa, she always used the term "Christian" rather than "Mormon" and she never mentioned the differences between the Mormon Church and mainstream Christianity, which would be difficult for me to understand as an outsider anyway. Chinese students also identified her as a Christian. So I followed her use in this chapter.
2. *Wuwei* is a Taoist term that is difficult to translate into English. Literally, it means nonaction, but it does not mean doing nothing; it means following the path of *Tao*. Essential to *Tao*, *wuwei* transforms everything but does not force any change. *Tao Te Ching* is full of teachings about the power of *wuwei* (e.g., Chapters 2, 3, 37, 43, 57, and 63). Also see Wang (2007, 2013) for further discussion.

3. The *Currere* project is an assignment I give to my students in various classes. This project follows William F. Pinar's (1975) original formulation of *currere*'s four steps—regressive, progressive, analytic, and synthetic steps—in which students reflect, imagine, analyze, and synthesize their educational experience in its political, social, and psychic dimensions to transform their psycho-social conditions for achieving a deeper understanding of what it means to be an educator. I ask students to devote one month to each step and write at least one hour a week. *Currere* is the Latin root of curriculum, and several decades ago Pinar, along with his colleagues (see Miller, 2005; Pinar & Grumet, 1976; Pinar, 1994; Pinar et al, 1995), used *currere* as a way of shifting the focus from techniques and instrumentalism to existential and social aspects of humanity and education in the field of curriculum studies. I have discussed how to use this method in teacher education elsewhere (Wang, 2010c; Wang & Olson, 2009). The class that my student in this story took used the *currere* method as an optional final project.

5

FOLLOWING THE FLOW

An Organic Approach to Research

Waking up early one autumn morning during my China trip, I went out for a walk. Grass was green, the singing of birds was clear, and a small child's smile was endearing. Perception was sharpened, consciousness was heightened, and the natural rhythm of the landscape and soundscape in the surroundings flowed into my interior world to smooth out ragged edges. I never imagined that a heightened consciousness would accompany my research process, but I felt a deepened sense of cross-cultural integration of personhood. The sense of flow that I experienced, I suspect, cannot be replicated in another time, another place, and another setting, not even for me. But following the flow in this cross-cultural research, I get in touch with a deeply uplifting human spirit that is embedded in our shared life.

In this chapter I tell research stories. An organic flow characterizes this study, although it does not mean that the research is a smooth process. It is full of interruptions, contradictions, and unpredictable turns, but an organic whole is formed through a process of curving and interweaving. This chapter first identifies defensive, disruptive, deconstructive, and dialogical moments in the research process to illuminate how these moments come together to dynamically weave research relationality. Secondly, I propose an organic approach to a qualitative, life history study. Drawing upon both the American qualitative research tradition and the Chinese scholarly tradition, I discuss the combination of inductive analysis, intuition, and revelation in this study, which follows the pathways of surprise, stillness, and spirituality to weave the web of research. Finally, I discuss the nature of this cross-cultural study in its dance with multiple languages and multiple cultures.

Research Moments

The frequency of the spontaneous moments of peace, revelation, and connection-making across time and place that happened in my four-month research in China surprised me. These moments were often accompanied by, or a result of, intensified feelings and thoughts. This research study has carried me beyond where I ever imagined going. In my time with the four participants, the rhythms of drama and stillness were also dialectical, interactive, and integrative. The temporality of human life and existence flowed through this research in serendipitous and mysterious ways. In this section, I focus on moments of research that brought me new insights and created twists and turns that enabled the flow of the research to follow nonlinear and complicated patterns. These four moments—defensive, disruptive, deconstructive, and dialogical—are also interconnected.

Defensive Moments

I first noticed defensive moments through my reactions to participants' stories and viewpoints. For instance, one of my first defensive moments was related to Fen's assertion that there was no distinctive line between Chinese thought and Western thought, which directly challenged the basic assumption of my research. After my initial reaction passed, I continued to inquire why Fen made such a statement, which eventually led me to an extensive study of Chinese philosophy and literature at the turn of the 20th century. The key to living with defensive moments is the ability, either on the spot of the actual conversation or afterwards, to look into "why" and switch from reacting to responding. To turn defensive moments into something productive, it is important for the researcher to notice them, to question the researcher's own assumptions, and further transform them into in-depth understanding.

Participants can also have defensive reactions. If the researcher notices such a moment on the part of the participant, the researcher may think about different ways of interaction that can help the participant to get past the defensiveness. On another occasion, Fen commented that Chinese women were more liberated than American women. My further conversation with Fen on the issue did not go into much depth on the spot, as her consideration was purely from whether or not women participated in the workforce. Ironically, many female writers' work, which Fen used in her teaching, focused much more on emotional rather than economical aspects of gender, but Fen only focused on the economical aspect. I suspect that Fen was reacting to my questions defensively intentionally or unintentionally by asserting Chinese women's advantaged status. I am not sure if she would make the same statement to her Chinese female colleagues, and I have not seen such an advantageous positioning of Chinese women in her writings. In any case, I do not feel that I was successful in reducing the defense; otherwise, my conversation with Fen about the role of gender could have been much deeper and more enriched.

Interestingly, when those moments were related to cross-cultural issues, I found different aspects of my cultural identity were provoked to react to participants' perspectives. For instance, my Chinese aspect sometimes reacted to Americans' viewpoints while at other times my American aspect reacted to Chinese's viewpoints, although such a categorization is too neat to capture the complexity of my shifting positioning. Throughout my conversations with Song, as you have seen in Chapter 3, I found myself reacting to his critiques of American culture. Song had a much stronger identification with Chinese culture even though he had had more extensive and longer life experiences in the USA than I had—double my own time of living in the USA at the time of the interview. Noticing this tendency, I reminded myself of the necessity to *respond* rather than *react* to his comments.

On the other hand, when David commented that the USA had an established field of China studies while China had no comparable field of American studies, my first reaction was: How can that be true? In my further research, I realize that David's perspective is shared by others (see Lautz, 2012). My second reaction was that objective investigation in any area was not part of the Chinese scholarship tradition, but David believed that Chinese intellectuals should establish such a field. With Teresa, it was her judgment related to Chinese society and Chinese youth that triggered my reactions. These defensive moments on my part were more or less related to my Chinese identity, but with Song, I was more critical of Chinese viewpoints.

Reaction mobilizes defensive mechanisms and easily provokes, implicitly or explicitly, aggressive postures to block conversation. A nonviolent response, however, is based upon understanding the other's position and where it comes from even though one may disagree with such a position. Based upon such an understanding, conversation can continue to reveal more nuances of participants' viewpoints. For cross-cultural interviews, researchers need to suspend their judgment, ask good questions, and contribute their own input without elevating it above the participant's viewpoint, so that dialogues and conversations can be ongoing to reach more breadth and depth.

Disruptive Moments

I define disruptive moments as participants' interruption of the researcher's assumptions and plan or the researcher's disrupting of participants' story lines. While defensive moments need to be reflected and worked through, disruptive moments may have both interruptive and constructive effects on the research process.

When Fen and I first met, at the end of the meeting she mentioned that the university track field would be a good place to do interviews because we could walk on the track while talking with each other. I had never considered such a possibility and was worried that her voice would not be clear enough with the background noise. Moreover, I could not jot down any notes if I was walking with her. But she was most comfortable with such a setting and actually insisted on it. It was a disruptive moment for me, but I understood that it was her preference, so I decided to go along. I asked her to hold the tape recorder in her hand to make her voice clearer, and she did not mind doing it. It turned out that such a nonconventional arrangement had a productive effect, since I could observe her interactions with others when occasions arose and her multitasking ability, although I could not observe her facial expressions. We did our first two interviews on the track field, and after the interviews, I immediately wrote down field notes.

Another disruptive moment happened at the end of my last interview with Fen. The interview took place in a quiet section of the library, but an acquaintance of hers appeared and asked to stay and listen, and Fen said it was fine with her. That person's presence was a disruption to me, especially since an administrator was expected to present a certain image of herself, of the university, and of China to an overseas scholar. But the discomfort was more on my part than on Fen's part. I ended the interview when our discussion about Western and Chinese intellectuals came to a certain sense of closure; since the disruption happened at the end, it did not influence the interview as a whole. The presence of the third person and my discomfort with it, however, now reminds me of my desire to capture "authentic" viewpoints, which may not be obtainable in the first place, as Fen was already always in a social situation even without others' physical presence.

When I asked David how his cross-cultural experiences influenced his teaching, we had a mutually disruptive moment. First, David disrupted my assumption that cross-cultural experience influences teaching by answering: "No, my teaching methods did not change due to my experiences in China." Then I asked David about how he taught in the classroom setting, and as he described what he was doing in teaching about China at an American university, I questioned him further, shifting the question about teaching to the teacher: "Your cross-cultural exchanges and studies must have some imprint on you as a professor, not just in terms of delivering the content." David then began to elaborate how his experiences in and understandings of China made him comfortable in showing students that China was not an exotic place but an interconnected part of the world. Our discussion led to the second layer of disruption: I disrupted David's assumption that teaching was simply a method or technique by inviting him to think about how his embodiment of a cross-cultural being influenced his teaching of American students about a different culture he had experienced but most students had not.

Interestingly, David's denial of any change in teaching methods was echoed by both Song and Teresa, who taught in cross-cultural settings. I suspect that for many university professors, especially those who are not in teacher education, teaching might be perceived as merely techniques that are separate from self-understanding. Teaching in a phenomenological sense (Aoki, 2005; van Manen, 1990), however, is intimately related to being, and higher education teaching should be oriented towards both knowing and *being* (Barnett, 2009). Teaching and teacher/professor cannot be separated; teaching is less about methods and more about the professor's existential orientation to the world. The mutually disruptive moment between David and me was beneficial for me in understanding more about the assumptions of college teaching and paying more attention to the site of personhood than the subject contents or methods of teaching.

While participants sometimes disrupted my research assumptions spontaneously, I framed my own disruption of their assumptions consciously in a gentler way, careful not to frame the situation or the issue at hand through only my own lens. At the same time, I also think inviting participants to leave the surface of their understandings and go deeper is important.

Deconstructive Moments

I define deconstructive moments as efforts on the part of the researcher or participants to unsettle what is taken-for-granted, to reveal and decenter its dualistic logic in order to loosen its grip. The unsettling effects of deconstructive moments open up language and research to new possibilities, yet do not lead to any easy new consensus.

In the film *Derrida* (Dick & Ziering, 2002), Derrida states, "One of the gestures of deconstruction is to not naturalize what isn't natural. To not assume that what is provided by history, institutions, or society is natural." Derrida responded to the interviewer's questions in a deconstructive way, refusing to offer straightforward answers to any taken-for-granted notions, such as love, hospitality, forgiveness, democracy, and justice. In Derrida's (1992) textual analysis, he reads a text critically to mark the contradictions within a discourse, destabilize the hierarchical thinking inherent in binary opposites, and to reveal the limits of metaphysical conceptualization.

Scholars have discussed the connections and differences between deconstruction and Taoism or Buddhism (Fu, 1992; Loy, 1992; Shepherd, 2007), and I cannot discuss them in detail here. But many (Burik, 2010; Deng, 2005; Park, 2005) agree that both deconstruction and Taoism/Zen question dualism. I think they nevertheless follow different scholarly traditions: Derrida's questioning of dualism follows the Western intellectual history of affirming dualism first in modern philosophy and then deconstructing dualism in post-structuralism; Taoist or Buddhist questioning of dualism first affirms the whole as the origin of human life and then uses an interconnected viewpoint to question dualism. While this distinction needs further discussion, here I use their intersection of deconstructing dualism to define a Taoist style of deconstruction, not as a practice of discourse analysis but as seeing through dualism to restore the view of a bigger picture. Derrida goes deeper into the structure of a discourse in order to deconstruct it from its interior logic, but a Taoist style of unlearning intends to disable the move to dichotomy through an intuitive understanding of human and ecological interdependence and to peel off layers of judgment to realize that opposite forces are not enemies but part of the same web of relationships.

The dialogues between Song and me in Chapter 3 demonstrate a few deconstructive moments. My tendency to split things into good and bad was reflected in various comments I made. For instance, when Song commented that his heart was like still water, not to be disturbed by the outside meaningless turbulence, I immediately responded that it would depend on if the water was dead or alive. Rather than using the Derridian style of going into a complicated analysis of a concept historically and institutionally, Song simply said, "water is water," which effectively deconstructed my mental image of good or bad and reminded me to see reality as it is. In a sense, to term such a moment as deconstructive is misleading, since it is about restoring the picture of the whole, but such restoration cannot happen without deconstructing the mentality of splitting reality into opposites with one side privileged. So in another sense, what has become "natural" for many of us is a split and fragmented world dominated by categories, concepts, and moral judgment, and cutting through such a dominant way of thinking requires nothing less than the denaturalization of the given, as Derrida demonstrates in deconstruction.

I also practiced decentering throughout my dialogues with Song. When he was overenthusiastic about the mystery and double meanings in the Chinese language, I brought to his attention that such a quality is shared among many linguistic systems in different forms. Derrida is famous for playing with the French language (for instance, conflicting double meanings of the French word *brisure* as both "joint" and "break," as Burik [2010] points out). In particular, I insisted on my preference of "zero" over "one" because the centering effect of "one" implies manipulative control and mastery. The discussion about "truth" and "life" was also important to me because centering truth can hardly be free from logocentrism, while the emphasis on life is more inclusive.

While deconstructive moments happened in actual conversations between Song and me, they are also created through my writings, including juxtaposing my emotional experiences as parallel to Song's pursuit of truth in Chapter 3 and juxtaposing my own stories of cross-cultural learning and teaching with Teresa's teaching stories in Chapter 4. When the excess that cannot be reduced into one storyline is demonstrated, different aspects of cross-cultural engagements can be highlighted. More importantly, what speaks silently between the different lines might be elements repressed within a particular culture that cannot be revealed without letting them speak along with a different storyline at the same time (Miller, 2005). Deconstructive moments also appeared in my interaction with Fen, who refused to reconcile conflicting aspects of her life, work, and teaching, including gendered aspects. Her comfort with ambiguity provided a deconstructive space for me to reexamine my own assumptions and rethink China–West intellectual engagement.

Dialogical Moments

I define dialogical moments as moments of interaction between the researcher and participants that lead to new awareness for both parties without necessarily reaching agreement. Bakhtin (Bakhtin, 1984; Morson & Emerson, 1990; Wang, 1997) brings the notion of polyphony into dialogue to unsettle the desire for a final closure. This sense of polyphony is important for framing dialogical moments in my study.

Such moments can be demonstrated visibly in the dialogue section in Chapter 3. While Song and I had a lot of resonance, we also mutually challenged each other on our cross-cultural readings of different issues. Sometimes we advanced each other's arguments by adding our own perspectives, sometimes we provided complementary insights to each other, and other times we disagreed with each other and offered alternative interpretations. In Song's nonattachment to concepts, he did not mind using my terms, such as "zero," and "life," to continue his thought process, although his faithfulness to truth—important to his life journey—did not seem to be changed. At the same time, I also accepted his challenges to my dualistic thinking, although it did not prevent me from following such a line of thinking on another occasion and being challenged again. The movement back and forth between us confirmed, clarified, enriched, questioned, and advanced our own viewpoints, and what happened in the middle space between us is a rich soil from which I can cultivate more understandings and insights in the years to come. It was and is still an ongoing dialogue without reaching any final agreement.

I appreciated Song's ability to follow the flow of conversation and not get stuck with conceptualization, even when it was essential to his thinking. I had dialogical moments with other participants as well in various different ways. My dialogues with Fen were mediated through my reading of her writings, from which I noticed the shift from her earlier pursuit of transcendence to her current concerns with living her daily life fully. Fen admitted that she herself had not noticed such a shift, but my observation did make sense. Our continual conversation did not reach any conclusion, but it left a lot for further thinking. Fen and I also had sustained dialogues about the role of gender, academic freedom, and what it means to be a leader.

In my first interview with David, an important dialogical moment happened when he described his profound reaction to the student movements in 1989 and the crackdown by the Chinese government: "I was always interested in China and studied it a lot, but that was the most psychological experience." I immediately responded: "It was traumatic." It was certainly traumatic for me, and I spontaneously brought my own feelings into the situation, but David quickly agreed: "Oh, yes, very, very traumatic." In the second interview when he referred to it, he said, "It was a trauma as you were saying." At the same time, he understood that the trauma he had "was not the same as the trauma of those students, who died, were injured, or arrested, but it felt like it was a trauma for the whole country." It was both a personal and national trauma, indeed. In later interviews I periodically returned to the issue of how he worked through it and answered his own burning question, "Why not democracy in China?" David formulated different responses to the question. Although no final answer could be offered to it, the question stirred an ongoing dialogue that kept opening up new possibilities.

Defensive, disruptive, deconstructive, and dialogic moments in my research were intertwined, sometimes mutually exchangeable, and on most occasions coexisted in a particular situation. The flow of my research has been enabled by these pauses, interruptions, and dialogues, and in this sense, the flow is both "natural" and "constructed," and efforts on the part of the researcher are essential for going deeper under the superficial mainstream and digging out new tunnels to reach beyond the given. Actually following the flow requires much mindfulness and attentiveness to twists and turns and working with them to facilitate an emergent process. These moments point to an organic approach to a qualitative study in which knowing, feeling, acting, and being form a dynamic process that gives birth to new insights for both the researcher and participants.

An Organic Approach to Research

Interestingly, my participants all embodied a sense of flow in their life journeys: David insisted that he followed a pathway in answering a calling that emerged from his previous experiences without his preplanning; Fen believed that she followed whatever came naturally to her and took advantage of opportunities; Teresa saw serendipity as the thread of her life; Song came back "home" as he followed his internal compass. At the same time, following the flow was never "easy," as each participant had invested her or his time, energy, and commitment and made great efforts to enable the emergence of her or his unique pathway. In following each participant's pathway, this study has become an organic process that integrates body and mind, knowing and being, and East and West to generate insights.

Life History as an Integrative Approach

Ellen Condliffe Langmann (2000) traces the history of American educational research—"an elusive science" as she titles the book—during the past century. It is clear from her historical analysis that the pursuit of scientific research through statistics and technology had dominated the field for the past century. The interpretive turn in philosophy and social sciences, however, has led to the flourishing of qualitative research in education since the 1980s, which questions the objective criteria of knowledge and the accurate representation of reality. Different from positivist research, qualitative research acknowledges and studies the complexity and ambiguity of human life. Petra Munro (1998) points out that the revival of life history methodology in sociology came about because of this new focus, through the interpretive or narrative (or linguistic) turn, on "acknowledging the subjective, multiple and partial nature of human experience" (p. 8).

However, at the beginning stage of qualitative research formulation, there was a tendency to follow the criteria of objectivity in positivist or quantitative research. As Guba and Lincoln (1989) acknowledge, the criteria they had proposed earlier to evaluate qualitative research was derived from quantitative research. But with its efforts to challenge modern dualism of mind over body in research traditions, qualitative research has moved to incorporate more aspects of humanity and transcend quantitative research in which the voices of the body are mostly silenced. In the current research landscape, there are various efforts to expand research horizons. For example, poetry has been adopted as a way to analyze and present data (Prendergast, Leggo, & Sameshima, 2009; Feldman, 2004); the roles of emotions in qualitative research has been explored (Gilbert, 2001; Hasebe-Ludt & Hurren, 2003; McLeod & Thomson, 2009); juxtaposition has been used as a way of showing contradictions within research, teaching, and life (Miller, 2005); and qualitative research has been experienced as a spiritual journey (Rosenblatt, 2001). The traditional separation between body, mind, and spirit for the sake of research objectivity has been disrupted in many different ways in order to demonstrate the complicated and messy nature of human experience.

Among the different qualitative methodologies, life history is more holistic and open-ended than other, more structured strategies, because it situates individual stories in social and cultural history and gives participants more freedom to tell whole stories in their own voices (Goodson & Sikes, 2001; Munro, 1998; Tierney, 2003). The positivist or post-positivist traces of objectivity in qualitative methods are least influential in life history research because life history is an account of a person's life in her or his own words, mediated through the interaction between a researcher and a participant.

I chose life history methodology for my study also because of its open-ended yet contextualized tendency and its potential match with the Chinese notion of personhood situated in history, place, and culture, although I did not expect that this potential match would eventually lead to the incorporation of Chinese scholarly traditions into the study. My study is a topical life history since its focus is not on a person's whole life but on a particular aspect of a person's life. A life history approach in general or in topical format allows an emergent and serendipitous pathway of research to follow its own natural course.

In *Life History Research in Educational Settings,* Ivor Goodson and Pat Sikes (2001) discuss their preference for "relatively unstructured, informal, conversation-type encounters" (p. 28) over structured, purposeful guidance of interviews. Petra Munro (1998) talks about the nondirected nature of interviews, which allows her participants to talk about what is central to their lives. I also started my conversation with each participant in an open way, and left the participants the choice of what to include in their storytelling, starting with childhood experiences. Without this openness, if I had specifically asked participants about their cross-cultural experiences in the beginning, I probably would not have gotten all the stories about Song's experiences in China or Teresa's tales of serendipity, all of which were foundational for their cross-cultural experiences and reflections. As participants had already been informed of the focus of my study, David moved smoothly from his childhood stories to the first turning point he experienced in China as a teenager without any prompting on my part.

For Goodson and Sikes (2001), the objective criteria of traditional empirical research do not fit into life history research, and researchers are expected to share part of their own perceptions with participants as a way of building a trusting research relationship. In my study, I shared my experiences and thoughts with participants throughout the interviews, especially with Song and Fen as they interacted with me in ways that evoked such responses from me. My dialogues with Song became a mode of co-dwelling in the tensionality of life dramas. With Song, my sharing was much beyond the purpose of building trust in a research relationship as it became, for some part of the interviews, a conversation between two collaborators in exploring a mutually interesting topic. To some degree, there are five participants in this study: I am the fifth participant. Four participants' stories are foregrounded, yet the background of my own cross-cultural life and teaching is essential for the whole picture to emerge.

I not only interacted with my participants in a more or less participatory way but also incorporated my own voices with participants' stories in my data analysis and subsequent writing. Moreover, in writing the chapter devoted to each participant, I came up with my analysis framework and presentation style according the nature of my participant's stories and the mode of my interaction with them. Thus, each chapter follows a writing style appropriate for each participant. Therefore analysis and writing also became an emergent process in which the writing mode was interdependent upon what emerged from the research process, yet at the same time my own scholarly co-creativity is clearly demonstrated.

The message of nonviolence came from serendipity and my painstaking effort to make sense of five participants' life histories, a message neither I nor participants expressed in the beginning of the study. But the "life-changing effects" (Goodson & Sikes, 2001, p. 26) of this study on me were crystallized in that particular revelatory moment when David shared his story about the Tiananmen Square tragedy in 1989. Sometimes I wonder: What if I had not found David on the Internet search to replace the other potential American participant? Would the message of nonviolence have spoken to me in this powerful and irreversible way? The truth is, I don't know. It may have taken me years of more work to fully embrace this vision, which was in me and in the world, and yet I had lost touch with it for a long time.

That moment was both serendipitous and revelational. I would not have had reached it if I had used only the conventional method of line-by-line, paragraph-by-paragraph, story-by-story thematic analysis (even though this method is also a useful strategy) in qualitative research. The accumulation of the analysis of parts may or may not lead to an insight into the whole picture. As Robert Atkinson (1998) suggests, "Life stories should be first read as a whole" (p. 67), and it was through reading each participant's stories as a whole and the interactions between the researcher's and participants' life journeys that the most significant meanings spoke to me. The message of nonviolence came from an organic process of deepening understanding, cultivating insights, and reaching revelation, a process in which not only intellect but also emotions and spirit participated. The message came from the whole-being experiencing of surprise, stillness, and spirituality.

Here, the role of spirituality in qualitative research needs to be discussed. In general, in the Western academy, the term "spirituality" is almost automatically under suspect since religion and spirituality are often perceived as interchangeable (Hendrix & Hamlet, 2009). As Ruth Hayhoe (2006) argues, there is a "general disregard for spiritual or religious knowledge in the social sciences" (p. 4), although political, social, and economic knowledge is privileged. Even in qualitative research, scholars are cautious about spiritual knowledge. But the spiritual dimension of life, however we define it, is part of human experience and should not be neglected.

Paul C. Rosenblatt (2001) discusses how his qualitative research over decades has become a spiritual journey for him. Interestingly, he started out as a quantitative researcher, but engaging in qualitative research unexpectedly over the years profoundly influenced him as a person and a researcher. As a result of his research process, he embraces spirituality both in its narrow and broad senses. He is from a Jewish background, and his research has brought him closer to his religion. But his sense of connection with participants across various backgrounds and different countries goes beyond any particular religion. Rosenblatt (2001) defines spirituality as:

> A sense of what is most important in life, what it means to be human, the most fundamental meanings of connections with other humans and with the universe, the meanings of life and death, and what is felt and known about certain things that are at the edge of or beyond rationality and immediate experience. I also think of spirituality as including the ways in which we are in oneness with others, awe as an experience and what causes feelings of awe, the ways we can find profoundly moving and transcendent experience in what might seem to many people to be ordinary, a sense of basic connection to lives and times in the past and in the future, and a sense of relationship with God, however one defines God. (p. 113)

In the broad sense of spirituality, it is difficult to imagine any qualitative research in education that lacks spiritual meanings. A broadly defined sense of spirituality is related to the Chinese sense of spirituality, which has historically influenced Chinese intellectual and aesthetic traditions. One's existence and one's relationship with the other and with the universe is the source of spirituality, with or without a particular notion of God. Not using the language of God, as a person, a researcher, and an educator, I have a profound sense of the spiritual. Similar to Rosenblatt (2001), I find the spiritual effect of this study on me is beyond words. Those profound moments of fusing temporality, places, and cultures into new awareness are simply beyond my pen to describe, although they stayed with me during the study and will always stay with me in my daily life. Their impact is beyond their immediate effect, as I imagine that they will influence me in many years to come in anticipated and unanticipated ways. Spiritual revelation is an important part of organic research.

Blending Chinese Scholarly Tradition with Western Methodology

When I started my research, I did not intend to integrate Chinese scholarship tradition into my research methodology, and only in the latter part of my research did I realize that the natural incorporation of Chinese tradition, not only in the topic of my study but also in its methodological orientation, had happened along the way. In my research design and protocol, I followed Western methodology, which emphasizes inductive analysis and logical reasoning, but my interactions with and understandings of each participant's life journey throughout the research process have been infused by Chinese ways of knowing and being in which intuitive understanding through a whole-being experience plays an important role.

I followed the general procedure of purposeful sampling in life history research (Goodson and Sikes, 2001; Munro, 1998) to find four participants with a balance of nationality and gender. I collected interview, observation, and document data from each participant to make triangulation possible. I kept a research journal that recorded the research process and provided reflective descriptions of researcher subjectivity. I also wrote down poetic thoughts or intuitive commentaries about my "home-"coming experiences in the journal. The transcription of interviews and narrative recordings of observation notes were completed word by word, including the information about participants' speech patterns such as pauses, emotional expressions, and bodily movements. I also checked on the accuracy of interview transcripts, shared book chapter drafts with the three participants who wanted to read them, and asked them to feel free to give or not give feedback. All these efforts were intended to collect thorough and adequate qualitative data for analysis and to meet the criteria for rigor in qualitative research (Guba & Lincoln, 1989).

Although there were moments of instant enlightenment in my interactions with Song during the interview process, the incorporation of the Chinese ways of thinking, awareness, and spirituality happened more intentionally during data analysis. In this process, my understanding of the qualitative data along with the revelation of new awareness led to a synthesis of knowing and being for me as a cross-cultural educator and researcher. There were moments when words just flowed out, effortlessly, into my research journal, and I felt like I was in touch with the underlying current of life: my ego was dissolved in the vibration of shared life energy, yet simultaneously I was affirmative of my own existence in this world. Everybody, everything, and every existence became connected in those moments of instant union that transcended the separateness of each entity—the manifestation of the existence of *Tao*. Openings to the sense of a mysterious interconnectedness beyond me yet influencing me blend logic, intuition, and revelation in my research.

I think it is significant, as you read in the beginning of this book, that I "saw" the structure of this book—the final product of my analysis—when I was transcribing my interview with Teresa. That moment at once fused my act of interview transcription (one of the most common tasks for a qualitative researcher in forming a relationship with empirical data) and my intuitive synthesis. My scholarly creativity blended the empirical pursuit of accurately transcribing participants' words with the imaginative integration at another level, even though the two tasks were not logically related to each other at that moment. That moment captured the spirit of this study: The process of interviewing the participants, my own cross-cultural encounters with history, culture, and the human psyche, and scholarly imagination and synthesis came together at the moment. Such moments happened throughout the research process as I made various unexpected connections within and across languages and cultures.

Interestingly, those moments of experiencing a rare connection with the whole directed me back to Chinese scholarly traditions, which I had not paid much attention to earlier. As a cross-cultural researcher, I was educated in both Chinese and American graduate schools, and both ways of thinking—if there are separate ways—must have been present in my (collective) unconsciousness and consciousness as I entered the research situation. Different from modern Western research traditions, which emphasize the pursuit of truth through scientific rationalism and empirical verification, Chinese scholars argue that the Chinese scholarly tradition is based upon an organic integration of knowledge, emotions, and spirit (Sun, 2006; Yang, 2005; Zhang, 1995). Awareness that mediates between reason and emotion (Yang, 2005) in which stillness plays a role, intuitive thinking that generates insights into the whole and sees the bigger picture beyond conflicts (Wang, 2007), and spiritual union with *Tao* (Sun, 2006) characterize the integrative quality of Chinese scholarship. While affirming these differences, almost all Chinese scholars argue for integrating Chinese and Western methodology, because they believe that the transformation of traditions on both sides is necessary for scholarly creativity in a new century.

My conversation with Song already touched upon this issue, although we did not necessarily frame it as an issue of methodology. With strong empirical training in the USA, Song discussed the Western emphasis on rational analysis and theory building, which is supposed to be value free. By contrast, Chinese scholarship tradition has not developed such an attention to objective accuracy and scientific pursuit of detailed analysis, but emphasizes the role of whole-being experiences and insights to reach new consciousness. Through conversing with Song, I realized that good research needs to incorporate all the elements of knowing, intuition, and revelation so that the detailed and reliable analysis of the parts and the insights into the whole can be integrated through insightful and "spirit-ful" (Doll, 1998) knowing. In other words, using both American and Chinese wisdom to conduct cross-cultural research unites both the means and end of research towards cross-cultural understanding, imagination, and collaboration.

At the end of the research, I can now appreciate the complementary contributions of both analytic strategies and integrative wisdom, and I refer to such a combination as "organic" since it heals the cultural and epistemological divide. The Western qualitative research tradition departed from empirical positivism half a century ago to explore alternative ways of research. At the same time, the Chinese scholarly tradition has struggled for more than a century with how to integrate Western and Chinese orientations into a more fruitful union. So there is no longer a categorical line between Chinese and American research methodology—just as contemporary Chinese thought has become a hybrid product as a result of encountering the West—and it would be misleading to sharply distinguish the two. But in my study, because participants include both Chinese professors and American professors, and the researcher is conscious of her cross-cultural identity, the sense of combination is more clearly demonstrated and realized.

If knowing is about understanding the details of a phenomenon from a certain distance, and intuition is about gaining insights into the whole through interbeing interaction (including with nonhuman beings), then revelation is about a moment of fusion of life energy flowing *through* artificial boundaries to achieve clarity into the interconnectedness of life. In an organic approach to research, integration of body, mind, and spirit is enabled by the unity of knowing, intuition, and revelation. But it is not a seamless unity; it is an interactive and polyphonic unity that emerges from the process rather than being pre-imposed. In such an approach, both the breadth and depth of research are strengthened. Here, breadth refers to clearing out conceptual barriers to reach an intuitive understanding of the whole, and depth refers to a thorough understanding of the parts to reach the whole. When breadth and depth meet, new insights emerge.

In such a research process, detailed analysis and the compatibility of techniques and methods are necessary. At the same time, integration cannot happen automatically with the mere accumulation of techniques, but must be situated in whole-being experiences to make meaningful connections among separate or fragmented elements knowledge. Differential knowledge of the parts and integrative insights of the whole interact with each other to achieve a higher level of understanding. Importantly, integration must be inclusive, not to establish a hierarchical system or an elitist model but to attend to the multiple. Here I prefer the metaphorical meaning of "zero," rather than a definite "one," to symbolize such integration (see the last Chapter 0), which is generative, dynamic, and open to differences. In this zero space, the triple aspects of scholarly creativity—logic, intuition, and revelation—come together organically. An organic approach to research is a non-violent approach.

Turns and Curves in Doing Cross-Cultural Research

Cross-cultural research is a broad concept, sometimes referring to different cultures within the same nation. For instance, negotiating with the mainstream culture, racial, ethnic, or gendered minorities have to do "cross-cultural" work. In my study, cross-cultural research refers to understanding participants' transnational engagements with another country, although their cross-cultural movements are intimately connected with their intra-cultural engagements with social differences. In particular, American professors' engagement with China and Chinese professors' engagement with the USA were situated in the history of the two countries' complicated relationships, which in the 20th century were often hostile. Both David and Song went to the other country when the two countries had just opened their doors to each other in the early 1980s. Fen's intellectual engagement and Teresa's teaching in China happened during a later, friendlier time, although during recent years, the tension between two countries seems to have grown. Such a background highlighted the dramatic national differences in ideology, cultural norms, and intellectual traditions. In bringing these four professors' life histories together, this international cross-cultural study is full of twists and turns. In the following sections, I reflect on and discuss two important issues in doing cross-cultural research: language and subjective positioning.

Language, Translation, and Cross-Cultural Research

The first obstacle to doing cross-cultural research is the language barrier. As a cross-cultural, bilingual person, my first advantage in doing this study is that I can comfortably use both Chinese and English, one of which is each participant's native language, although translation can still be an issue. With Teresa, I basically used English since she did not speak Chinese; with Fen, I used Chinese since she did not speak English. I transcribed interviews in the original languages the participants used. I did not translate everything in Fen's interviews into English during my data analysis because I did not want to lose the bigger holistic picture of her stories. When I read and interpreted Fen's stories, the language I used to process my own thought was Chinese, compatible with her linguistic—and cultural—expressions. But later I had to write her stories in English. My writing of Chapter 2 went through an internal translation from Chinese into English, and when I wrote her stories, I processed my thoughts mostly in English.

For David, I think his Chinese is as good as my English, if not better. So before we started, I asked him which language he would like me to use for the interviews. He said whatever I preferred was fine. Perhaps because he is American, somehow I felt more comfortable talking with him in English. He used Chinese, however, once in a while when phrases were difficult to translate into English or when he was referring to the names of Chinese places and universities. Those Chinese phrases reflected unique Chinese situations or Chinese thought, and it was interesting for me to observe when he used the Chinese language, which often suggested these phrases' incompatibility with English.

With Song, the situation was a bit different; the major difference was his awareness of the role of language in thought, and he played with Chinese language to show its wisdom and mystery. Song is bilingual, but we naturally communicated in Chinese, although occasionally he used English to express his ideas, much more than David used Chinese. And when occasions called for it, I also used English as well. Interestingly, when Song started out narrating his stories in China, he seldom used English, but during the later interviews when he switched to reflect on the events, he began to use English much more often. To a great degree, his thought process, after two decades of studying and teaching in the USA, was already bilingual. I transcribed my interviews with him using both languages, faithful to Song's own language choice.

In our conversations about Chinese language, Song revealed several ways in which Chinese characters originally implied a meditative sensibility that might have been lost in the contemporary use. First, the same Chinese word can carry mutually contradictory meanings. For example, the Chinese character *guang* (光) has a double meaning of both light and emptiness. Song commented that light is a unique, zero mass but carries energy, so the double meaning of the word implies that enlightenment is achieved by emptiness. Second, phrases that originally had positive meanings now have negative connotations, for example, *deyiwangxing* (得意忘形). Song interpreted *yi*—the second word in this four-word phrase—as consciousness and explained the phrase's original meaning as "When one reaches consciousness, one forgets the matter's form." It was originally a positive term that indicated the liberating effects of meditative consciousness, but in the contemporary age it has come to mean that one is too elated to remember reality. Third, the combination of seemingly contradictory words can indicate the best state of consciousness one can reach. For instance, *liao* (了) and *de* (得) can form different phrases to indicate similar meanings. For Song, *liao* (了) is about Buddhist emptiness and *de* (得) is about the Taoist approach to obtaining *Tao*. They seem to be in contradiction since one is about getting rid of attachments while the other is about getting in touch with *Tao*. He explained to me that they were both from the same source but demonstrated different facets, so they were actually compatible with each other. When the two are used together with the bridge of negation, *bu* (不), *liaobude* (了不得), or *budeliao* (不得了), the term refers to a superior state. Such linguistic play not only reflects Chinese philosophy, in which opposites come from the same source, but also indicates that the contemporary transformations of meanings have a tendency to downplay the role of meditative intuition.

Even for a researcher like me who is familiar with two languages, translating Chinese into English as I write up these chapters is difficult. After translating Fen's and Song's stories and thoughts, I know that some meanings are lost or there is an element of displacement, and the worst part is that there is not much that I can do to bridge the gap, a gap not only linguistically but also intellectually and culturally unbridgeable. Some journals in China now include English abstracts for Chinese articles, but I can see how the self-translated English words cannot capture the spirit of the Chinese thought either. The fun Song had with the Chinese language and our shared laughter are simply impossible to convey in English. Yet I must find a way, as many cross-cultural persons do, to translate in this globalizing, transnational, and intercultural world. Dwelling on the unbridgeable bridge in Aoki's (2005) terms, translation is a creative and co-creative activity, contributing to the transformation of language, thought, and culture, as Chapter 2 demonstrates, that translation played a transformative role in modern China.

Researchers who don't know "the language of the other" (Ng-A-Fook, 2009) are linguistically uncertain about the match between the translated words and the original. But researchers who know the other language, like me, are actually more aware that an exact match in translation is impossible, and yet I must find a way to translate. The language of the other is not only linguistic but also national and cultural. As Mei Wu Hoyt and I (Wang & Hoyt, 2007) argue elsewhere, intercultural and cross-cultural creativity dwells in the multiple tensionality of linguistic and cultural translation. Translations *"work* those relationships most often in the gaps created by tension, rupture, disjuncture" (Miller, 2005, p. 213) to extend to the other horizon without being able to reach it in full embrace. The tensionality of translation is a generative space where differences are both highlighted and mediated, and when a bridge is made, it can never be fully settled but is always open to new playful acts. Cross-cultural research is situated in this unsettling yet generative space.

Complexity of Subjective Positioning

In a cross-cultural study, the researcher must negotiate multiple languages and cultures with participants who also have multiple identities. In my study, not only is the researcher doing a cross-cultural study, the participants also live cross-cultural lives. My subjective positioning in relationship with participants' subjectivity becomes complicated and messy, but in embracing this complexity I let the situation and each participant's unique positioning influence my own research positioning. However, following the intersubjective flow does not mean giving up the researcher's responsibility; it means affirming my research subjectivity using an emergent approach to make an original scholarly contribution.

Qualitative research does not pretend to be neutral and objective, but it has a general commitment to letting participants' voices come through and having deep respect for participants' own perspectives. Yet at the same time, much of narrative inquiry and life history methodology literature (Connelly & Clandinin, 1990; Hole, 2007; Munro, 1998) encourage researchers to have a collaborative relationship with participants as a way of dealing with difficult issues of representation, voice, authority, and ethics. I see the orientation of attending to participants' own viewpoints and the orientation of collaboration as potentially conflicting. Collaboration is more than people working together. It must include an element of mutuality or even equality. If the research is collaborative, it not only means that the researchers share their own life stories one way or another but also implies a relationship of back and forth movement of thoughts and feelings between the researcher and participants to achieve a certain degree of mutuality. Collaboration potentially leads to collaborators on both sides changing their perspectives. If such changes occur, what count as participants' own authentic voices?

Petra Munro (1998) discusses her collaborative intention in her life history research with female teachers but finds that such an intention did not match the expectations of her participants—"life historians," she called them—and they resisted such a collaborative effort. She discusses in detail various dilemmas related to feminist collaborative life history research. For example, collaboration makes it difficult to spare life historians from being subject to the researcher's analytic framework. "Getting 'too' close" (p. 128) has its risk of not allowing life historians to fully speak in their own voices, but Munro's goal of using life history methodology is to "validate women's voices and experiences as truth" (p. 129) in a feminist narrative inquiry. While not reaching a resolution, she questions to what degree research relationships with participants can be collaborative.

I started this life history project without assuming a collaborative position but adopted an emergent approach: What emerges from the research process is not totally up to the researcher but depends on participants as well. For me, a truly collaborative project cannot follow the typical qualitative research protocol, which requires anonymity—with rare exceptions (See Ruth Hayhoe's [2006] portraits of influential Chinese educators)—because participants should have substantial influence over not only the research process but also the presentation of the research in writings and publications. When ultimately the researcher assumes sole authorship, to what degree can such research be called collaborative? I don't think I assumed much of an authority position during the interview process since my participants, as mature and established university professors, actually held more authority than I did in their respective fields and I perceived myself as a student, but my authorship of this book gives me an authority position that I simply must accept with a sense of responsibility.

Song was acutely aware of this issue when we discussed the chapter focusing on his stories. He commented: "It is not my story." He knew that it would be a story told through my own interpretative lens regardless of what or how I wrote. But he showed much interest in what I was going to write and wanted to read it. He provided brief comments on the first draft of the chapter, commending its creativity and pointing out the inaccuracy of some translations of political terms, but he did not respond further when I sent another draft. I also talked with him about nonviolence as an educational theme in the last interview, and he acknowledged that the theme was at the level of the human existential conditions and beyond the political systems he was familiar with. While all other participants asked me one way or another whether our interviews served the purpose of my study, Song was the only participant who did not have such concerns, and when he felt he had finished with his stories in 2009—even though there was much more to tell—he did not want to meet face to face again for the follow-up interview, although he was happy to meet me when I traveled to China in 2011. However, the collaborative nature and mutual influence of our conversations is the strongest among the four participants. Even with such mutuality, Song's acknowledgment that "it is not my story" still rings true to a great degree. It *is and is not* his story.

An emergent approach does not set a predetermined agenda—not even with the good intention of collaboration or empowerment—but it follows the principle of respecting participants and treating them ethically. Before I started the research, I was clear that I wanted to learn from my participants and that what I would learn would also benefit my own cross-cultural life. I did not feel the need to "empower" participants, but I knew the interaction process might have certain effects. In our interactions in the research process, I followed the preferred pattern of each participant. I shared my stories or my perspectives when I perceived that participants would like to hear them or the research situation asked for it. But I did not perceive sharing my own stories as something inherently more ethical than not sharing, because it depended on participants' interests and contexts, and whether my sharing matched the flow of the research. The life history approach involves a lot of time and energy on the part of participants, so I wanted to give participants freedom to decide to what degree they wanted to contribute, and I built an element of choice into the informed consent form as well.

Among the four participants, I shared the least with Teresa during the interviews because she was so enthusiastic about telling all her stories, and I did not often interrupt her storytelling. She seemed to assume that my study was about her, not about me, but at the end of the study, she invited me to share my own stories. I told David a little bit about me as he asked a few questions during the process, but I did not share anything substantial with him, as his questions were passing comments rather than real openings for my own stories. He had a very tight schedule, so I also felt the urgency to capture his stories as much as possible. Even though I told him that the student movements of 1989 influenced me a great deal, I did not discuss anything in detail with him as he was immersed with making sense of that painful experience all over again during the interviews. I did insert the term "trauma" that David had not used but later adopted. In general, I withheld myself more with Teresa and David than with the Chinese participants, although it was not intentional on my part; it was a result of particular interactions with different participants.

I was more tentative in asserting myself into my interactions with American participants also because the tradition of American research implies a more objective position (David did a lot of archival research). I was relatively at ease with the Chinese participants, even though I had not met Fen before and there was not necessarily any sense of rapport between us when I was doing this research. During the third interview, before we said goodbye to each other, Fen was pleased to know that I planned to get married that year and commented, "That is really important. I don't care about your career, but having a family is really good news." Here the research relationship gave way to friendship. Both Teresa and Fen addressed me as a friend at the end of the research, but Fen assumed a position of a friend even before the interview started. When we first met, she said that she saw me as "an insider," which in Chinese society means somebody she can trust and be frank with (see Chu & Liao [2007] for a discussion of the insider/outsider in Chinese tradition). Moreover, since many of the conversations I had with her were about intellectual issues, I needed to insert my own thoughts during the interview process to generate questions. By comparison, listening to Teresa's story in its holistic flow did not demand such insertions.

As we saw in Chapter 3, Song commented that the interpersonal boundary was thin in Chinese society. Because of this relative lack of a substantial distinction between the private and the public, and self and other, I interacted with both Fen and Song in a more mutual way. In reflecting on such a difference in subjective positioning, I realize that "code switching" (Caughey, 2006, p. 68) not only happens in cross-cultural life but also in cross-cultural research, especially when the researchers themselves live cross-cultural lives. In other words, I was more like a Chinese with Chinese participants and more like an American with American participants. Such a switch was not necessarily an intentional research act, but happened as a response to the situation and as a result of my preference for "following the flow" rather than setting up an agenda to be applied to all participants. Is such differential treatment fair to participants? For such qualitative cross-cultural research, I believe that treating all participants the same would be less fair, because it would ignore linguistic, social, and cultural differences.

However, such a portrayal presents too clear-cut a picture; code switching is only one mode of making intercultural connections in this study. Three of the participants had substantial cross-cultural life experiences, so participants also have a different degree of integrated subjectivity. Both David and Song used two languages in their interviews with me, and both of them have an American aspect and a Chinese aspect—if we can separate the two aspects in one person's subjective landscape. On most occasions, two cultural aspects cannot be separated, since we all integrate both into our own subjectivity in various ways of blending and detaching. Moreover, social, historical, and cultural contexts influence a person's life but do not determine a person's identity or subjective positioning. For instance, even though there is a sharper distinction between the private and the public in American society, such a distinction collapsed in Teresa's storytelling.

Teresa, as an American participant, shared some of her life stories that most would consider "private." She was the only participant who volunteered her love stories, for instance. Fen shared a little bit about her husband, daughter, and parents-in-law's and their roles in her life, but in a brief manner, but Teresa told her stories all at once without any hesitation. Both David and Song mentioned nothing about their significant others, a topic I did not feel comfortable asking about due to gendered considerations. While Teresa was the oldest among the participants and her age might contribute to such a candid expression, I believe it was her openness and enthusiasm that contributed the most to the fuller range of her life stories. Thus, cross-cultural study needs to be cautious about subsuming a person into a general cultural tendency.

In terms of research procedure, cross-cultural issues emerged more with Fen than with any other participant. Adopting a Western protocol did not lead to any substantial issues with Teresa, David, or Song, although they did not care much about the formal procedure of informed consent forms (they all signed them). Fen did not understand what the informed consent was, and after I explained the rationale, she still did not see much value in it. Later she also found it curious that I used a pseudonym for her in telling her stories. She assumed that in such a study, I would use her real name, and I realized later that she took pride in the fact that I had selected her as one of two Chinese participants and the only person in the north part of China. In China, researchers using narrative inquiries or life history methodology tend to select participants who are highly respected in society and often the participants' real names are used. Fen felt it was an honor to be chosen for participation and did not see why anonymity was needed to protect participants' rights.

In China, building relationships is not only important for the process of research but is also important before the research starts. As I mentioned in the opening Chapter 0, I recruited Fen through personal networking after I found her information through an Internet search. Another professor hosted a dinner for both of us as our initial contact. While American research tradition may see such a way of recruitment as having the potential to interfere with the authenticity of the later data collection, the mediating professor, who did not know Fen personally but contacted her through another person, made the suggestion, and I readily accepted it since it followed the Chinese tradition for introducing two strangers. Forming research relationships in different cultural contexts can be different, from the initial recruitment to the end of the research.

An organic approach to research, however, does not lead to neat conclusions or seamless unity. As the different modes of presentation and analysis for each participant's stories from Chapter 1 to Chapter 4 show, each participant walks her or his own unique pathway, and I have co-traveled along their memory lane to experience the spirit of their respective life journeys. The central thread of nonviolence is not the only thread that holds the study together, but it is the message that speaks most strongly to me. The temporality (both external and internal) of this study also played an important role in giving birth to this message. Immediately after finishing the first three interviews with Song, when my mind was more open and receptive, I traveled to interview Teresa first and then David. Teresa's story about the death of her parents and David's story of the 1989 tragedy combined with my own memory of the life-or-death situation produced a revelatory moment when the vision of nonviolence was clearly revealed to me. There is a way to die peacefully (Fowler, 2005) and there is a way to live meaningfully in the midst of death (Pinar, 1992).

Weaving together participants' stories, however, I claim the vision of nonviolence as my own "synthesis," the final moment of *currere* (Pinar, 1975 [1994]): I relocated the meaning of the present through the thread of nonviolence after studying five cross-cultural pathways. Except for discussing with Song the existential significance of nonviolence, I have not had a chance to share this theme with any other participant. Because of Teresa's affirmation of love and peace, I imagine she would support it. She referred to Jesus' teachings of the message of love in the world, "not with the sword, but in totally peaceful, non-violent ways." And she acknowledged that Gandhi's formulation of nonviolence was a result of studying Christianity and Judaism along with Hinduism and Buddhism. David denounced the violence of the communist revolution and affirmed the moral center of history in justice, but I did not have an opportunity to discuss with him whether his notion of justice is compatible with the message of nonviolence.

Following the flow of this cross-cultural research, I circle back to a zero space of nonviolence. In the next chapter, which is again numbered Chapter 0, I elaborate a playful curriculum of nonviolence.

0
A PLAYFUL CURRICULUM OF NONVIOLENCE IN A ZERO SPACE

Ideas and thoughts cross national borders. (Fen)

Every situation was a great opportunity in another way if you think about it. (David)

Play is transcendent. (Song)

Serendipity is the theme of my life. And that is the way I teach. (Teresa)

We have traveled with four participants on their cross-cultural pathways and now circle back to a zero space, full of possibilities. Is it a full circle? The number four is Carl Jung's favorite number because it is close to a circle figuratively and it symbolizes balance and wholeness. We can clearly see his preference in his drawing of a mandala[1] and the use of its symbolism in individual case analysis (Jung, 1969, pp. 355–391). Both Taoist and Jungian symbolism is marked by the circle with no beginning and no ending, indicating the perpetual circular movement of life (Rosen, 1996). But I don't envision enclosing a zero space as a full circle because openings to alternative pathways are important to keep the circle alive (see the diagram later in this chapter). In circling back and moving forward, I discuss the multiplicity of cross-cultural pathways in their intersections and divergence, depict a zero space of educational dynamics, and compose lyrics of playful curriculum about, through, and for nonviolence.

Multiple Cross-Cultural Pathways

By now, we have heard four cross-cultural professors' intriguing stories. From the resonance, dissonance, and juxtaposition of their life histories, we not only glimpse a bigger picture of China–US engagement but also witness each individual's creativity and singularity in their unique journeys. Individuality, relationality, and national and cultural contexts interact to form a complicated, ever-shifting landscape of cross-cultural life and education. Here I highlight several aspects that have important implications for nonviolence education.

Temporality

Temporality is an important existential and educational theme (Huebner, 1999; Pinar, 2004), particularly for life history research (Caughey, 2006). It not only refers to external time, which is chronological and linear, but also to internal time, which is experienced and nonlinear (Wang, 2010c). While the boundary between the external and internal is arbitrary and they are always intertwined rather than separate, they indicate different dimensions of temporality. The notion of time is also culturally situated. According to Liu (1974), the Chinese sense of time is more circular, whereas the Western sense of time is more linear. Just like a circle, "time, for the Chinese, is forever flowing, without beginning or end" (p. 146). Jon Smythe's (2012) study of Peace Corps volunteers' experiences also indicates that part of Americans' culture shock was related to a different sense of time in Africa, Asia, and Eastern Europe.

Both internal and the external time played a role in my participants' stories, although what is most interesting for me is their internal experiencing of temporality in different places and situations. Their stories mainly involve the past and the present, but they all gesture openness to the future. Fen and David were born in the same year, while Song is one generation and Teresa two generations older. Such a difference in external time is related to changes in social and cultural contexts, so their stories reflect more or less a historical change. But internal experiencing of time can be stuck at a particular site while external time moves forward, regardless of a person's inner difficulties. We can be frozen in the past collectively and individually due to historical and personal trauma, and most of the time we don't even realize such an effect of the past. Such an internal time can stretch back and forth to prolong its impact if we don't attend to and work through those psychic attachments to difficulty. Thus here I focus on my participants' relationships with difficult memories in which individual and collective time intersect.

David's traumatic experiences in 1989 set him on a voyage to further engage China in China–US educational exchanges. In this process, he gradually let go of the original difficulty and shifted his lens intellectually and cross-culturally. He recursively returned to his burning question and continued making more sense of it. Such a nonlinear movement of inner time worked in David's life history for intellectual and personal growth. While he laughingly admitted that he had not figured it out yet, I believe it was an ongoing, interminable process in which the original difficulty had been transformed into a generative site to carve out new possibilities. His recursive efforts marked his willingness and capacity to work through difficulty in productive ways. Aware of the temporality of cross-cultural learning, which is not flat but has depth, David cultivated pedagogical patience for his students' learning process. Giving students enough time and room to work out their own problems, David was attuned to pedagogical temporality.

Song's stories show another example of working through trauma for enlightenment, not in the modern Western sense of Enlightenment but in a Buddhist sense of emptying out rational categorical thinking to reach wisdom. The temporality of Song's life was also recursive, as his return to China re-affirmed his roots, yet such a return was not a repetition, since his relationship with the Chinese situation was changed irreversibly after his journey in the USA. The comfort that scientific reason initially provided him in his American doctoral studies, soothing the wound of the Cultural Revolution, gradually gave way to a search for a lost language of his own—also a lost language within China during its modernization and Westernization in the past century. It was Zen and Taoist meditations—stillness of time—that reconnected Song with his homeland, dissolving the psychic, emotional, and bodily barriers that blocked his reception to life energy. My work with him has also touched a part of me usually not visible in the busy-ness of everyday life, a part existing long before I was born, and in being touched, I have sensed a deeper integration of my cross-cultural personhood. In David's and Song's stories—and my stories—dwelling and crossing are integrated.

Teresa's stories were different. While David's and Song's senses of time were socially and individually situated, her sense of time was universal because of her religious belief. While nursing her parents and witnessing their passing away was deeply emotional for her, she felt that it was a relief for them to go to Heaven after suffering from illness. Her belief in God seemed to provide a comfort to shield her from experiencing any insoluble sadness. When she was a teenager, longing for freedom from family responsibility, she once tried to run away but was brought back home immediately. She mentioned this incident in a passing comment and did not see it as significant. Teresa appeared to be always optimistic and did not let bad things get to her. Her universal approach to time was also related to her universal approach to life in general. Liu (1974) argues that the Greek philosophers searched for the unchangeable and that the Christian tradition promises eternity, whereas the Chinese tradition of time is about change according to situations. Teresa's concept of universal time followed the Christian tradition, and her sense of temporality was not influenced by the Chinese concept during her stay in China.

For Fen, her father's unexpected death when she was becoming an adult must have had an impact on her. Louise W. Knight (2010) believes that Jane Addams' early loss of her father was devastating, especially because she did not have a chance to work through her relationships with him as an adult. While Addams was close to her father, Fen was not close to her father. But Fen also did not have a chance to form a relationship with her father as an adult, so such a premature ending to the relationship might have left a lingering effect. Fen said her father's sudden death was like a dream. This sense of unreality might also have been related to her underdeveloped relationship with him. Fen acknowledged her mother's strong influence over her, but her mother passed away early as well. Like Teresa, Fen did not dwell on any difficulties, even as a child. She did not have much material comfort when she was young, yet she found space in nature for playing. Different from Teresa, however, Fen's sense of time was not universal, and she acknowledged the influence of aging on her perspective on life.

The flow of temporality in these participants' life and cross-cultural engagements is informative for intercultural education, since the experiencing of time is individually and culturally contextualized. A nonviolent relationship with temporality in education and pedagogy is also a nonviolent relationship with students' sense of being and becoming.

Engagement With Differences

As I discuss elsewhere, how a person becomes open to a different culture depends on both personal and social contexts (Wang, 2009). As we saw in Chapter 2, at the turn of the 20th century many Chinese intellectuals and scholars were expected to be open to Western thought and culture, although they approached the West in different ways. As Li (2010) comments, because of the influences of Western literary theory in the 1920s and 1930s, Chinese scholars "had more distance from Chinese traditional literary criticism" (p. 118) than from Western theories. The influx of liberal Western thought stopped in 1949 when the New China officially adopted a Marxist ideology, but reemerged after the 1980s when the open door policy was implemented. Song was among the first groups of Chinese to go to the USA after the Cultural Revolution. When Fen started her doctoral studies, this trend had already intensified in the Chinese intellectual field. At the turn of the 21st century, how to integrate Western and Chinese learning is still a major challenge for Chinese intellectuals.

Fen's research of the Western literary theory, philosophy, and cultural studies were less intentional on her part as an individual person and more due to the Chinese intellectual context, which required Western learning. Like the May Fourth generation, she had to encounter the West intellectually even though not experientially. Eleven years older than Fen, Song chose to go to the USA in his quest for truth and for an alternative to the Chinese political model. At that time, Song believed that everything would be better, if not perfect, in the USA. It took considerable effort on Song's part to initiate his journey to the USA and enroll himself at an American university. In other words, Chinese professors have had to encounter the West intellectually since the 1980s, even though the degree of personal initiative may be different.

The new waves of globalization since the 1990s have centered in Euro-American economic, social, and cultural forces, which further intensified global dissemination of Western thought (Smith, 2003a, 2008). Although the recent rise of China as a world power has begun to draw more American attention than before, the China–West relationship in the past century was mainly one-directional, making it necessary for Chinese professors to encounter the West. However, whether scholars are proactive in engaging a different thought may influence the depth of their engagement, as we can see in that the qualities of Fen's and Song's engagements with American or Western thought were different.

Examining the other side of the ocean for the past century, on the other hand, we know that it took something special for an American or a Westerner to become truly interested in Chinese culture and Chinese thought. At the beginning of the 20th century, the image of China fell to an all-time low in Europe (Pohl, 2003). Although Western intellectuals began to show interest in Taoist pacifist traditions after World War I, such interest stayed at the margin. Sometimes it took nothing less than a rebellious posture against European traditions to be oriented toward the East, as Allan Watts' stories show (Watts, 1972; Wang, 2009).

After the 1980s, David's and Teresa's entrances into China were not marked by rebellion. David's chance to go to China as a teenager was based upon his father's decision to take a political risk. For young David, politics was not a concern but going to another country excited him. His cosmopolitan childhood experiences gave him a solid foundation for taking advantage of an unexpected opportunity. Here, his cosmopolitan lens was not marked by asserting similarity or universality but by attending to the cultural and social differences in another nation. Although many things were dramatically different and the material conditions were miserable, David respected his Chinese peers and their ability to live and study in a difficult situation. His cosmopolitan lens was marked by the "comprehension of alterity" (Pinar, 2009, p. vii). As Pinar (2009) argues, a cosmopolitan curriculum needs to negotiate between the local and the global, with a commitment to understanding others in their own contexts and situations. A cosmopolitan approach well-immersed in experiencing the international in David's approach did not meld diversity and multiplicity into one lens.

Teresa went to China following a serendipitous phone call from her friend inviting her to teach English in China in 2000. Similar to David, this chance came to her, and she had the wisdom to embrace a new opportunity. When Teresa went to China, however, China had already changed from the early 1980s when David went there. The material, social, cultural, educational conditions of China had progressed dramatically during those two decades. It is interesting to observe here that David had more appreciation of Chinese culture and his Chinese peers than Teresa who, for instance, felt that Chinese youth were less mature than American youth. Perhaps their first encounters produced similar qualitative effects regardless of the degree of the gap, but I also think that their different orientations made a difference. In Teresa's approach, the universal Christian lens does not necessarily consider Chinese culture fully equal; let's not forget that China was perceived as a notoriously pagan culture by Christian missionaries (Lin, 1959). So David's and Teresa's openings to China were not quite the same, and their age differences during their first encounters with China might have played a role as well.

The intersections and divergence in the ways these four professors were open to another culture influenced their modes of sustained engagement through dramas, turning points, gradual sinking-in, transformative learning, and sustained engagement in stillness. Teresa approached different cultures through the notion of universal love, but interestingly, her cultural and pedagogical difference made her teaching particularly appealing to Chinese students. Fen approached differences through her refusal of categorization, but she did not deny the concrete and specific differentiation between Chinese thought/culture and Western thought/culture. David was comfortable in international settings, bilingual and with dual citizenship, but he did not hold a universal approach like Teresa. He embodied differences *within himself,* so his engagement with differences was threaded through an organic relationship that acknowledges but does not radicalize the role of difference. Song approached difference first through understanding and affirming differences and then through dissolving boundaries of differences into a shared sense of humanity. While affirming interconnectedness, he still values cultural differences and identified himself more as a Chinese, even though identity is no longer an issue for him. The four participants' cross-cultural pathways also demonstrated their own individuality and creativity as they negotiated with the multiple and followed serendipitous winding roads.

In these cross-cultural engagements, life and thought do not necessarily coincide. There was clearly a gap in Fen's stories for which she refused to make an explicit connection. Experiences alone do not necessarily lead to insights, but without lived experiences it is difficult for new thought to emerge. David's deepened intellectual growth emerged from his experiences, but it was his devotion to working on his painful experiences that led to an ongoing process of learning, unlearning, and relearning. Thus new insights generated along the way cannot be reduced to experiences. In Teresa's teaching, experience is privileged over intellectual engagement. Song felt that his life and thought had become united in a full circle after his journey, although it seems to me that it was a partial unity because he did not bring a body-mind integrative orientation to his teaching in China.

Engaging difference also requires not reifying difference. To the degree that the East and the West are different, difference becomes the shadow of each other in a Jungian sense (Mayes, 2005), and a fuller realization of human potential relies on our ability to recognize and integrate the shadow within ourselves through encountering the other. Through the history of the China–US relationship, we have seen on both sides how the other has been portrayed as what the self rejects, or desires, or a mixture of both, and the self-other relationship has been determined by one's own lens no matter whether it projects the image of the other as negative or positive. But if we work *within* ourselves *with* the other, we may see different or even opposing sides of ourselves, and only when the self-self relationship is simultaneous with the self-other relationship can a creative and compassionate cross-cultural relationship be built for the benefit of both the self and the other.

In the West, for the past few decades the role of difference has been the topic of much discussion. To simplify a highly complex picture, I summarize several influential approaches: In a liberal approach, difference is pushed away in the pursuit of equality; in a pluralist approach, difference is treated as a separate entity, but what remains at the center still holds an authority position; in a critical approach, difference is essentialized into social identities opposed to one another while the marginalized are called upon to unite and challenge hegemony; in a post-structural approach, difference is radicalized as unknowable otherness that cannot be assimilated into the self. All these approaches can be useful in certain contexts. But in a nonviolent approach, I argue, difference is not suppressed, nor separated, nor essentialized, nor radicalized, but considered an organic part of interconnected life. Depending on the situation, whether difference needs to be highlighted or needs to be transcended, improvisation of a nonviolent relationship with both the self and the other respects but does not objectify difference. I have learned the simultaneity of such a respect and refusal (to objectify) from my participants in their various cross-cultural endeavors. While intercultural and cross-cultural encounters may bring uncommon assumptions to the foreground, a nonviolent engagement with difference approaches the unknown within the self and in the other as inexhaustible potentiality that can enrich the quality of our shared life in an ongoing process.

Power

These four participants shared a lack of interest in power struggles. This lack forms an interesting contrast to the overinvestment in power discourses in the field of American curriculum studies (Pinar, 2012). Even though the Foucaultian, postmodern notion of power is more fluid, complicated, and relational than the modern notion of power, the proliferation of power discourses, often related to identity politics, runs the risk of losing the educational focus on the whole person to a focus on political struggle. There has certainly been a power relationship between China and the USA, and the nature of this relationship oriented participants differently. But in the participants' life stories, power issues were never primary.

As David acknowledged, his passion for China studies was a calling, and he enjoyed his work getting people involved in cross-cultural exchanges and understandings. Specifically, he mentioned that such enjoyment was "not so much being the boss as to get to arrange things so that people can have interesting experiences" and make connections. His doctoral program was intellectually intense and his financial resources were quite limited, while his friends worked on Wall Street. It was not money or fame or status that drove his pursuit, but his deep care and commitment. He told his American students that if they wanted to be in this field, they also had to care deeply.

Song's concerns with truth were genuine, and his studies at an American university were oriented by this fundamental interest, without any concern for external rewards. As he formed a calm and nonattached approach to life in general, he also approached power issues between the USA and China in a peaceful way.

He commented that events in politics were like big or small waves in the sea, and since we all ultimately came from and returned to the same source of life energy, competing for power was utterly meaningless. Although he believed that imperialism, colonization, and Euro-American-centered globalization pressured other countries to comply, I did not discern any over-invested resentment on his part. He also believed that the West had more potential to transcend the material and mental levels to reach a higher level of consciousness, while his sympathy belonged to ordinary Chinese people whom he perceived as the disadvantaged.

In Teresa's world, it was love, not power, that connected people and connected humanity and God. She was also aware of the abuse of power on the part of Christian authorities or churches. Making a difference in students' lives and in society was her pedagogical purpose, not power struggles but spreading out Christian universal love. In Fen's story, administrative work was not about being the boss, similar to David, but about making the connection between the academic life of the university and the concerns of the society. Fen also made it clear that she was not interested in power games and would not sacrifice her own perspectives or way of life in order to pursue a higher position.

My participants were not interested in the issue of power and authority positions but were more committed to cross-cultural learning, teaching, and living. Certainly power structures and relationships had influenced their lives, but their commitment and focus were not on power but on life. A nonviolent relationship cannot be formed if involved parties are locked into the pursuit of power and ego-satisfaction. In nonviolent activism, this point is also made clearly. In Liberia's women's peace movement, which forced out the dictator and ended the civil war in 2005, those women had the wisdom to not appear politically oppositional in their mass demonstrations but insisted that all they wanted was peace (Disney & Reticker, 2008; Gbowee, 2011). They stayed away from "politics" to enact a successful social campaign for peace. Gandhi (1942 [2007]) also commented that the nonviolent movement is "not a program of seizure of power" but "a program of transformation of relationships" (p. 40). Orienting relational dynamics in educational settings—not staging political struggles for authority—has the most potential to spread out the transformative power of nonviolence.

College Teaching

A quick glimpse at the topics of articles published in the journal *College Teaching* since 2000 shows that college teaching is conceptualized mainly as teaching methods, content development, and assessment. These topics include methods to encourage active learning, grading, and self-assessment, how to combine art and science in interdisciplinary contents, small group activities or class discussion or lectures; and how to establish a classroom climate, prepare effective assignments, choose textbooks, use technology, encourage attendance and motivation, design syllabi, and teaching critical thinking. With a few exceptions, the journal's main focus is on strategies and methods.

In such a context, it is not a surprise that most of my participants initially did not think that their cross-cultural engagements had influenced their teaching because they did not change their methods in any substantial way. But curriculum is more than content, and teaching is more than method. While curriculum studies have been reconceptualized since the 1970s (Miller, 2005; Pinar, et al., 1995), college curriculum and teaching also need to shift the focus from methods and techniques to personal cultivation and growth. As Ronald Barnett (2009) points out, "knowledge—and more specifically the process of coming to know and to form an understanding (whether theoretical or more practical)—has implications for the student's *being*" (p. 437; emphasis in the original). Barnett traces the shift from the focus on knowledge to the focus on skills in Western universities, but he further argues that neither knowledge nor skills, which deal with known situations, are adequate for educating students who are expected to engage purposively with the world and live in the midst of today's complexity and uncertainty. Students' orientations to the global society and their capacity to deal with novel and unstable situations in intercultural contexts cannot be cultivated by teaching knowledge and skills alone.

Thus modes of being and modes of being-with-others emerge on the stage of higher education in cross-cultural and international contexts. Such an attention to students' being cannot be cultivated without instructors' attention to their own being. It was at the site of personhood that my participants offered the most important insights into cross-cultural higher education curriculum and pedagogy work. The embodiment of cross-cultural journeys in professors' teaching was not (merely) about methods, but about the modes of organic relationality and creative personhood. At the same time, attentiveness to modes of being can be accompanied by the changes of methods. For instance, Fen was explicit about the influence of Western constructivism on her teaching methods. My own teaching methods have been transformed by my cross-cultural journey, and my attention to personhood has led to my various efforts to redesign pedagogy.

David's presence as a cross-cultural being was what he was teaching in an American liberal arts college. His embodied experiences in China and his teaching about China were guided by his fundamental orientation to learning *from* the other for mutual benefit, as was his public work as a leader of educational exchange programs. From his own learning process, he understood the importance of lived experiences for American students, and he designed and implemented such a learning program not only in the classroom but also outside of the classroom by bringing students to China. His students were guided to examine and imagine another part of the world through affirming a shared sense of humanity in the classroom first and then engaging in "embodied learning" (McClelland, Dahlberg, & Plihal, 2002, p. 5) through their experiences in China for their personal growth.

Song's paradoxical affirmation of de-education for education was not about method either, but about the importance of unlearning. His meditative wisdom and non-dual approach were not reflected in the content of his teaching, but in the presence of the instructor as an unorthodox person. For Teresa, her strength lay in creating experience-based learning opportunities, and other professors emphasize the role of lived experience in higher education (Grauerholz, 2001; McClelland, Dahlberg, & Plihal, 2002). In a way, Teresa's and Song's teaching approaches seemed to be opposite, as one was proactive and outward while the other was meditative and inward. I think curriculum for peace and nonviolence in higher education needs to combine both inward and outward movements so that self-cultivation and social transformation can go hand in hand.

Teaching the whole person involves integrating intellect and emotions and promoting students' physical, intellectual, emotional, aesthetic, moral and spiritual growth. In other words, teaching is for "deep learning" (Grauerholz, 2001). I appreciate the term "deep" because engaging in activities itself is not necessarily transformative and can be superficial especially in cross-cultural contexts. Experiences without critical reflection can lead to biased or even prejudiced descriptions and interpretations of another culture, but an integrated mode of learning not only reflects knowledge about other cultures, but also reflects modes of being and being-with for reaching in-depth intercultural awareness and understandings. When both the left and right brains are engaged—much of higher education privileges the left brain—deep learning can happen. Fen's student-centered approach, which integrates aesthetic sensitivity and poetic understanding, can contribute to students' deep learning.

Discipline-based knowledge, skill acquisition, and personal growth need to go hand in hand. Teaching and learning through the site of personhood must go beyond a cognitive approach, and it cannot be linear or directly effective. As Liz Grauerholz (2001) points out, "No activity or professor can guarantee that students will experience deep learning. What instructors can do, however, is to create fertile conditions" (p. 45). Creating opportunities and conditions for students' growth in intercultural awareness and cross-cultural understanding can take many forms, as my participants demonstrated in their universities. And their own presence as professors who embody cross-cultural personhood in various ways is an important condition itself.

Now, to return to my questions that initiated this project: How did university professors' life experiences contribute to their cross-cultural engagements and how did such engagements influence their educational work in universities? While this entire book is the answer, I would like to highlight three facets. First, participants' intra-cultural and intercultural experiences within their own country had an intimate relationship with their cross-cultural engagements. Those life experiences situated in local and national contexts and their intellectual and spiritual working with those experiences already oriented them to border-crossing with capacity and compassion. Both serendipity and their preparedness led them onto cross-cultural paths, although each participant's specific mode of opening and engagement was uniquely and singularly her or his own. Second, the site of professors' cross-cultural personal transformation was essential for them to enact educational approaches that created conditions in which students were also encouraged to initiate and sustain cross-cultural and intercultural learning. Their abilities to integrate fragmentation, heal traumas, and accept ambiguity within themselves laid a cornerstone for sustainable educational work that profoundly influenced students' subjective and intersubjective landscapes. Third, different modes of engaging the other (and the self) in cross-cultural experiences lead to different ways of engaging educational work, whether as a professor or an administrator, including their relationships with time, power, difference, and teaching orientation, as I discussed earlier. The individuality of each professor in her or his unique journey is not only contextualized in history and culture but also goes beyond the constraints of a particular culture, so we need to be mindful of the interplay between individual and culture and an individual person's combination of different cultures within her or his subjectivity.

Engaging Differences in a Zero Space of Nonviolence

What is zero? Zero is nothing, most would say. Is zero nothing? Mathematically, zero is neither positive nor negative, yet a sense of number would not exist without it. Philosophically in the East, zero is both empty and full. Figuratively, zero can dance without ever being upside down. Meditatively, zero is both still and moving. As a wheel of life, zero can go either right or left without being wrong. In other words, zero is beyond either/or, beyond win or lose, and beyond right or wrong. Beyond the categorization of language, zero is difficult to speak about; we designate it as nothingness, yet from nothingness everything is born.

In Taoism, the interaction between *yin* and *yang* gives birth to the universe, mediated through the balancing act of three. The number three indicates a sense of going beyond binary oppositions and thus serves as a transcendent function. As Jeffrey C. Miller (2004) points out, "The number three and the third have a long cultural, religious, and mythical history" (p. 112) in various settings. I was in search of a third space in my previous work (Wang, 2004). As I finished the book *The Call from the Stranger on a Journey Home: Curriculum in a Third Space*, I realized that in my struggles with cultural and gendered dualism and opposites, I stopped short at the third to reach further into zero. A zero space is more playful, fluid, and inclusive. For Carl Jung, although the third is important in the process of synthesizing the opposite two, the number four is the symbol of unity and wholeness: "The transformation of the three leads to the wholeness of the four" (Miller, 2004, p. 111). Four leads to a circle or a sphere, a zero both figuratively and metaphorically. Zero symbolizes the wholeness of life and the source of creativity.

In my dialogues with Song, I insisted that zero was more fundamental than one in symbolizing the unity of life because its nonattachment to anything fixed can destabilize the potential of unification for violence. The fluidity of zero includes rather than excludes, and this inclusion is beneficial for enriching a network of human life. Zero is playful with the constraint of language since language in its defining power tends to categorize, but categorization can seldom capture each lived moment of human experience. Christopher D. Morris (2007) argues that the *Tao* that cannot be spoken is paradoxical since *Tao Tè Ching* makes an effort to speak about it. However, as Song also acknowledges, I think that to speak about the unspeakable is to invite everybody to experience *Tao* in living, co-becoming, and being. Without the effort to speak, there is no journey, and there is no circle.

A zero space of nonviolence is not an abstract concept but is experienced by each person in each lived moment in each context. I use the term "space" to include both the temporality of life history and cross-cultural stories in specific places as well as a specific individual's responses to her or his own time and place. Here, time, place, culture, and internal experiencing form an intricate web of connections and circular movements in a space. As we have seen, each individual participant's trajectory in engaging the other culture is unique. Here, the term *the other* culture indicates difference and the need to mediate between two different cultures. Just as the opposites of *yin* and *yang* exist individually and cosmically in a person's life, a zero space moves through conflicting life energies, which can be intensified by cross-cultural encounters, to build nonviolent relationships with the self, the other, and the world. Engaging differences, a zero space is not flat but holds both depth and breadth, incorporating the role of differentiation yet not reinforcing fragmentation. Engaging differences in a zero space of nonviolence is an ongoing process of releasing the creativity of each singular component while making connections between split parts to renew and rejuvenate the communal and ecological whole. Each individual is a knot with its singular pattern in this web and creative individuality makes the formation of a dynamic, nonviolent community possible.

The following diagram depicts a zero space of nonviolence. Five essential aspects of nonviolence are indicated in the circle: organic relationality, non-instrumental engagement, serendipitous play, spiritual openness, and de/education. Four *Taiji* symbols with different positions of *yin* and *yang* (The *Taiji* symbol is one and inseparable, but specific dynamics can be different in different situations) are used to anchor these aspects through circular movements. The circle is not a full circle and I intentionally add a fold into it. Leaving the circle open indicates an ongoing opening to different pathways and new possibilities. The fold inside also indicates the temporality of nonviolence: It takes time to see visible effects of nonviolence on both individuals and communities.

168 Nonviolence and Education

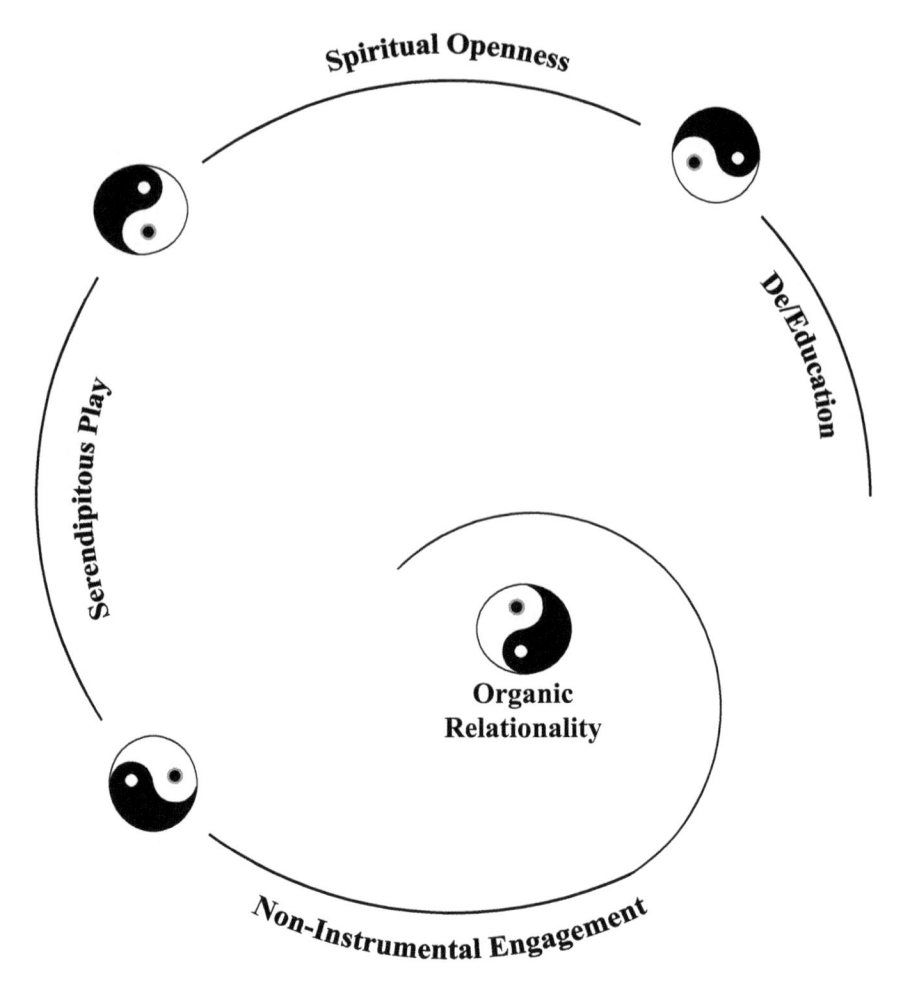

FIGURE 1 A Zero Space of Nonviolence

(Spiritual Openness, De/Education, Non-Instrumental Engagement, Serendipitous Play, Organic Relationality)

In the following, I briefly describe the five essential aspects of a zero space of nonviolence, especially in the context of higher education.

Organic Relationality

Organic relationality refers to both cultivating the organic integration of body and mind within oneself and promoting compassionate self-other relationships. While Teresa paid much attention to self-other relationships in her teaching, David's teaching was based upon his personal journey of integrating different elements in cross-cultural encounters. Organic relationships are not necessarily smooth and conflict-free, but as David's stories show, working through difficulty is an essential part of enabling organic healing for productive cross-cultural relationality. Living through trauma, Song's meditative experience of a Kundalini awakening led him onto a new path. The moment of experiencing the unity of mind and body changed his relationship with himself and with others, but it was his prolonged practice of stillness on a daily basis that gradually transformed his inner landscape. Song described his relationship with others as non-contesting and noncompetitive, including those who struggled at the bottom of society, whose smiles and happiness had become his smiles and happiness. As I think about my own life as a cross-cultural person and educator, I realize that I have a better relationship with others when I have a better relationship with myself.

Organic relationality lies at the heart of nonviolence. It emphasizes the interconnectedness of life and sees differences not as enemies but as partners. It incorporates tensions and conflicts and builds layered relationships among fragments both within the inner world of personhood and in the external world of society. It is not about subsuming diversity into uniformity, as the existence of any network depends not only on visible connections but also empty spaces (Fleener, 2002), entangled knots, or even dead-ends. The organic relationality of nonviolence welcomes differences and does not avoid conflicts because it has the ability to stretch, transform, and reconnect.

In today's world, developing global citizenship is often perceived as an important challenge for higher education (Stearns, 2009). While multiple dimensions such as the personal, the interpersonal, and the organizational are often included in new initiatives for global citizenship, they are often positioned as separate realms. The atomistic adding-up of parts—knowledge, skills, and dispositions—to depict global competency is not uncommon, but such an aggregative approach cannot capture the dynamics of organic relationality. The process of educating for the whole person with international awareness and understanding needs to connect organically both within and across self, other, and community. We need not abandon analytical thinking and in-depth understanding of parts; however, we need to understand that the patterns of higher-level interconnections that emerge from the interplay of individual components and their contexts may not resemble the parts but have a qualitative difference.

Non-instrumental Engagement

Organic relationality cannot be formed without non-instrumental engagement. Instrumental thinking once dominated curriculum theories and teaching practices at school levels in its objective-oriented, ends-justifying-means curriculum development approach. For the past few decades, the reconceptualization movement has transformed the scholarly landscape of American curriculum studies, although standardization and accountability have been imposed upon school practices by mostly noneducational forces. In the field of higher education, however, curriculum development models that are oriented by objectives and assessment have largely remained the norm (e.g., the special issue of *New Directions for Teaching and Learning,* 2007, No. 112, and publications in *College Teaching*), although some areas related to identity and diversity have been more theorized.

My participants' cross-cultural learning and teaching tell different stories. Song asserts that personal cultivation must transcend ideas/concepts/rationality and instrumental thinking to reach a higher level of existential awareness. David's pursuit of engagement with China was driven by non-instrumental concerns, and he passed the message of caring in intercultural encounters to his students. Teresa followed the flow of serendipity in her teaching as she did not attempt to control the process and outcome of students' learning but worked with what emerged in and outside of the classroom. Fen combined both structure and surprise in her teaching, which led to astonishing outcomes for both students and instructor. None of them have pursued a predetermined goal in their teaching, although they may have started with a broad sense of what they intended to accomplish. Their life stories are marked by the absence of pursuing power; it was the inherent appeal of another thought or another life that drew them onto cross-cultural pathways.

Non-instrumental engagement or engagement without attachment to a predetermined goal is difficult to imagine in today's accountability age, but I think it is important for educators. Engagement without attachment means engaging students' learning and growth without trying to control the outcome. As Pinar (2012) points out, controlling the outcome is impositional, not educational. In higher education, the instructor's passion and commitment can encourage students' pursuit of their *own* pathways, but the instructor must keep a certain distance from students to protect their own explorations; otherwise, ideas or values can be imposed. When ideas do not touch students' internal landscape, they don't have any long-term pedagogical effects. As much as educational work is political, professors are not politicians whose goals are to rally mass movements towards a certain political purpose. The professor's educational work, if situated at the site of personal cultivation, must grant students their own intellectual freedom. In teaching nonviolence, I always remind myself of the need for pedagogical distance (Pitt, 2003; Taubman, 1992) and the necessity of allowing students to disagree with nonviolent principles.

Serendipitous Play

When engagement is not instrumental, it opens up a space for serendipitous play. In one way or another, my participants all perceived their life pathways as following what came to them, although they all put effort into their cross-cultural encounters. Teresa expressed her faith in God as the guiding principle for her serendipitous play both in life and in teaching, but David's sense of following the calling of his life, Fen's decision to take on new tasks, and Song's unexpected return to China all indicate the lack of a predetermined goal. They were open to what life might bring. Thus the combination of improvisation, openness, and effort was demonstrated in their serendipitous pathways.

While there are studies about the positive role of humor in college teaching (Hellman, 2007; James, 2004), serendipitous play is more than using humor as an instructional tool. Serendipitous play anchors a sense of flow in achieving a connection between professors/students and what they are teaching/learning in a community of learners. In such a flow, students are immersed in their activities, focus completely on the task, work creatively and collaboratively with their classmates, and forget about time (Grauerholz, 2001, p. 45). In other words, they lose themselves in their involvement with the task at hand while at the same time experiencing satisfaction and enjoyment. Play is not just about hands-on activities in the classroom; it is also about being playful with subjects, ideas, and relations (Doll, 2012). Learning is usually perceived as serious study that cannot mix well with play. But as Doll (1990 [2012]) points out, "Seriousness quickly overpowers our sense of alternative possibilities; it locks us in to the already tried; it limits our perspective" (p. 148). By contrast, play can unlock our imagination, encourage us to explore new pathways, and stretch boundaries for reaching new insights into the whole. Flow can also happen in social relationships, when playing with tensions rather than fighting over conflicts, to energize the rhythm of communal life.

Play keeps knowledge alive (Doll, 2005 [2012]) and brings people to work together. Playing with ideas is important in higher education because creative intelligence is beyond cognition and knowledge, and new scholarship is generated by playing with subjects and disciplinary boundaries and by understanding or building surprising relationships that cannot be perceived on the surface. In serendipitous play, the mechanism of control gives way to the process of complex emergence, which is nonlinear and circular (Doll, 2012). It does not reject ambiguity, uncertainty, and complexity but welcomes them for generating new possibilities. Nonviolent relationships are playful, joyful, and humorous and encourage hybrid cross-fertilization of ideas and connections. Reta Ugena Whitlock (2012) comments that activists for peace and nonviolence are delightful persons to be around. Transcending boundaries and seeing through tensionality to look at the bigger picture, nonviolence workers can let go and play and inspire others to also become playful.

Spiritual Openness

Play and spirituality are related, according to Song's contemplative wisdom. Spirituality is a highly contextualized concept in this study, as the Chinese notion of spirituality is quite different from the American notion of spirituality. Spirituality is important to both Teresa and Song, although for Teresa it is deeply rooted in her religious faith, whereas for Song the spiritual is beyond religions and lies in deeper, non-dualistic understandings of human and ecological life. Fen's sense of spirituality as transcendent had been set as opposite to the secular, but in recent years she has realized that the spiritual and the secular are more integrated. I did not have a chance to discuss spirituality with David, but his sense of moral center as a historian and his engaged relationship with the other can be perceived as spiritual in a broad sense. Whether the participants used this particular language or not, they demonstrated a strong sense of spiritual openness in their cross-cultural pathways.

Spirituality is a contested concept with various interpretations and meanings (Hendrix & Hamlet, 2009a, 2009b; Speck, 2005). American higher education, with its modern pursuit of science and technology and its contemporary adoption of business and corporate models, has shifted from its earlier concerns with religious education and civic engagement to today's separation between spirituality and the pursuit of knowledge and skills (Murphy, 2005). This separation is also reinforced by the principle of separation between church and state. College professors at public universities often feel the need to stay away from spirituality in teaching. Those who make an effort to incorporate spirituality into college teaching define it broadly as "a way of being in the world that incorporates beliefs, values, attitudes, emotions, behaviors, and insights" (Hendrix & Hamlet, 2009b, p. 4), and through lived experiences, both students and professors search for their better selves in their transformation as spiritual beings. Although I don't think that better selves are necessarily "discovered," cultivating compassionate aspects of humanity within oneself to transcend binary thinking and to connect with the shared life energy makes nonviolence a spiritual space.

Aware of the constraint of religious dogmas in the notion of spirituality, I emphasize the necessity of spiritual *openness;* we cannot abandon the spiritual aspect of human life, without which nonviolence is impossible. I first define spiritual openness as a way of being in the world that is emergent rather than permanent. As William E. Doll, Jr. (2002 [2012]) points out, "Our accepted concepts of God, religion, spirituality assume a type of permanence—a cosmology of permanence as it were—we no longer find valid" (p. 35). Such a sense of permanence can easily lead to dogmas that exclude rather than include, but an emergent sense of spirituality is dynamic and fluid, bringing life-affirmative energies to all participants. Second, spiritual openness is rooted in organic relationality, which leads individual persons to go beyond ego and engage ecological and cosmological spirituality that is grounded in "patterns that connect" (Doll, 2002 [2012]). These patterns that connect within and across human and ecological realms require open eyes to see both visible and invisible links. Bringing fragmented or split parts back to the organic whole, spiritual openness is restorative.

Third, spiritual openness is both transcendental, reaching beyond the given, and embodied, attuned to specific human situations. Yoshiharu Nakagawa (2008) argues that Eastern wisdom is twofold, involving not only the efforts to climb the mountain to reach enlightenment but also "full engagement with everyday life" with awareness (p. 236). Here, the spiritual is not only about aspiring beyond but also about awakening to the profound meanings of our ordinary lives. Fourth, spiritual openness is also intimately linked to meditative stillness, which suspends one's judgment and loosens one's own attachments so that one can look at the world as it is and engage the world peacefully. Furthermore, spiritual openness inspires individual and collective pursuits of what is good in life but does not try to control or produce fear or anxiety through religious dogmas. Especially in intercultural and international contexts, spiritual openness is important for building connections across specific faith traditions. As Janice D. Hamlet (2009) points out, spirituality in the context of higher education strives "to maintain an ongoing openness toward new and diverse ways of letting people learn, but especially toward letting oneself learn how to let others learn" (p. 31). That is indeed the position of teaching—to enable students to learn.

Doubling Education with De-Education (De/Education)

Spiritual openness is linked with de-education, which requires emptying out presumptions, categorical thinking, and instrumental pursuit. De-education is a term that Song used, although other participants had similar teaching stories. David's teaching of American students about China challenged their biases and stereotypes, and there is necessarily an element of unlearning on the part of students as they learn about China and learn from Chinese experiences. Teresa's teaching challenged Chinese students' conventional notions of learning as dominated by left-brained activities. Song's notion of de-education was not only related to going beyond instrumental reason but also intimately connected with self-education. While personal cultivation and self-education for new insights, awareness, and relationships cannot be taught directly, pedagogical and educational conditions can be created for enabling students to participate in such a process. The instructor's modeling of personal and professional growth is part of such a condition. My participants' lived experiences and/or intellectual engagement with another culture and their embodiment of cross-cultural orientations made unique contributions to what and how they taught in the classroom. Their self-education of learning *from* the other was a living testimony of what it meant to live, learn, and teach in an international, cross-cultural, global society.

The paradoxical doubling of education and de-education, which I term as de/education, is particularly important in higher education. While primary and secondary students are more open to educational influence, as they are in the process of self-formation, college students have formed more stable viewpoints and value orientations. Higher education can challenge students' previous assumptions and beliefs when critical thinking is encouraged. It is not unusual to hear a college student or a graduate student comment that it has taken going to college for them to understand the self and the world in a different light. In a sense, de-education demands more effort than education; different from presenting a system of knowledge and values to students, challenging students' existing perspectives often provokes resistance. Without this capacity for unlearning, however, can students take in new knowledge and develop new awareness? To educate, thus, goes hand in hand with to de-educate.

However, de-education does not necessarily mean self-interrogation, as we sometimes assume, but can be embodied through students' lived experience. David Kahane (2009) proposes contemplative pedagogy to "help students to understand the habits of thought, judgment, and reaction that keep them trapped in the cocoon of their own privilege, which is also to say their own suffering" (p. 59). Specifically Kahane uses meditation, free-writing, and mindful reading/seeing in his philosophy class on global citizenship and justice. He makes the connection between disassociation with other's suffering and the relationship we have with ourselves and argues that alienation from our own internal world cannot be treated by rational reflection but requires "the ability to observe our own present-moment experience with a certain degree of compassionate detachment" (p. 53). Being gentle with oneself is necessary for being gentle to others.

All five aspects discussed above are intertwined, and their circular, nonlinear, and complicated movements form a zero space of nonviolence. As a cautionary note, however, I don't want to position nonviolence as a utopian vision but, to avoiding the pitfalls of idealization, approach "violence-nonviolence as a continuum" (Weigert, 1999, p. 16) rather than a binary. I also don't want to pit nonviolence against other visions of shared life for the common good, such as democracy or social justice, as long as they are inclusive and restorative, following the principle of nonviolence (Wang, 2010a). Furthermore, the notion of nonviolence does not deny the existence of psychic and social violence; instead, violence must be continually worked through in nonviolence education. But I insist that we resist any message that normalizes violence as if it is "natural" and given. Arguing about whether violence or nonviolence is human nature is not particularly fruitful, because we have seen plenty of both in individual, family, and social life. Human nature is not an essentialized notion. I don't think it is given, or mainly biological, but it is, individually and collectively, in an ongoing process of formation. If human nature is plastic and shapeable through social and cultural processes, then what we should pursue becomes imperative.

Committed to nonviolence education, we must acknowledge and transform violence in an ongoing process because there is no guarantee that a community of nonviolence can be built and maintained in any static sense. Since in our daily life nonviolence and violence are often mixed, our task is to create educational conditions in which nonviolence is advocated and cultivated and violence is analyzed and challenged so that we can move continually towards the pole of nonviolence. Nonviolence education is a daily practice for educators both in and out of the classroom.

Curriculum Dynamics of Nonviolence

I used to move quite often. In leaving, important relationships were uprooted and I often felt torn apart from unspoken or unspeakable attachments, imagined or realistic, even though I chose to leave. The irony of choice—choosing to leave—is that leaving was accompanied by a feeling of being left. Feeling rootless, I kept on moving. The summer of 2010 when I visited my parents in Harbin was different: The city began to feel like a hometown for me for the first time. Harbin was very noisy and dirty as the subway construction was underway. Worst of all, it was unbearably hot, beyond all my imagination, even though Harbin usually has the coolest summer in China. But somehow everything began to come together, and I felt right at home. And the power of such coming together was so overwhelming that I almost lost my way in the midst of the noise and heat. Somehow it was only after my hometown felt like a home was I able to feel rooted in other places, feeling homelike in my American home.

I taught Madeleine R. Grumet's (1988) book *Bitter Milk* in a graduate seminar the next summer. Right after I finished the class, I had a dream. In the dream I attended a conference with Dr. Grumet, and she was showing me a huge egg with harmonious patterns on the shell. When I woke up, I naturally linked the egg with the maternal discussed in her book. Now as I reimagine it, the root is in the egg, in the maternal creativity that grows out of the relational. We as human beings are all rooted in the maternal, in the union of the feminine and the masculine, in the harmonious dance of opposite cosmic forces. For years I had felt stuck professionally and personally in an age of accountability, but making the effort to crack an opening in the ground where I stood and find a footing helped me to move towards new possibilities. Only through dwelling in life lived deeply enough could I move towards what was yet to come. In digging into the crack of difficulty, I did find my footing in a long-standing shared human heritage of nonviolence, the maternal[2] force that incorporates both the feminine and the masculine, which spoke the most to my heart.

Along the way, I have become more playful and more spontaneous in life, and a sense of flow has emerged more often in my teaching. A class I taught on gender and teaching is a good example. I used three textbooks for that class, one from a sociological perspective (Johnson, 2005), one from a personal perspective (Doll, 1995), and another one addressing differences within the group of women and intersections between gender and race, class, and sexuality (hooks, 2000). Students were very engaged in discussions and a flow emerged in the class. However, not until the last class meeting did I realize how much the flow meant for students. When students took turns sharing what they had learned from the class, they each talked about how this class had profoundly influenced them personally and changed their interactions with their families and their students. I was moved by their testimonies. And best of all, I did not feel I did anything special! Upon reflection, I can see several aspects that contributed to changes in students' perspectives, feelings, and actions: letting go of centralized control on the part of the instructor, combining textbooks in an organic way to address both the particular and the whole, giving students freedom to make connections with texts and with their classmates through both inner and outer engagement, and leaving room for ambiguity and contradictions without judgment. This approach enacts the Taoist *wuwei*, teaching without a central authority (Wang, 2007).

This sense of flow was marked by students' concentrated involvement with texts and with one another. I was so fully attentive to what was under discussion and engaged with students that I forgot my own ego. But the class was not absent of students' struggles with ideas and their emotional working through gender issues in their lives and in their teaching. In a sense, flow needs bumps in order not to stay flat or become a linear stream. Against the mainstream hierarchical gendered system, the emergence of vibrant flow came not through following the taken-for-granted paths but through digging under the hardened surface of biased societal constraints to let the stream of life come forward, and the opening of fountains worked its magic over time in unexpected ways. Many university professors occasionally experience such a moment of flow in teaching, and the question is how to create conditions for it to emerge more often.

Paradoxically, in my story, finding a footing and being able to release flow go hand in hand. The ability to crack through and dwell in difficulty paves the way for getting in touch with the most generative life energy. Students' engagement with the text and with one another is both rooted in their own experiences and connected to the rhythm of the class they cocreated. Finding more ground in my cross-cultural teaching, I became more rooted and more playful at the same time.

Dynamic Interplay

The curriculum dynamics of nonviolence involve a complicated interplay between and among professor, student, text/context, and community. To acknowledge the role of difference in such dynamics, the "strangeness" of both the text/context and the student needs to be recognized so that the professor is receptive to unfamiliar lenses and does not unintentionally "colonize" students' own thoughts (Huebner, 1999; Wang, 2002). To approach students as the stranger is to respect their ways of knowing and being and to invite them to join in a shared search for meanings, purposes, and new possibilities. To approach the subject matter or text as the stranger is to ask students to experience the text rather than approaching it as an object to master. When students are guided to approach what is different—whether this difference comes from texts or from classmates or from the world—with openness and conversational serendipity, they participate in the continual creation of the world nonviolently. To know is to be in relation with and to educate is to lead students out onto their own journeys. In cross-cultural encounters, both the courage to venture into the unknown—what might be excluded by one's own culture—and the ability to empty out the preconceived notions of another culture are necessary for forming meaningful relationships. The complex contours of engaging difference may lead students back to see the other side of their own culture. As a result of integrating differences, they become fuller in the "wholeness" of individuation in a Jungian sense.

In nonviolent relationality, individual and community are interdependent. In nonviolence educational traditions, as I discuss elsewhere (Wang, 2013b), there are individual-oriented, relationality-oriented, and community-based approaches. In the first approach, individual equality and democratic values are the underlying principles for nonviolence, such as in human rights education and conflict resolution education (see Muller, 2002; Tibbits, 2008). In the second approach, non-duality and interconnectedness are the bases for reaching inner and outer peace (see Kaneda, 2008; Lin, 2008). In the third approach, community-based activism is the key to nonviolence education, such as various community efforts inspired by Gandhi or Martin Luther King, Jr. (for more information, see such community organizations' websites such as www.thekingcenter.org and www.mettacenter.org). All these approaches can be effective, especially in combination. Whether the starting point is individual rights, or relationality cultivation, or community building, the key is to shift relational dynamics towards non-dualistic cultivation of self and society. Like a sphere in which self and culture cannot be separated (Tung, 2000), individual creative improvisation and communal serendipitous effort are both essential for forming an organic whole. Responsible, courageous, fluid, and creative individuality that does not do violence to either the self or the other is the cornerstone of nonviolence. However, a separate sense of the individual that privileges the self (whether in a personal sense, a group sense, or a national sense) against the shared life must be challenged in order to form nonviolent relationships, without which an open-minded and loving community cannot emerge.

Can community be built not upon commonality but upon difference? Drawing upon different schools of thought, Ewa Płonowska Ziarek (2001) articulates feminist ethics of *dissensus*, which "redefine freedom in relational terms as an engagement in transformative praxis motivated by the obligation for the Other" (p. 2) to enable both self-creation and nonviolent relationships with the other. Such ethics highlight the role of difference and hold individuality and relationality in both tension and coexistence. Julia Kristeva (1993) proposes the notion of a polyvalent community that "respects the strangeness of each person" (p. 35) and connects members not through unity but through shared vulnerability. Janet Miller (2010) discusses curriculum communities without consensus, which acknowledges the importance of constructing a communal space but refuses any universal notion of the self or the collective. Instead, her vision of such communities without consensus is "composed of 'selves' and versions of curriculum work that re-form daily and differently in response to difference and to the unknown" (p. 96).

What runs through these discussions is the effort to acknowledge that a community is not marked by commonality or sameness but by both recognition of difference and embodied bridge-building within, between, and among differences. I also contend that a community without consensus is not merely tied together by working *against* the normative violence but also by working *for* a shared principle, and I advocate nonviolence as such a visionary principle to hold individuals and communities together, even though specific endeavors can be different.

The underlying basis for internal nonviolence is the unity between body and mind, so the very possibility of nonviolence depends on our capacity to work through difficult emotions to achieve inner peace. Influenced by post-structural thought, the curriculum field has embraced the role of tensions, contradiction, and ambiguity (Aoki, 2005; Doll, 2012; Fleener, 2002; Miller, 2005), but I think emotional struggles with tensions and conflicts need more attention. Tensions unsettle psychic attachments, *dissensus* of community complicates the individual's sense of belonging, and the pains of uprooting, exile, and alienation in a global society can cause both internal and external splits. The postmodern embracing of fragmentation, antagonism, and uncertainty must be coupled with emotional and psycho-spiritual working through of difficult feelings. Otherwise, repressed psychic residues will come back to enact various barriers for individuals or communities. Curriculum dynamics in higher education, especially in cross-cultural contexts, must engage emotional work in the classroom.

The role of the body is often neglected in higher education since the university is usually perceived as an institution of intellectual advancement. In the classroom, the spatial arrangement for large-class lectures symbolizes the disembodied mode of teaching and learning. But the human body is the site for knowing and living, and teaching and learning are embodied activities. As Freema Elbaz-Luwisch (2009) points out, feeling, imagination, and the body play important roles in encounters of difference and students' cross-cultural learning. In her narrative approach to teacher education, she designs various ways of creating room for the body in the classroom to bring together students from diverse backgrounds—both Arabs and Israelis in Israel—in their storytelling and sharing. When intense feelings are expressed authentically in small group settings, they tend to draw students together rather than splitting them apart. Embodied experience is a key to cultivating students' capacity for building connections across differences and even hostility.

With increasing migration, immigration, and mobility, oppositions can accompany persons' explorations into new places, and each nation has its own embodied memories of conflict, antagonism, and war, which are imprinted in individual bodies consciously or unconsciously. Even for those who migrate voluntarily, these memories do not disappear with cross-cultural and transnational moves, but become more complicated and entangled. Cross-cultural and international encounters—both face to face and virtual—can be oppositional in today's polarized world (Li, Conle, & Elbaz Luwisch, 2009), and professors and students are challenged to envision an international community not based upon sameness but upon difference. Polarization can happen in various contexts and may intensify in the post-September 11 era. Examining that era, Judith Butler (2004) posits "the body as the site of a common human vulnerability," even though this vulnerability is differentiated through "norms of recognition" (p. 44). The issue of whose bodies can be valued or erased in the public memory and recognition is necessarily linked with nationalism and the history of colonization. But the body is inevitably relational as every*body* is born into primary care, or lack of primary care.

Nonviolent responses to national trauma require an acknowledgement of such a shared bodily vulnerability. Embodied education beyond rational discussions may organically heal the wounds.

While it is important to incorporate bodily movements in the classroom, stillness to achieve unity between body and mind is also necessary for cultivating cross-cultural and intercultural understanding. Mindful breathing, mindful seeing, or mindful reading does not require the body to move but requires meditative sensitivity and the capacity to center the self in stillness (Kahane, 2009; Schoeberlein & Sheth, 2009; Smith, 2008). Situated at the intersection between the self and the world, mindfulness is an activity embodied through the relational. When teaching a college class on the environment, Sid Brown (2008) asked each of her students to form a relationship with a plant of their choice. Each student spent an hour a week with a tree, talking with it, writing under it, studying it, or simply sitting with it. Gradually, not only did the students feel something in their relationship with a tree but the tree started to speak back to them in various ways. Being fully present to listen to the voice of the tree, which cannot speak for itself, students were learning how to form a loving relationship with the environment. Embodied curriculum and teaching can take various forms in higher education, and we need to remember that the mind of the university and its students cannot be separated from the body of the university and its students.

The Non-dual Nation in a Global Society

Nonviolent curriculum dynamics enacted at the cross-cultural and international level need to be based upon a non-dual notion of the nation, similar to a non-dual notion of the individual, as the two intersect through national identity. There are different approaches to affirming such non-duality, for instance, the Taoist and Buddhist approach that I have discussed throughout the book, which emphasizes the role of underlying interconnectedness across individuals and nations. Here I would like to briefly comment on another approach: the Kristevian (1993) approach of "nations without nationalism," which refuses to see an enemy in the other nation. In Kristeva's psychoanalytic approach, the figure of the foreigner is important. For her, "in the long run, only a thorough investigation of our remarkable relationship with both *the other and strangeness within ourselves* can lead people to give up hunting for the scapegoat outside their group" (p. 51; emphasis in the original), and this coming to terms with the nation's collective unconsciousness is the basis for building constructive connections with both foreigners and other nations.

In other words, foreigners are not only outside of us but also inside of us, and our interaction with foreigners outside can help us to integrate our own otherness within. The notion of a "nation without nationalism" suggests that we recognize our national origins and claim our identification with pride, yet at the same time transcend national identity to reach out to others so that the repressive or exclusive function of nationalism can be avoided. In such an account, national borders are simultaneously affirmed and transcended. Thus a non-dual relationship curves through difference to build connections. The dualism of "us" versus "them" has played a violent role in international relationships, and going beyond dualism is important for cross-cultural curriculum, teaching, and education.

As Terrance R. Carson (2009) points out, "Curriculum studies is customarily contained within national and local boundaries in the form of educational practices that are embedded in local and national histories and cultures" (p. 145). But the challenge of the past two decades in higher education is the tide of globalization and internationalization that not only requires policy change but also calls for reexamining curriculum design, pedagogy, and learning (Luxon & Peelo, 2009). Internationalizing curriculum for either sustainable development or global citizenship in response to contemporary world circumstances encourages local efforts to promote global learning and competencies (see Anderberg, Norden, & Hansson, 2009; Gray-Donald & Selby, 2004; Stearns, 2009). While these efforts have flourished, creating organic relationships within and across the local, the national, and the global, in the midst of conflicts and tensions, is essential for enacting nonviolent relationality in higher education curriculum.

Nonviolence is a tradition shared by many cultures, nations, and religions. We have seen its role in Chinese and American philosophical and activist traditions. Although I have no intention of perceiving what has emerged from this China–US cross-cultural study as universal, the nonviolence tradition has existed worldwide throughout human history. Indigenous peace-making has had a long tradition in North America (Smith-Christopher, 2007); the African notion of *ubuntu*, which emphasizes relationality and restorative justice played an important role in the work of the Truth and Reconciliation Committee in South Africa (Tutu, 1999); and women's particular contributions to peace and nonviolence have long been acknowledged (Harris, 2008; Knight, 2010; Pinar, 2009). In major world religions, there is a strong message of nonviolence, including in Islam, which is often portrayed as violent in the West (Harris, 2007).

I see nonviolence as part of the best human heritage across spiritual, cultural, and national boundaries and therefore as having the potential to heal the divide between East and West, or the first, second, and third world. Nonviolence is essentially an educational project because internal nonviolence with the self is the bridge to external nonviolence with others, as demonstrated in my participants' journeys. Many nonviolence activists—Jane Addams (Knight, 2010), Nelson Mandela (1994 [2003]), Leymah Gbowee (2011)—also went through internal transformation as the basis for their public work. Nonviolence education, as I advocate here, is defined in a broad sense as cultivating nonviolent orientations from within, transforming internal negative energies into positive, life-affirmative awareness, and creating compassionate relationships with others within and across national/cultural borders. From the personal to the international dimensions, if we embrace traditions of nonviolence, the non-dual notion of the individual and of the nation can lead us to dynamic curriculum interplay between and among the autobiographical, the local, the national, and the global.

A Playful Curriculum of Nonviolence

Since violence in various forms is present to an alarming degree in the contemporary age (now digital violence becomes another form of a human-made commodity, which this book does not discuss), educational scholars offer critical analyses of violence. But I think it is time for us to shift our attention to nonviolence for a moment, to see nonviolence rather than violence as the foreground, to envision what it might be like to educate about, through, and for nonviolence. Foregrounding violence may unintentionally reinforce its message while the proactive educational work of nonviolence promises to dissolve the mechanism of violence from its root. When the background and foreground of violence and nonviolence are switched, the educational landscape becomes different.

A playful curriculum about, through, and for nonviolence unites teaching content and methods and educational means and end. Transforming the content of studies, we should teach the fundamental role of nonviolence in life. When control and mastery are portrayed as the driving force of human history, alternative possibilities of nonviolent coexisting and inter-being are excluded. As Loewen (1995) points out, in earlier colonial periods, there were cohabitant communities of colonists and indigenous people, but when such portraits are excluded from textbooks, students only can see an inevitable route of cross-cultural conquest. Loewen discusses the secondary school curriculum, but university textbooks are not much better. However, professors have more freedom to introduce critical or experientially based materials, and we need to actively seek opportunities to teach students about nonviolence.

Nonviolence literature in universities currently appears in peace studies programs that emerged after World War II (although it is usually treated only as a nonviolent means of political uprising). But we should systematically and comprehensively integrate the message of nonviolence into university curriculum, including humanities, liberal arts, social science, and ecological studies, and even natural science and engineering can benefit from contemplating its meanings. If students have not learned about nonviolence in their earlier education, then they should encounter such alternative possibilities in universities, to unlearn the mechanism of domination in taken-for-granted assumptions. General education is a good site for reengaging human stories and possibilities, while specialized courses can deepen students' understandings.

The transformation of China Studies as a field, as we read in Chapters 1 and 3, and the ever-changing landscape of the Chinese intellectual field, as we read in Chapter 2, indicate a tendency to move towards a more nonviolent intellectual relationship between China and the West. The intellectual field of the West has in general moved towards acknowledging the value of non-Western knowledge systems since the late 1960s and the early 1970s. So to some degree, knowledge across cultures is now more fluid and less centralized. When knowing about the world becomes more mutual and less dominant in international studies, students have better opportunities to learn from the other.

While the missing voice of nonviolence in curriculum is an issue, educational methods that are transmission-oriented rather than inspirational cannot embody the spirit of nonviolence. As Anthony Herrington and Jan Herrington (2006) point out, formal teaching in higher education is by and large characterized by transmitting "theoretical knowledge devoid of context" (p. 2). Typically, "textbooks and lecture notes are the main resources for study, with the practice of 'cramming' for exams a common learning strategy" (p. 2). Such an approach does not lead to "deep learning," as Grauerholz (2001) argues. The notion of text is rich in historical, social, and cultural contexts, which have a lived quality that can be educationally experienced. Deep learning must be personally engaged in both in solitude and in community. It is not unusual for general education classes at American universities to have unbelievably large class sizes. To cope with such classes, most professors adopt a lecture style of teaching, by which it is difficult to touch students' inner landscape.

Nonviolence is both a means and an end of education. Professors cannot impose their own agenda, even when such an agenda is oriented to the common good such as social justice. As Crews (1999) points out, in social justice teaching some faculty members are more interested in orienting students to values to which professors are committed rather than to values that students are encouraged to nurture themselves. He argues, "Teaching the whole person demands that we respect one another, i.e., that we allow our students the same intellectual and moral freedoms we expect for ourselves" (p. 27). Orienting students to social justice does not mean teaching a set of values but means providing opportunities for students to engage in their personal transformation. Moving students as whole persons toward transcending themselves, rather than directly teaching what students do not want to learn, I have developed a nonviolent approach to social justice education (Wang, 2013c). An impositional means cannot achieve a nonviolent end.

The purpose of education varies for different types of universities and for different students. While Nel Noddings (2003) asks why happiness is never an explicit purpose of education in the prevailing instrumental approach, I advocate nonviolence as an important goal of education. When I teach nonviolence in teacher education, most of my students are skeptical about such possibilities, because in encountering strangers, violence rather than nonviolence is still the norm in our society. But nonviolence is a visionary and *playful* work for educators, as we play with the limit to let compassionate relationality grow. We may not realize its effects immediately, but the internal value of nonviolence in uplifting human dignity with self-cultivation and compassion calls for our dedicated engagement, and it takes generation after generations for its influence to spread.

Such a sense of end is not instrumental but existential and transcendent. As an end, nonviolence is an essential thread in the daily fabric of educational work in which we engage, including cross-cultural and international education. When the integrative power of nonviolence plays its role in multiple dimensions of education, infuses the network of curriculum dynamics, creates a community of *dissensus,* and nurtures individual creativity, the university becomes a site of educating for the best human possibilities.

Now, as I write closing words, permit me to come back to the beginning of this study when I returned to my hometown.

When I went back to my hometown in 2009, my mother insisted that I visit a doctor (introduced by my father's friend) specializing in traditional Chinese medicine to treat my insomnia. I did not believe any magic would appear, as I had struggled with it for years, and I had begun to feel that my body could no longer restore its natural rhythm. But I went to see the doctor, so as not to disappoint my mother. While the maternal is important in many cultures, mother occupies a special place in Chinese culture (Kristeva, 1977; Wang, 2004), although such a value has historically not been free from the grip of patriarchy. Fen credited her mother's strength and Song credited his mother's affections. Kristeva (1996) asks us to imagine the maternal as creative, a mode of maternity negotiating between the singularity of womanhood and the relationality of enabling the child's growth towards freedom. Motherhood embodies a co-creative and creative relationship that leads to the birth and growth of the other.

My mother was wise. I was astonished to find out that I could actually get back in touch with the natural flow of my body and mind with the help of the traditional Chinese medical treatment. Within 10 days of intensive treatment combining acupuncture, herbs, and massage, I was able to sleep well. The disturbance of my emotional life—incidentally I encountered one of those falling-off-the-cliff feelings during the time of treatment—was balanced by the process of organic healing. One of the differences between Western medical treatment and traditional Chinese treatment is that the Western method treats the part of the body where symptoms appear while the Chinese method treats the whole body to relieve symptoms. Each approach has its own advantages and limits, and it seems to me that the promise lies in combining both analytical accuracy and organic holism, although a particular problem may have a preference for a particular method. The organic healing I experienced in those 10 days released me from where I was stuck, and released me into movement, to listen more attentively to my inner voice.

When I walked into Dr. Tang's office the first time, I noticed that it was a peaceful place for handling different tasks simultaneously. His patients, assistants, colleagues, and students (he was also a university professor) walked in and out of the office as he provided treatment, or advice, or teaching. Calligraphy with words "simplicity and sincerity" hung on the wall along with a painting of the Chinese ideograph of "love," whose symbolic meanings were conveyed well in the spirit of the room. Dr. Tang performed acupuncture treatment, and as I sat in the chair each time, I had a chance to observe his interactions with different people. What impressed me the most was his calm attitude towards everyone, using a calm voice no matter whether the person was his boss, a colleague, a student, or a patient. Perhaps because my mind was intense, he had a calming effect on me in our brief encounter each day.

The curriculum I experienced in that treatment center (attached to a medical university)—which was struggling due to the decline of Chinese traditional medicine in comparison to Western modern medicine—was a curriculum of nonviolence. There is a "heart" in the Chinese ideograph of "love," and love lies at the heart of nonviolence. A zero space of nonviolence is filled with all-inclusive, life-affirmative energy that sustains loving relationships in the midst of difficulty, antagonism, loss, crisis, cruelty, and violence. In our conflict-ridden global society, it takes a lot of commitment, courage, compassion, and creativity to carve out pathways towards such a vision of nonviolence. And that is the calling of education.

As the book ends, may we listen to the call of nonviolence together?

Let's attend to nonviolence as a spiritual aspiration to foreground our educational work. Let's cultivate organic relationality—not calculations of power—to mobilize communal dynamics of difference for both individual creativity and social imagination. Let's patiently get in tune with our internal temporality with patience so that time flows through us to open new horizons. Let's weave organic patterns of serendipitous paths to welcome the unexpected on the less traveled roads. And let's play—play with ideas, play with boundaries, play with relations, and play with our own shadows. We play at the limit to enter the circle of nonviolence, dancing with smiles, tears, and passions. To dance the circle, in our unique steps individually, in our emergent patterns of relationships collectively, we move towards what is yet to be imagined. Following cross-cultural pathways of surprise, stillness, and spirituality, can we seek from within the courage, capacity, and compassion to get in touch with the most generative rhythm of life and curve our roads onto nonviolence together with our students? The roads under construction will be bumpy, with many unanticipated twists and turns, and may not lead to our desired destination in a short time, but do we have another choice in an age of "nonviolence or nonexistence" (King, 1960, p. 39)?! Developing educational pathways of nonviolence starts with our daily work of "here and now." No matter where you are at this moment, when you close this book, could you think about what nonviolence means for you here and now?

Notes

1. Mandala, in Sanskrit, means a magic circle without beginning and without end. For Carl Jung, Mandala symbolizes the wholeness of the Self. It is the path to individuation. He drew mandalas to portray his own psychic states for self-understanding and used

such a method in individual analyses of his patients, who drew mandalas in therapy to depict their dreams or fantasies.
2. Here the notion of the maternal I refer to is metaphorical rather than literal. In a literal sense, a mother is a woman, and in my study, all my participants, especially Chinese participants, referred to their mothers positively. However, not all children experience their mothers positively and some mothers can be controlling and aggressive. In Jungian psychology (Mayes, 2005), along with the Great Mother, there is the Devouring Mother. But the metaphorical sense of the maternal is not necessarily tied to the biology of sex. Just as *yin* and *yang* do not correspond to woman and man, respectively, and every person has both elements within, the maternal function can also be played by both woman and man. The particular appeal of the metaphorical sense of the maternal for me is its creative power that is embedded in the relational through negotiating between the feminine and the masculine, independence and interdependence, and the subjective and the intersubjective. In this sense, nonviolence and the maternal are intricately and internally connected through relationality.

REFERENCES

Addams, Jane (2002). *Peace and bread in time of war.* Champaign, IL: University of Illinois Press. (Original published 1922).
Addams, Jane (2007). *Newer ideals of peace.* Champaign, IL: University of Illinois Press. (Original published 1906).
Allan, Sarah (1997). *The way of water and sprouts of virtue.* New York: State University of New York Press.
Anderberg, Elsie, Norden, Birgitta, & Hansson, Birgit (2009). Global learning for sustainable development in higher education. *International Journal of Sustainability in Higher Education, 10*(4), 368–378.
Aoki, Ted T. (1981). Toward understanding curriculum. In Ted T. Aoki (2005), *Curriculum in a new key* (William F. Pinar & Rita L. Irwin, Eds.) (pp. 219–228). Mahwah, NJ: Lawrence Erlbaum.
Aoki, Ted T. (1987). Revisiting the notions of leadership and identity. In Ted T. Aoki (2005), *Curriculum in a new key* (William F. Pinar & Rita L. Irwin, Eds.) (pp. 349–355). Mahwah, NJ: Lawrence Erlbaum.
Aoki, Ted T. (1990). *Sonare* and *Videre*. In Ted T. Aoki (2005), *Curriculum in a new key* (William F. Pinar & Rita L. Irwin, Eds.) (pp. 267–276). Mahwah, NJ: Lawrence Erlbaum.
Aoki, Ted T. (1992). Layered voices of teaching. In Ted T. Aoki (2005), *Curriculum in a new key* (William F. Pinar & Rita L. Irwin, Eds.) (pp. 187–197). Mahwah, NJ: Lawrence Erlbaum.
Aoki, Ted T. (1993). The child-centered curriculum? In Ted T. Aoki (2005), *Curriculum in a new key* (William F. Pinar & Rita L. Irwin, Eds.) (pp. 280–289). Mahwah, NJ: Lawrence Erlbaum.
Aoki, Ted T. (2005). *Curriculum in a new key* (William F. Pinar & Rita L. Irwin, Eds.). Mahwah, NJ: Lawrence Erlbaum.
Atkinson, Robert (1998). *The life story interview.* Thousand Oaks, CA: Sage Publications.
Bai, Heesoon, & Cohen, Avraham (2008). Breathing Qi (Ch'i), following Dao (*Tao*). In Claudia Eppert & Hongyu Wang (Eds.), *Cross-cultural studies in curriculum* (pp. 35–54). New York: Routledge.

Bai, Heesoon, Scott, Charles, & Donald, Beatrice (2009). Contemplative pedagogy and revitalization of teacher education. *The Alberta Journal of Educational Research, 55*(3), 319–334.

Bakhtin, Mikhail (1984). *Problems of Dostoevsky's poetics* (Caryl Emerson, Ed. and Trans.) Minneapolis, MN: University of Minnesota Press.

Barnett, Ronald (2009). Knowing and becoming in the higher education curriculum. *Studies in Higher Education, 34*(4), 429–440.

Bergere, Marie-Claire (1990). Tiananmen 1989. In Jeffrey N. Wasserstrom (Ed.) (2002). *Twentieth-century China* (pp. 239–255). New York: Routledge.

Bernstein, Richard J. (1991). *The new constellation.* Cambridge, MA: MIT Press.

Bjune, Irma Vazquez (1995). Serendipity. *English Journal, 84*(2), 64–65.

Brouwer, Daniel C., & Squires, Catherine R. (2003). Public intellectuals, public life, and the university. *Augmentation and Advocacy, 39*, 201–213.

Brown, Sid (2008). *A Buddhist in the classroom.* New York: State University of New York Press.

Burik, Steven (2010). Thinking on the edge. *Philosophy East & West, 60*(4), 499–516.

Butler, Judith (2004). *Precarious life.* London: Verso.

Capra, Fritjof (2010). *The Tao of physics.* Boston, MA: Shambhala. (Original published 1975).

Carson, Terrance R. (2009). Internationalizing curriculum. *Curriculum Inquiry, 39*(1), 145–158.

Caughey, John L. (2006). *Negotiating cultures & identities.* Lincoln, NE: University of Nebraska Press.

Chan, David B. (1991). The China syndrome. In Jonathan Goldstein, Jerry Israel, & Hilary Conroy (Eds.), *America views China* (pp. 183–192). London: Associated University Press.

Chapman, Nancy E., & Plumb, Jessica C. (2001). *The Yale-China Association.* Hong Kong: The Chinese University Press.

Chen, Xunwu (2010). Fate and humanity. *Asian Philosophy, 20*(1), 67–77.

Chu, Haonan, & Liao, Jianqiao (2007). Qingnianren dui zijiren he wairen xinren de xingbie chayi yanjiu [A study on gender differences on youth's sense of trust for insiders and outsiders]. *Qingnian Yanjiu, 11*, 43–49.

Chu, Paochin (1991). The American view of China, 1957–1982. In Jonathan Goldstein, Jerry Israel, & Hilary Conroy (Eds.), *America views China* (pp. 171–182). London: Associated University Press.

Chuang Tzu (n.d.). *Wandering on the way.* (Victor H. Mair, Trans. and Intro.). Honolulu, HI: University of Hawai'i Press.

Cohen, Paul A. (2010). *Discovering history in China.* New York: Columbia University Press. (Original published 1984).

Connelly, Michael F., & Jean Clandinin, D. (1990). Stories of experience and narrative inquiry. *Educational Researcher, 19*(4), 2–14.

Conroy, France H. (1991). Democracy spring. In Jonathan Goldstein, Jerry Israel, & Hilary Conroy (Eds.), *America views China* (pp. 194–209). London: Associated University Press.

Crews, Robin J. (1999). Peace studies, pedagogy, and social change. In Kathleen Maas Weigert & Robin J. Crews (Eds.), *Teaching for justice* (pp. 23–32). Washington, DC: American Association for Higher Education.

Cui, Dahua (1992). *Zhuangxue yanjiu* [Studies on Zhuangzi's school of thought]. Beijing, China: People's Press.

Cui, Zhiyuan (2008). Zhongguo xiandai wenxue piping fanxing yu xinshiqi wenxue piping xingtai [Paradigms of literary criticism in Chinese modern literature and forms of literary criticism in the new era]. *Chuangzuo yu Lilun, 5*, 18–24.

Cunningham, Philip (2009). *Tiananmen moon.* Lanham, MD: Rowman & Littlefield.

Davies, Gloria (Ed.) (2001). *Voicing concerns.* Lanham, MD: Rowman & Littlefield.
Deng, Shaoqiu (2005). Delida jieguo lun yu daojia shengtai shenmei guan [Derridian deconstruction and Taoist ecological aesthetics]. *Jiangxi Shehui Kexue, 7,* 68–70.
Derrida, Jacques (1990). Privilege. In Jacques Derrida (2002), *Who is afraid of philosophy?* (Jan Plug, Trans.). Stanford, CA: Stanford University Press.
Derrida, Jacques (1992). *The other heading* (Pascale-Anne Brault & Michael B. Naas, Trans.). Bloomington, IN: Indiana University Press.
Dick, Kirby, & Ziering, Amy (Directors). (2002). *Derrida* [Motion Picture]. United States: Jane Doe Films.
Disney, Abigail (Producer), & Reticker, Gini (Director). (2008). *Pray the devil back to hell* [Film]. Sausalito, CA: ro*co Films Educational.
Doll, Mary A. (1995). *To the lighthouse and back.* New York: Peter Lang.
Doll, Jr., William E. (1990). Post-modernism's utopian vision. In William E. Doll, Jr. (2012), *Pragmatism, post-modernism, and complexity theory* (Donna Trueit, Ed.) (pp. 144–152). New York: Routledge.
Doll, Jr., William E. (1998). The spirit of curriculum. *Early Childhood Education, 31,* 3–7.
Doll, Jr., William E. (1999). Reflections on teaching. In William E. Doll, Jr. (2012), *Pragmatism, post-modernism, and complexity theory* (Donna Trueit, Ed.) (pp. 207–221). New York: Routledge.
Doll, Jr., William E. (2002). Struggles with spirituality. In William E. Doll, Jr. (2012), *Pragmatism, post-modernism, and complexity theory* (Donna Trueit, Ed.) (pp. 33–42). New York: Routledge.
Doll, Jr., William E. (2005). Keeping knowledge alive. In William E. Doll, Jr. (2012), *Pragmatism, post-modernism, and complexity theory* (Donna Trueit, Ed.) (pp. 111–119). New York: Routledge.
Doll, Jr., William E. (2008). Looking back to the future. In William E. Doll, Jr. (2012), *Pragmatism, post-modernism, and complexity theory* (Donna Trueit, Ed.) (pp. 23–32). New York: Routledge.
Doll, Jr., William E. (2011). Our mistake is in our thinking. Keynote speech at the 32th Bergamo Conference on Curriculum Theory and Classroom Practice, Dayton, Ohio, October 13–15, 2011.
Doll, Jr., William E. (2012). *Pragmatism, post-modernism, and complexity theory* (Donna Trueit, Ed.). New York: Routledge.
Doll, Jr., William E., & Gough, Noel (2002). *Curriculum visions.* New York: Peter Lang.
Durka, Gloria (2002). *The teacher's calling.* Mahwah, NJ: Paulist Press.
Duszynski, Donald W. (2008). Acceptance of the Clark P. Read Mentor Award. *The Journal of Parasitology, 94*(6), 1202–1208.
Easwaran, Eknath (1997). *Gandhi the man.* Tomales, CA: The Blue Mountain Center of Meditation. (Original published 1972).
Edgerton, Susan Huddleston (1996). *Translating curriculum.* New York: Routledge.
Elbaz Luwisch, Freema (2009). Feeling, imagination, and the body in encounters of difference. In Xin Li, Carola Conle, & Freema Elbaz Luwisch (Eds.), *Shifting polarized positions* (p. 219–244). New York: Peter Lang.
Eppert, Claudia, & Wang, Hongyu (Eds.) (2008). *Cross-cultural studies in curriculum.* New York: Routledge.
Esherick, Joseph W., Pickowicz, Paul G., & Walder, Andrew G. (Eds.) (2006). *The Chinese Cultural Revolution as history.* Stanford, CA: Stanford University Press.
Eyre, Richard M. (2008). *The three deceivers. The three alternatives.* Fairfax, VA: Meridian.
Fairbank, John King (1986). *The great Chinese revolution.* New York: Harper & Row.

Feldman, Rhoda (2004). Poetic representation of data in qualitative research. *Journal of Critical Inquiry into Curriculum and Instruction, 5*(2), 10–14.
Feng, Youlan (2004). *A memoir of Feng Youlan.* Beijing, China: People's University Press. (Original published 1984).
Fitz-Gibbon, Andrew (Ed.) (2010). *Positive peace.* Amsterdam, Netherlands: Rodopi B. V.
Fleener, Jayne (2002). *Curriculum dynamics.* New York: Peter Lang.
Forcey, Linda Rennie, & Harris, Ian Murray (Eds.) (1999). *Peacebuilding for adolescents.* New York: Peter Lang.
Foucault, Michel (1977). *Discipline and punish* (Alan Sheridan, Trans.). New York: Pantheon Books.
Foucault, Michel (1982). Sex, power, and the politics of identity. In Paul Rabinow (Ed.) (1997), *Ethics* (pp. 163–173). New York: The New Press.
Fowler, Leah C. (2005). *A curriculum of difficulty.* New York: Peter Lang.
Freedman, Sarah Warshauer (2001). Teacher research and professional development. In Ann Lieberman & Lynne Miller (Eds.), *Teachers caught in the action* (pp. 188–208). New York: Teachers College Press.
Fu, Hongchu (1992). Deconstruction and Taoism. *Comparative Literature Studies, 29*(3), 296–321.
Furth, Charlotte (2002). Intellectual change. In Merle Goldman & Leo Ou-Fan Lee (Eds.), *An intellectual history of modern China* (pp. 13–96). Cambridge, UK: Cambridge University Press.
Gandhi, Mohandas K. (1993). *An autobiography* (Mahadev Desai, Trans.). Boston, MA: Beacon Press. (Original published 1927 & 1929 in two volumes).
Gandhi, Mohandas K. (2007). *Gandhi on non-violence* (Thomas Merton, Ed.). New York: New Directions. (Original published 1942).
Galtung, Johan (1964). An editorial. *Journal of Peace Research, 1*(1), 1–4.
Galtung, Johan (2009). *The fall of the US empire—then what?* Basel, Switzerland: TRANSCEND University Press.
Gay, Geneva (2010). *Culturally responsive teaching* (2nd ed.). New York: Teachers College Press.
Gazetas, Aristides (2003). Re-constituting pedagogies. In Donna Trueit, William E. Doll, Jr., Hongyu Wang, & William F. Pinar (Eds.), *The internationalization of curriculum studies* (pp. 103–115). New York: Peter Lang.
Gbowee, Leymah (2011). *Mighty be our powers.* New York: Beast Books.
Ge, Zhaoguang (2006). Chengwei Zhongguo Na Yidai de zhishi fenzi [Becoming a Chinese intellectual of that generation]. *Dushu, 6,* 47–56.
Gilbert, Kathleen R. (Ed.) (2001). *The emotional nature of qualitative research.* Boca Raton, FL: CRC Press.
Giordano, Peter J. (2010). Serendipity in teaching and learning. *Journal on Excellence in College Teaching, 21*(3), 5–27.
Goodson, Ivor F. (1998). Storying the self. In William F. Pinar (Ed.), *Curriculum* (pp. 3–20). New York: Garland.
Goodson, Ivor F., & Sikes, Pat (2001). *Life history research in educational settings.* Buckingham, UK: Open University Press.
Gough, Noel (2003). Thinking globally in environmental education. In William F. Pinar (Ed.), *International handbook of curriculum research* (pp. 53–72). Mahwah, NJ: Lawrence Erlbaum.
Grauerholz, Liz (2001). Teaching holistically to achieve deep learning. *College Teaching, 49*(2), 44–50.
Gray-Donald, James, & Selby, David (2004). Through the (not so) green door. *Ekistics, 71*(427/428/429), 203–212.
Greene, Maxine (1973). *Teacher as stranger.* Belmont, CA: Wadsworth.

Grumet, Madeleine R. (1988). *Bitter milk*. Amherst, MA: University of Massachusetts Press.
Guba, Egon G., & Lincoln, Yvonna (1989). *The fourth generation evaluation*. Newbury Park, CA: Sage Publications.
Guo, Jian, Song, Yongyi & Zhou, Yuan (2006). *Historical dictionary of the Chinese Cultural Revolution*. Lanham, MD: Scarecrow Press.
Hall, Bradford "J" (2009). Serendipity and stewardship. *New Directions for Teaching and Learning, 120,* 37–45.
Hall, David L., & Ames, Roger T. (1987). *Thinking through Confucius*. New York: State University of New York Press.
Halpern, Nina (1993). Studies of Chinese politics. In David Shambaugh (Ed.), *American studies of contemporary China* (pp. 120–137). New York: Woodrow Wilson Center Press.
Hamlet, Janice D. (Winter, 2009). Engaging spirituality and an authentic self in the intercultural communication class. *New Directions for Teaching and Learning, 120,* 25–33.
Han, Minzhu (1990). *Cries for democracy*. Princeton, NJ: Princeton University Press.
Harding, Harry (1991). From China, with distain. In Jonathan Goldstein, Jerry Israel, & Hilary Conroy (Eds.), *America views China* (pp. 244–272). Cranbury, NJ: Associated University Presses.
Harris, Ian (2008). History of peace of education. In Monisha Bajaj (Ed.), *Encyclopedia of peace education* (pp. 15–24). Charlotte, NC: Information Age Publishing.
Harris, Rabia Terri (2007). Nonviolence in Islam. In Daniel L. Smith-Christopher (Ed.), *Subverting hatred* (pp. 107–127). Maryknoll, NY: Orbis Books.
Hasebe-Ludt, Erika, & Hurren, Wanda (Eds.) (2003). *Curriculum intertext*. New York: Peter Lang.
Hayhoe, Ruth (2001). Lessons from the Chinese academy. In Ruth Hayhoe & Julia Pan (Eds.), *Knowledge across cultures* (pp. 323–347). Hong Kong: Comparative Education Research Centre.
Hayhoe, Ruth (2006). *Portraits of influential Chinese educators*. Hong Kong: Comparative Education Research Center.
He, Ming Fang (2000). *A river forever flowing*. Greenwich, CT: Information Age Publishing.
Hellman, Stuart V. (2007). Humor in the classroom. *College Teaching, 55*(1), 37–39.
Hendrix, Katherine Grace, & Hamlet, Janice D. (Eds.) (Winter, 2009a). As the spirit moves us [Special Issue]. *New Directions for Teaching and Learning, 120.*
Hendrix, Katherine Grace, & Hamlet, Janice D. (Winter, 2009b). Introduction. *New Directions for Teaching and Learning, 120,* 3–7.
Hendry, Petra Munro (2012). *Engendering curriculum history*. New York: Routledge.
Herrington, Anthony, & Herrington, Jan (2006). What is an authentic learning environment? In Anthony Herrington & Jan Herrington (Eds.), *Authentic learning environments in higher education* (pp. 1–13). Hershey, PA: Information Science Publishing.
Hershock, Peter D. (2005). *Chan Buddhism*. Honolulu, HI: University of Hawai'i Press.
Hershock, Peter D. (2009). Ethics in an era of reflexive modernization. In John Powers & Charles S. Prebish (Eds.), *Destroying Mara forever* (pp. 151–164). Ithaca, NY: Snow Lion.
Hershock, Peter D. (2012). *Valuing diversity*. New York: SUNY Press.
Hershock, Peter D., Mason, Mark, & Hawkins, John (Eds.) (2007). *Changing education in a world of complex interdependence*. Hong Kong: The University of Hong Kong Press.
Herzfeld, Michael (2012). Passionate serendipity. In Alma Gottlieb (Eds.), *The restless anthropologist* (pp. 100–122). Chicago, IL: The University of Chicago Press.
Hole, Rachelle (2007). Working between languages and cultures. *Qualitative Inquiry, 13*(5), 696–710.

Hong, Zicheng (2007). *A history of contemporary Chinese literature* (Michael M. Day, Trans.). Boston, MA: Brill. (Original published 1999).

hooks, bell (2000). *Feminism is for everybody*. Cambridge: South End Press.

Hu, Minggui, & Yang, Jianmin (2008). Zhongguo xiandai wenxue piping fadong de wenhua puxi yanjiu [Cultural genealogical studies of Chinese modern literary criticism]. *Fujian Luntan, 10,* 94–100.

Hu, Yipeng (2011). *Zhongguo yinshi* [Hermits in China]. Beijing, China: Shehui Kexue Xueshu Chubanshe.

Huang, Jiande (2007). *Xifang zhexue de chuanru yu yanjiu* [Introduction and studies of Western philosophies]. Fuzhou, China: Fujian Renmin Chubanshe.

Huebner, Dwayne (1967). Curriculum as concern for man's temporality. In Dwayne Huebner (1999), *The lure of the transcendent* (Vikki Hillis, Ed; William F. Pinar, Intro.) (pp. 131–142). Mahwah, NJ: Lawrence Erlbaum.

Huebner, Dwayne (1985). Religious metaphors in the language of education. In Dwayne Huebner (1999), *The lure of the transcendent* (Vikki Hillis, Ed; William F. Pinar, Intro.) (pp. 358–368). Mahwah, NJ: Lawrence Erlbaum.

Huebner, Dwayne (1993). Education and spirituality. In Dwayne Huebner (1999), *The lure of the transcendent* (Vikki Hillis, Ed; William F. Pinar, Intro.) (pp. 401–416). Mahwah, NJ: Lawrence Erlbaum.

Huebner, Dwayne (1999). *The lure of the transcendent*. (Vikki Hillis, Ed.; William F. Pinar, Intro.). Mahwah, NJ: Lawrence Erlbaum.

Humphreys, Christmas (1968). *Sixty years of Buddhism in England (1907–1967)*. London: Buddhist Society.

jagodzinski, jan (2002). The ethics of the "real" in Levinas, Lacan, and Buddhism. *Educational Theory, 52*(1), 81–96.

jagodzinski, jan (2008). The gaze of the teacher: Eye-to-eye with Lacan, Derrida, and the Zen of Dôgen and Nishitani. In Claudia Eppert & Hongyu Wang (Eds.), *Cross-cultural studies in curriculum* (pp. 137–169). New York: Routledge.

James, David (2004). A need for humor in online courses. *College Teaching, 52*(3), 93.

Jhally, Sut (Executive Producer & Director) (1999). *Tough guise* [Motion picture]. USA: Media Education Foundation.

Ji, Xianlin (2006). *Ji Xianlin tan rengshen* [Ji Xianlin talking about life]. Beijing, China: Dangdai Zhongguo Chubanshe.

Johnson, Allan G. (2005). *The gender knot* (2nd ed.). Philadelphia, PA: Temple University Press.

Johnson, Steven (2010). *Where good ideas come from*. New York: Riverhead Books.

Jung, Carl (1969). *The archetypes and the collective unconscious* (2nd ed.) (R. F. C. Hull, Trans.). Princeton, NJ: Princeton University Press.

Kahane, David (Summer, 2009). Learning about obligation, compassion, and global justice. *New Directions for Teaching and Learning, 118,* 49–60.

Kaneda, Takuya (2008). Shanti, peacefulness of mind. In Claudia Eppert & Hongyu Wang (Eds.), *Cross-cultural studies in curriculum* (pp. 171–192). New York: Routledge.

Kenyon, Cynthia L. (2008). *Reframed teacher leadership*. Unpublished doctoral dissertation, University of Northern Iowa.

King, Jr., Martin Luther (1960). Pilgrimage to nonviolence. In James M. Washington (Ed.) (1986), *The essential writings and speeches of Martin Luther King, Jr.* (pp. 35–40). New York: HarperOne.

Kingston, Maxine Hong (1989). *The woman warrior*. New York: Vintage Books.

Knight, Louise W. (2005). *Citizen*. Chicago, IL: The University of Chicago Press.

Knight, Louise W. (2010). *Jane Addams*. New York: W.W. Norton & Company.
Ko, Dorothy (1994). *Teachers of the inner chamber*. Stanford, CA: Stanford University Press.
Kohl, Herbert (1993). *I won't learn from you!* Minneapolis, MN: Milkweed Editions.
Kress, Cathann (2006). Twenty-first century leaning after school. In Erik Schwarz & Ken Kay (Eds.), *The case for twenty-first century learning* (pp. 133–140). San Francisco, CA: Wiley.
Kristeva, Julia (1977). *About Chinese women* (Anita Barrows, Trans.). New York: Urizen Books.
Kristeva, Julia (1987). *Tales of love* (Leon S. Roudiez Trans). New York: Columbia University Press.
Kristeva, Julia (1991). *Strangers to ourselves* (Leon S. Roudiez, Trans.). New York: Columbia University Press.
Kristeva, Julia (1993). *Nations without nationalism* (Leon S. Roudiez, Trans.). New York: Columbia University Press.
Kristeva, Julia (1996). *Julia Kristeva: Interviews*. New York: Columbia University Press.
Kristeva, Julia (2000). *The sense and non-sense of revolt* (Jeanine Herman, Trans.). New York: Columbia University Press. (Original work published 1996).
Ladson-Billings, Gloria (1995). Toward a theory of culturally relevant pedagogy. *American Educational Research Journal, 32,* 465–491.
Langmann, Ellen Condliffe (2000). *An elusive science*. Chicago, IL: The University of Chicago Press.
Laozi [Tao Te Ching] (1992). Changsha, China: Hunan University Press.
Lautz, Terry (August 12, 2010). China's deficit in American studies. *Chronicles of Higher Education,* Retrieved May 10, 2012, from http://chronicle.com/article/Chinas-Deficit-in-American/123884/
Lee, Leo Ou-Fan (2002). Literary trends. In Merle Goldman & Leo Ou-Fan Lee (Eds.), *An intellectual history of modern China* (pp. 196–266). Cambridge, UK: Cambridge University Press.
Lewis, Magda (Ed.) (2010). Knowledge commodified and the new economies of higher education [Special Issue], *the Journal of Curriculum Theorizing, 26*(3).
Levinas, Emmanuel (1987). *Time and the Other and additional essays* (Richard A. Cohen, Trans). Pittsburgh, PA: Duquesne University Press.
Li, Fengwei (2010). 1917–1937: Xifang wenxue lilun yinjie yanjiu Chutan [1917–1937: An initial study of the introduction of Western literary theories]. *Xinyang Shifan Xueyuan Xuebao, 30*(3), 118–122.
Li, Xin (2002). *Tao of life stories*. New York: Peter Lang.
Li, Xin (2005). A *Tao* of narrative. *Curriculum Inquiry, 34*(3), 339–366.
Li, Xin, Conle, Carola, & Elbaz Luwisch, Freema (2009). *Shifting polarized positions*. New York: Peter Lang.
Lin, Jing (1991). *The Red Guards' path to violence*. New York: Praeger.
Lin, Jing (2006). *Love, peace, and wisdom in education*. Lanham, MD: Rowman & Littlefield.
Lin, Jing (2008). Constructing a global ethic of universal love and reconciliation. In Jing Lin, Edward J. Brantmeier, & Bruhn, Christa (2008). *Transforming education for peace* (pp. 301–315). Charlotte, NC: Information Age Publishing.
Lin, Xiaoqing (2005). *Peking University*. New York: State University of New York Press.
Lin, Yutang (1959). *From pagan to Christian*. Cleveland, OH: The World Publishing Company.
Liu, Jincai (2002). 1917–1927: Zhongguo xiandai wenxue piping lilun ziyuan de yinjin [1917–1927: Introduction of theoretical resources in Chinese modern literary criticism]. *Zhongzhou Xuekan, 3,* 69–73.

Liu, Shu-Hsien (1974). Time and temporality, *Philosophy East and West, 24*(2), 145–153.
Loewen, James W. (1995). *Lies my teacher told me*. New York: Touchstone.
Loy, David (1988). *Nonduality*. New Haven, CT: Yale University Press.
Loy, David (1992). The deconstruction of Buddhism. In Harold Coward & Toby Foshay (Eds.), *Derrida and negative theology* (pp. 227–253). New York: SUNY Press.
Loy, David (2009). *Awareness bound and unbound*. New York: State University of New York Press.
Lu, Hsun (2007). What happens after Nora leaves home? In Ling Ding (Ed.), *The Power of weakness* (pp. 84–93). New York: The Feminist Press. (Original published 1923).
Luce-Kapler, Rebecca (2009). Serendipity, poetry and inquiry. In Monica Prendergast, Carl Leggo, & Pauline Sameshima (Eds.), *Poetic inquiry* (p. 75–58). Rotterdam, Netherlands: Sense.
Luo, Zhitian (2006). *Zaizao wenming de changshi* [The attempt to recreate civilization]. Beijing, China: Zhonghua Shuju.
Luxon, Tony, & Peelo, Moira (2009). Internationalisation. *Innovations in Education and Teaching International, 46*(1), 51–60.
Ma, Junjie, & Wu, Jun (2011). Han "yuanfen" de wenhua fuzaici fanyi [On the translation of the culturally-loaded word of "yuanfen"]. *Longdong Xueyuan Xuebao, 22*(4), 79–81.
Macdonald, James B. (1995). *Theory as a prayerful act*. New York: Peter Lang.
MacFarquhar, Roderick, & Schoenhals, Michael (2006). *Mao's last revolution*. Cambridge, UK: The Belknap Press of Harvard University Press.
Mandela, Nelson (2003). *Long walk to freedom*. London: Abacus. (Original work published 1994).
Mann, Susan (2000). Myths of Asian womanhood. *The Journal of Asian Studies, 59*(4), 835–862.
Martin, Mike W. (2007). *Creativity*. Plymouth, UK: Lexington Books.
Mayes, Clifford (2005). *Jung and education*. Lanham, MD: Rowman & Littlefield.
McClelland, Jerry, Dahlberg, Karin, & Plihal, Jane (2002). Learning in the ivory tower: Students' embodied experience. *College Teaching, 50*(1), 4–7.
McLeod, Julie, & Thomson, Rachel (2009). *Researching social change*. Los Angeles, CA: Sage.
Merrill, Martha C. (1999). Learning about peace. In Kathleen Maas Weigert & Robin J. Crews (Eds.), *Teaching for justice* (pp. 125–135). Washington, DC: American Association for Higher Education.
Miller, James (1993). *The passion of Michel Foucault*. New York: Simon & Schuster.
Miller, Janet L. (2005). *Sounds of silence breaking*. New York: Peter Lang.
Miller, Janet L. (2010). Communities without consensus. In Erik Malewski (Ed.), *Curriculum studies handbook* (pp. 95–100). New York: Routledge.
Miller, Jeffrey C. (2004). *The transcendent function*. New York: State University of New York Press.
Mitter, Rana (2004). *A bitter revolution*. New York: Oxford University Press.
Moon, Seungho (2011). Rethinking culturally-responsive pedagogy. *Multicultural Education Review, 3*(2), 69–102.
Morris, Christopher D. (2007). *The figure of the road*. New York: Peter Lang.
Morson, Gary Saul, & Emerson, Caryl (1990). *Mikhail Bakhtin*. Stanford, CA: Stanford University Press.
Muller, Jean-Marie (2002). *Non-violence and education*. Paris: UNESCO.
Muller, Thor, & Becker, Lane (2012). *Get lucky*. San Francisco, CA: Jossey-Bass.
Munro, Petra (1998). *Subject to fiction*. Buckingham, UK: Open University Press.
Murphy, Christina (Winter, 2005). The academy, spirituality, and the search for truth. *New Directions in Teaching and Learning, 104*, 23–29.

Muskopf, Beth A. (1998). *Women, education, and leadership.* Unpublished doctoral dissertation, Miami University, Oxford, Ohio.
Nagler, Michael (2004). *The search for a nonviolent future.* Maui, Hawai'i: Inner Ocean.
Nakagawa, Yoshiharu (2008). Eastern wisdom and holistic education. In Claudia Eppert & Hongyu Wang (Eds.), *Cross-cultural studies in curriculum* (pp. 227–245). New York: Routledge.
Ng-A-Fook, Nicholas (2009). Toward understanding a curriculum of being inhabited by the language of the other. *Transnational Curriculum Inquiry, 6*(2), 3–22.
Noddings, Nel (2003). *Happiness and education.* New York: Cambridge University Press.
Odin, Jaishree K., & Manicas, Peter T. (Eds.) (2004). *Globalization and higher education.* Honolulu, HI: University of Hawai'i Press.
Oldmeadow, Harry (2004). *Journeys East.* New York: World Wisdom.
Palmer, Parker J. (2007). *The courage to teach.* San Francisco, CA: John Wiley & Sons. (Original published 1998).
Park, Jin Y. (2005). Notes on comparative philosophy. *The International Journal of Fieldbeing, 2*(2). Retrieved May 10, 2013, from www.iifb.org/ijfb/JYPark-4–5
Pinar, William F. (1972). Work from within. In William F. Pinar (1994), *Autobiography, politics and sexuality* (pp. 7–11). New York: Peter Lang.
Pinar, William F. (1975). The method of *currere.* In William F. Pinar (1994), *Autobiography, politics and sexuality* (pp. 19–27). New York: Peter Lang.
Pinar, William F. (1976). The trial. In William F. Pinar (1994), *Autobiography, politics and sexuality* (pp. 29–61). New York: Peter Lang.
Pinar, William F. (1979). A voyage out. In William F. Pinar (1994). *Autobiography, politics, and sexuality* (pp. 117–150). New York: Peter Lang.
Pinar, William F. (1992). Cries and whispers. In William F. Pinar & William M. Reynolds (Eds.), *Understanding curriculum as phenomenological and deconstructed text* (pp. 92–101). New York: Teachers College Press.
Pinar, William F. (1994). *Autobiography, politics, and sexuality.* New York: Peter Lang.
Pinar, William F. (2001). *The gender of racial politics and violence in America.* New York: Peter Lang.
Pinar, William F. (2003a). Introduction. In Donna Trueit, William E. Doll, Jr., Hongyu Wang, & William F. Pinar (Eds.), *The internationalization of curriculum studies* (pp. 1–13). New York: Peter Lang.
Pinar, William F. (Eds.) (2003b). *International handbook of curriculum research.* Mahwah, NJ: Lawrence Erlbaum.
Pinar, William F. (2004). *What is curriculum theory?* Mahwah, NJ: Lawrence Erlbaum.
Pinar, William F. (2009). *The worldliness of cosmopolitan education.* New York: Routledge.
Pinar, William F. (2010). *Curriculum studies in South Africa.* New York: Palgrave MacMillan.
Pinar, William F. (2012). *Curriculum studies in the United States.* New York: Palgrave Macmillan.
Pinar, William F., & Grumet, Madeleine R. (1976). *Toward a poor curriculum.* Dubuque, IA: Kendall/Hunt Publishing Company.
Pinar, William F., Reynold, William, Slattery, Patrick, & Taubman, Peter (1995). *Understanding curriculum.* New York: Peter Lang.
Pitt, Alice (2003). *The play of the personal.* New York: Peter Lang.
Pohl, Karl-Heinz (2003). Play-thing of the times. *Journal of Chinese Thought, 30*(3&4), 469–486.
Porche-Frilot, Donna (2002). A perspective on "the call from the stranger: Dwayne Huebner's vision of curriculum as a spiritual journey." In William E. Doll, Jr. & Noel Gough (Eds.), *Curriculum visions* (pp. 300–303). New York: Peter Lang.

Posner, Richard A. (2003). *Public intellectuals*. Cambridge, MA: Harvard University Press.
Prendergast, Monica, Leggo, Carl, & Sameshima, Pauline (2009). *Poetic inquiry*. Rotterdam, Netherlands: Sense Publishers.
Raphals, Lisa (2003). Fate, fortune, chance, and luck in Chinese and Greek. *Philosophy East & West, 53*(4), 537–574.
Reardon, Betty A. (1988). *Comprehensive peace education*. New York: Teachers College Press.
Roschelle, Anne R., Turpin, Jennifer, & Elias, Robert (1999). Student contributions to public life: Peace and justice studies at the University of San Francisco. In Kathleen Maas Weigert & Robin J. Crews (Eds.), *Teaching for justice* (pp. 65–71). Washington, DC: American Association for Higher Education.
Rosen, David (1996). *The Tao of Jung*. New York: Penguin Books.
Rosenblatt, Paul C. (2001). Qualitative research as a spiritual experience. In Kathleen R. Gilbert (Ed.), *The emotional nature of qualitative research* (pp. 111–128). Boca Raton, FL: CRC Press.
Said, Edward W. (1994). *Orientalism*. New York: Vintage Books. (Original published 1979).
Sawyer, Richard (1998). *Teachers who evolve as curriculum makers*. Unpublished doctoral dissertation, Teachers College, Columbia University, New York.
Scarritt, James R., & Lowe, Seana (1999). The international and national voluntary service training program (INVST) at the University of Colorado at Boulder. In Kathleen Maas Weigert & Robin J. Crews (Eds.), *Teaching for justice* (pp. 83–90). Washington, DC: American Association for Higher Education.
Schoeberlein, Deborah, & Sheth, Suki (2009). *Mindful teaching and teaching mindfulness*. Boston, MA: Wisdom Publications
Schratz, Michael, & Walker, Rob (1999). Service-learning. In Kathleen Maas Weigert & Robin J. Crews (Eds.), *Teaching for justice* (pp. 33–46). Washington, DC: American Association for Higher Education.
Schwartz, Benjamin I. (2002). Themes in intellectual history. In Merle Goldman & Leo Ou-Fan Lee (Eds.), *An intellectual history of modern China* (pp. 97–141). Cambridge, UK Cambridge University Press.
Shambaugh, David (2009). Reflection on the American study of contemporary China. *Far Eastern Affairs, 37*(4), 151–158.
Shen, Keyong (2004). *Fenxi xinlixue* [Analytical psychology]. Beijing, China: Shenghuo• Duzhe• Xinzhi.
Shepherd, Robert J. (2007). Perpetual unease or being at ease?—Derrida, Daoism, and the "metaphysics of presence." *Philosophy East and West 57*(2), 227–243.
Shi, Feishang (2010). Ershi shiji yilai guoneiwai yinshi yanjiu qingkuang zongsu [Chinese and oversea studies about hermit in China since the 20th century: An overview]. Retrieved March 15, 2012, from www.sanw.net/oblog/user1/5/7720.html
Smith, David Geoffrey (1996). Identity, self and other in the conduct of pedagogical action. *JCT: An Interdisciplinary Journal of Curriculum Theorizing, 12*(3), 6–11.
Smith, David Geoffrey (2003a). Curriculum and teaching facing globalization. In William F. Pinar (Ed.), *International handbook of curriculum research* (pp. 35–51). Mahwah, NJ: Lawrence Erlbaum.
Smith, David Geoffrey (2003b). The specific challenges of globalization for teaching . . . and vice versa. In Donna Trueit, William E. Doll, Jr., Hongyu Wang, & William F. Pinar (Eds.), *The internationalization of curriculum studies* (pp. 293–318). New York: Peter Lang.
Smith, David Geoffrey (2008). "The farthest West is but the farthest East." In Claudia Eppert & Hongyu Wang (Eds.), *Cross-cultural studies in curriculum* (pp. 1–33). New York: Routledge.

Smith-Christopher, Daniel L. (2007). *Subverting hatred*. Maryknoll, NY: Orbis Books.
Smythe, Jon (2012). *Culture shocked*. Unpublished doctoral dissertation, Oklahoma State University, Stillwater, Oklahoma.
Sobol, Joseph Daniel (1999). *The storytellers' journey*. Urbana, IL: University of Illinois Press.
Speck, Bruce W. (Winter, 2005). What is spirituality? *New Directions for Teaching and Learning, 104*, 3–13.
Spector, Barbara Solomon (2006). Serendipity. In Samuel Totten & Jon E. Pedersen (Eds.), *Researching and teaching social issues* (pp. 181–206). Oxford, UK: Lexington Books.
Spence, Jonathan D. (1990). *The search for modern China*. New York: W.W. Norton & Company.
Spence, Jonathan D. (1992). Looking East. In Jonathan D. Spence (Ed.), *Chinese roundabout* (pp. 78–90). New York: W.W. Norton & Company.
Stearns, Peter N. (2009). *Educating global citizens in colleges and universities*. New York: Routledge.
Sun, Meitang (2006). Chongjian zhongguo xueshu zhi wojian [My perspective on how to reconstruct the Chinese scholarship]. *Xueshujie, 4,* 69–81.
Taubman, Peter (1992). Achieving the right distance. In William F. Pinar & William M. Reynolds (Eds.), *Understanding curriculum and phenomenological and deconstructed text* (pp. 216–233). New York: Teachers College Press.
Taylor, Jeremy (2009). *The wisdom of your dreams*. New York: Penguin.
Teng, Jinhua Emma (1996). The construction of the "traditional Chinese woman" in the Western academy. *SIGNS, 22*(1), 115–151.
Thich, Nhat Hanh. (2009). *The heart of understanding*. Berkeley, CA: Parallax Press. (Original published 1989).
Tibbits, Felisa (2008). Human rights education. In Monisha Bajaj (Ed.). *Encyclopedia of peace education* (p. 99–108). Charlotte, NC: Information Age Publishing.
Tierney, William G. (2003). Undaunted courage. In Norman K. Denzin & Yvonna S. Lincoln (Eds.), *Strategies of qualitative inquiry* (pp. 292–318). Thousand Oaks, CA: Sage Publications.
Todd, Sharon (2003). *Learning from the other*. Albany, NY: State University of New York Press.
Tolle, Eckhart (2003). *Stillness speaks*. Novato, CA: New World Library.
Tolle, Eckhart (2004). *The power of now*. Novato, CA: New World Library. (Original published 1999).
Tu, Wei-Ming (1979). *Humanity and self-cultivation*. Berkeley, CA: Asian Humanities Press.
Tung, May Paomay (2000). *Chinese Americans and their immigrant parents*. New York: The Haworth Clinical Practice.
Tutu, Desmond (1999). *No future without forgiveness*. New York: Doubleday.
van Manen, Max (1990). *Researching lived experience*. New York: State University of New York Press.
Vokey, Daniel (2008). Hearing, contemplating, and meditating. In Claudia Eppert & Hongyu Wang (Eds.), *Cross-cultural studies in curriculum* (pp. 287–312). New York: Routledge.
Walder, Andrew G. (2009). *Fractured rebellion*. London: Harvard University Press.
Walter, Katya (1994). *Tao of chaos*. Shaftesbury, UK: Element.
Wang, Hongyu (1997). Curriculum as polyphonic authoring. *Journal of Curriculum Theorizing, 13*(4), 20–24.
Wang, Hongyu (2002). The call from the stranger. In William E. Doll, Jr. & Noel Gough (Eds.), *Curriculum visions* (pp. 287–299). New York: Peter Lang.
Wang, Hongyu (2004). *The call from the stranger on a journey home*. New York: Peter Lang.

Wang, Hongyu (2007). Interconnections within and without. In Peter Hershock, John Hawkins, & Mark Mason (Eds.), *Changing education in a world of complex interdependence* (pp. 273–296). Hong Kong: The University of Hong Kong Press.

Wang, Hongyu (2008). The strength of the feminine, the lyrics of the Chinese woman's self, and the power of education. In Claudia Eppert & Hongyu Wang (Eds.), *Cross-cultural studies in curriculum* (pp. 313–333). New York: Routledge.

Wang, Hongyu (2009). Life history and cross-cultural thought. *Transnational Curriculum Inquiry, 6*(2), 37–50.

Wang, Hongyu (2010a). A zero space of nonviolence. *Journal of Curriculum Theorizing, 26*(1), 1–8.

Wang, Hongyu (2010b). Intimate revolt and third possibilities. In Erik Malewski (Ed.), *Curriculum studies reader* (pp. 374–386). New York: Routledge.

Wang, Hongyu (2010c). The temporality of *currere*, change, and teacher education. *Pedagogies: An International Journal, 5*(4), 275–285.

Wang, Hongyu (2013a). Confucian self-cultivation and Daoist personhood. *The Frontier of Education in China, 8*(1), 62–79.

Wang, Hongyu (2013b). A nonviolent perspective in internationalizing curriculum studies. In William F. Pinar (Ed.), *International handbook on curriculum research* (2nd ed.) (pp. 69–76). New York: Routledge.

Wang, Hongyu (2013c). A nonviolent approach to social justice education. *Educational Studies, 49* (6), 485–503.

Wang, Hongyu, & Hoyt, Wu Mei (2007). Sounds of silence breaking. *Journal of the American Association for the Advancement of Curriculum Studies, 3*. Retrieved May 1, 2012, from www2.uwstout.edu/content/jaaacs/vol3/wang.htm

Wang, Hongyu, & Olson, Nadine (2009). *A journey to unlearn and learn in multicultural education.* New York: Peter Lang.

Wang, Xiaozhao, & Chen, Kai (2009). Wusi yundong jiben jingshen dui zhongguo xiandai zhexue de qidi [The fundamental spirit of the May Fourth movement and its lessons for Chinese modern philosophy]. *Zhejiang Xuekan,* 39–43.

Watts, Alan (1972). *In my own way (1915 -1965).* New York: Vintage Books.

Wei, Yixia (2010). *Zhongguoren de mingyun zhexue* [A Chinese philosophy of fate]. Harbin, China: Heilongjian Jiaoyu Chubanshe.

Weigert, Kathleen Maas (1999). Moral dimensions of peace studies. In Kathleen Maas Weigert & Robin J. Crews (Eds.), *Teaching for justice* (pp. 9–21). Washington, DC: American Association for Higher Education.

Weigert, Kathleen Maas, & Crews, Robin J. (Eds.) (1999a). *Teaching for justice.* Washington, DC: American Association for Higher Education.

Weigert, Kathleen Maas ,& Crews, Robin J. (1999b). Introduction. In Kathleen Maas Weigert & Robin J. Crews (Eds.), *Teaching for justice* (pp. 1–8). Washington, DC: American Association for Higher Education.

Wen, Qingyun (2009). *Intellectuals in caves* [Yanxue zhi shi: Zhongguo zaoqi yinyi chuantong]. Shangdong, China: Shangdong Illustrated Magazine Press.

Weston, Timothy B. (2006). Beijing University as a contested symbol. In Joseph W. Esherick, Wen-hsin Yeh, & Madeleine Zelin (Eds.), *Empire, nation, and beyond* (pp. 275–291). Berkeley, CA: Institute of East Asian Studies, University of California.

White III, Lynn T. (2009). Chinese political studies. *Journal of Chinese Political Science, 14*(3), 229–251.

Whitlock, Reta Ugena (2012). "All we are saying . . ." *The Journal of Curriculum Theorizing, 28*(1), 227–230.

Wimmer, Randolph John (2003). *Stories of teacher educators*. Unpublished doctoral dissertation, University of Alberta, Edmonton, Alberta, Canada.
Xie, Xinhong (2002). Cong "mianzi" deng yu de yingyi kan fanyi de shizhi [Essence of translation revealed from the English translation of Chinese terms such as "face"]. *Huizhou Xueyuan Xuebao, 22*(1), 87–92.
Xu, Yuzhen (2005). Xunzhao kecheng yanjiu de disan kongjian [In search of the third space in curriculum studies]. Presentation at the Conference on the Internationalization of Curriculum Studies, Capitol Normal University, Beijing, China, May 9–10.
Yang, Yi (2005). "Ganwu" de xiandaixing zhuanxing [A modern transformation of "awareness"]. *Xueshu Yuekan, 11,* 112–119.
Yeh, Wen-hsin (2006). History in modernity. In Joseph W. Esherick, Wen-hsin Yeh, & Madeleine Zelin (Eds.), *Empire, nation, and beyond* (pp. 292–307). Berkeley, CA: Institute of East Asian Studies, University of California.
Yu, Moj Chiu, & Harrison, J. Frank (Eds.) (1990). *Voices from Tiananmen Square*. Montreal, Canada: Black Rose Books.
Yue, Daiyun (2001). On Western literary theory in China. In Gloria Davies (Ed.), *Voicing concerns* (pp.109–122). Lanham, MD: Rowman & Littlefield.
Zha, Qiang (2012). Intellectuals, academic freedom, and university autonomy in China. In Hans G. Schuetze, William Bruneau, & Garnet Grosjean (Eds.), *University governance and reform—policy, fads, and experience in international perspective* (pp. 205–226). New York, NY: Palgrave Macmillan.
Zhang, Zhilin (1995). Zhongxi kexue "yanjiu chuantong" de chayi yu huitong [The differences and intersections between Chinese and Western scientific "traditions of study"]. *Kexue Jishu yu Bianzhengfa, 4,* 31–34.
Zhou, Tiandu (1984). *Cai Yuanpei zhuan* [A biography of Cai Yuanpei]. Beijing, China: Renmin Chubanshe.
Ziarek, Ewa Płonowska (2001). *An ethics of dissensus*. Stanford, CA: Stanford University Press.

INDEX

4-H 109, 110, 111, 114

academic freedom 52, 64, 113, 118, 140
activism 6, 106, 177; nonviolence activism 115–16, 132, 163; pedagogical 11, 109, 112; political 51–2;
Addams, Jane 1, 115, 116, 117, 119, 158, 180
aesthetics 29, 45, 65, 97
Ahimsa 12
alterity 160
ambiguity 43, 54, 56, 66, 115, 139, 141, 166, 171, 175, 178
American culture 9, 80, 83, 117, 119, 124, 130, 136
American scholarship 31, 81, 82, 85, 96
American thought 42, 84
American values 119, 130
Ames, Roger T. 5, 63
anarchy 50, 92, 93
Aoki, Ted T. 8, 25, 26, 38, 39, 68, 89, 94, 100, 126, 132, 137, 150, 178
Atkinson, Robert 143
autobiography 5, 7, 9, 43, 46, 67, 91, 106, 181
awareness 1, 20, 34, 64, 72, 76, 112, 122, 127, 139, 144, 165, 170, 180

Bai, Heesoon 6, 13
balance 14, 35–6, 56–7, 62, 87, 156
Bakhtin, Mikhail 139
Barnett, Ronald 7, 137, 164
Bateson, Gregory 35
Beauvoir, Simone de 67
Beijing University 52, 78

binary 8, 138, 166, 172, 174
body 17, 86, 87, 88, 100, 147, 178–9, 183; and mind 13, 35, 103, 120–2, 141, 142, 161, 168, 169, 178
Brecht, Bertold 29
Brown, Sid 179
Buber, Martin 29
Buck, Pearl 108, 117
Buddhism 3, 12, 18, 47, 63, 75, 86, 90, 91, 103, 138, 155
Butler, Judith 178

Cai, Yuanpei 52
calligraphy 87, 97, 183
capitalism 89
Capra, Fritjof 30
carefree 58–60, 68
Carson, Terrance R. 180
categorical thinking 13, 14, 67, 92, 100, 158, 173
categorization 136, 161, 166, 167
Chairman Mao 88, 92, 93, 95, 98, 103n4
chaos and complexity theory 30, 124
Chen, Duxiu 51, 53
Chen, Xunwu 62
China and the West 2, 31, 33, 46, 57, 181
China studies 2, 9, 23–4, 29, 69, 103, 136, 162; in history 30–3; in political science 71, 94–5; shifting lenses of 16, 25, 181
China-US relationship 17, 33, 156, 157, 161
Chinese culture 6, 104, 117, 129, 136, 160, 183; critique of 22, 46–7, 51, 53

Chinese intellectual 4, 25, 46–51, 65–6, 136, 137, 144, 159, 181
Chinese learning 49, 51, 65, 159
Chinese literature 43–7, 49, 54
Chinese scholarship 82, 136, 145, 146
Chinese Students' Movement 22; May Fourth 51–3; in 1989 9, 17, 24, 35, 82, 83, 140, 143, 152
Chinese thought 2, 48, 63, 97, 135, 147, 149, 160, 161
Christian 34, 119, 160, 163; culture 33; philosophy 49; religion 50; theology 50; tradition 158
Christianity 17, 29, 33–4
circle 15n2, 88, 155, 157, 166, 167; full 90, 102, 156, 161; of life 80; of nonviolence 184; Taoist 3, 4
class struggle 51, 76
Cohen, Avraham 13
Cohen, Paul 30, 31, 32, 35, 38, 40, 49
Cold War 95
colonization 12, 47, 163, 178; half- 47
commercialization 7, 60
commonality 32, 132, 177
community 10, 12, 37, 38, 40, 88, 105, 119, 124, 167, 169, 176; -based education 112, 114, 115, 117, 177; building 114; of *dissensus* 177, 178, 183; of learners 171; planetary 13; service 105, 109, 110, 111, 114; world 35, 114, 178
compassion 13, 37, 129, 165, 182, 184
Connelly, Michael F. 150
Confucian thought 29, 37, 47, 52–3, 59
Confucianism 47, 52, 63, 64, 90, 126; and gender 59
consciousness 5, 88, 134, 138, 146, 149, 163; dualistic 13, 41; political 76, 94
constructivism 9, 67–8, 164
context 5, 6, 29, 40, 47, 49, 58, 90, 91, 101, 112, 152, 160, 169, 176, 178, 182; American 125; Chinese 61, 67, 159; cross-cultural 123, 165, 178; cultural 154, 157, 182; of higher education 5, 168, 173; historical 31, 43, 50; international 164, 173; political 12
contradiction 1, 40, 43, 56, 58, 66, 92, 100, 101, 134, 138, 142, 149, 175, 178
control mentality 112, 118
conversation 6–8, 59, 126, 136, 152; informal 11, 72, 142; intercultural 7; international 8; research 11, 55, 71, 135–6, 139–40, 143, 146, 152–3; pedagogical 129
cosmic cycle 36

cosmopolitan 7, 9, 17, 21, 39, 71, 96; curriculum 160; experience 17, 20, 160; lens 71, 82, 160
creativity 18, 87, 113, 118, 126, 167, 184; co-, 143, 150, 183; individual 63, 156, 161, 183; intercultural and cross-cultural 150; literary 53; maternal 175; scholarly 143, 146, 147
cross-cultural 8, 40, 55, 71, 72, 79, 91, 94, 102, 111, 123, 134, 140, 161, 170, 183; assumption 47; education 33, 58; educator 28, 35, 145; encounter 6, 19, 20, 39, 79, 146, 162, 167, 170, 176; engagement 1, 2, 7, 11, 14, 16, 22, 26, 39, 118, 139, 161, 165; exchange 29, 107, 162; experience 16, 26, 102, 132, 137; 142, 166; imagination 42, 69; journey 5, 38, 89, 101, 164; pathway 7, 21, 40, 72, 83, 96, 101, 155, 156, 161, 170, 184; studies 5–8, 26; teaching 106, 120, 176; thought 2, 66; understanding 28, 165, 179
crossing and dwelling 8, 26, 158, 175
cultural history 66, 72, 91, 142
Cultural Revolution 9, 33, 36, 47, 71–3, 77, 91–4, 98, 99, 103n1, 103n3, 103n4, 158, 159; and big-character posters 78, 103n4; and Cadre's Camp 73–5, 103n2; and counter-revolutionary 73, 92; and Red Guards 73, 74, 92, 93, 98; and struggle meeting 73, 74, 77, 93, 100
cultural studies 42, 45, 47–8, 55–6, 65, 66, 159
culture shock 26, 80, 81, 84, 157
Currere 5, 127–8, 133, 154
curriculum 5, 8, 14, 27, 67, 86, 107, 120, 131, 164, 177, 180, 184; cosmopolitan 160; creativity; playful 155, 156, 181; development 170; higher education 7, 8, 164, 165, 180, 181; theorizing 8; theory 81, 120, 169; as a third space 4, 166
curriculum studies 8, 15; as a field 5, 162; in higher education 8; internationalization of 6, 7; reconceptualization of 8, 164, 169

deconstruction 30, 47, 81, 99, 138, 139
de-education 102–3, 173–4
de/education 103, 167, 173
democracy 1, 9, 23, 51, 78, 88, 97, 138, 174; American 3, 38, 86, 118; and China 25, 34, 98, 140; and difference 116, 119; European 29; in-the-making 98;

liberal 29, 52; notion of 41; system of 83, 85; Western 34, 93, 95–6
Derrida, Jacques 4, 27, 132, 138, 139
Dewey, John 42, 50, 51
dialogue 5, 49, 72, 99, 136, 137; East/West 6; global 7; intercivilzational 6; polyphonic 139–40; research 139–41, 143, 167
difference 4, 17, 27, 40, 48, 66, 72, 150, 166, 175, 184; commonality and 32, 132, 177; connections across 27, 41, 178; cultural 6, 13, 20, 32, 81, 131; engagement with 159–62, 167; gendered 119; national 148; negotiating 54, 64, 81, 131, 176; openness to difference 116, 147; play with 84; as positive 55, 126; religious 86; social 7, 148, 153, 160
"differing for" 13, 40
difficult knowledge 122
discourse analysis 68, 138
disillusion 3, 10, 31, 33, 36–8, 51, 71, 85, 94–7, 102, 117
dissonance 128, 156
Doll, Mary Aswell 175
Doll, Jr., William E. 2, 14, 35, 171, 172, 175, 178
double texts 106, 120
double stories 72
dualism 4, 13, 14, 38, 55, 61, 86, 92–4, 99, 101, 138, 142, 166, 180
dualistic 13, 36, 41, 99, 138, 140

Easwaran, Eknath 1, 14, 91
East and West (East/West) 5–8, 30, 46, 48, 54, 63, 141, 180
ecological 13, 15, 35, 57, 138, 167, 171, 172, 181
Edgerton, Susan Huddleston 27, 130
educational exchange 11, 64, 164; Chinese and American 16, 23, 28, 157
Elbaz-Luwisch, Freema 178
embodied 26, 39, 60, 98, 112, 122, 141, 172; curriculum 179; difference 161; education 111, 179; experience 63, 177; learning 164
emergence 5, 8, 141, 171, 176
emotion 26, 71, 72, 75, 82, 87, 91, 102, 119, 123, 129, 165, 172; difficult 36, 83, 178; in research 142, 144, 146
emotional work 13, 84, 122, 176, 178
Emperor Ashoka 12
emptiness 3, 63, 77, 80, 149

energy 4, 18, 56, 73, 87, 88, 96, 149, 184; creative 18; life 3, 86, 90, 97, 123, 145, 147, 158, 163, 172, 176; of stillness 96
Enlightenment 63, 145, 149, 158, 172
Eppert, Claudia 6
Ethnocentrism 31, 32
Eyre, Richard M. 112, 125, 126

Fairbank, John King 93
feminism 45, 57, 58, 59, 67
feminist 11, 33, 47, 58, 64, 68, 115; ethics 177; teaching 131; research 151
Feng, Youlan 46, 51, 52
Fleener, Jayne 169, 178
flow 3, 14, 54, 55, 61, 68, 100, 112, 123, 125, 171, 176, 183; feminine 96; following 134, 140, 141, 150, 171; of interplay 14; natural 61–2, 121, 183; organic 134; of research 141, 152, 153, 155; a sense of 84, 87, 134, 141, 175, 176; of temporality 159
Foucault, Michel 34, 62, 98, 126, 162
Fowler, Leah 40, 154
Furth, Charlotte 50, 52, 53

Galtung, Johan 114, 118
Gandhi, Mohandas K. 1, 12, 14, 15n2, 91, 131, 155, 163, 171
Gay, Geneva 128
Gbowee, Leymah 163, 180
gender 4, 56, 57, 119, 140, 166, 176; construction of 64; and education 129, 175; equality 58; norm 54, 59; oppression 116
general education 181, 182
Giordano, Peter J. 124, 127, 128
global citizenship 7, 169, 174, 180
global competency 6, 169
global learning 6, 7, 180
globalization 6–8, 98, 101, 159, 163, 180
Goodson, Ivor 7, 142, 143, 145
Gough, Noel 2, 6
Grauerholz, Liz 165, 171, 182
Greene, Maxine 20
Grumet, Madeleine 5, 133n3, 175
guilt 38, 83, 89

Hall, Bradford 125, 126
Hall, David L. 5, 63
Hamlet, Janice D. 144, 172, 173
harmony 36, 62, 63, 66, 107
Harris, Ian 180
Hayhoe, Ruth 131, 144, 151

He, Mingfang 6
healing 13, 56, 71, 122; organic 35, 36, 169, 183
Heidegger, Martin 29
Hendry, Petra Munro 115, 116, 119
hermit 71, 90, 98, 101; -style 10, 99; tradition 97–8
Hershock, Peter 3, 5, 6, 13, 40
Hesse, Hermann 29
higher education 5–8, 60, 68, 101, 127, 164, 165, 168, 169–73, 178–80, 182
hooks, bell 175
Hoyt, Mei Wu 150
Hu, Shi 50, 51, 53
Huebner, Dwayne 4, 18, 20, 28, 126, 157, 176
Hull House 115, 116
humanism 53, 63
Humphreys, Christmas 18

I Ching 35
identity 5, 66, 68, 82, 83, 94, 153, 170; Chinese 47, 136; cross-cultural 147; cultural 81, 138; and difference; intellectual 72, 97; national 179; non- 94; -oriented 8; politics 7, 162; self- 65; the notion of 15n1
immanence 4, 63, 64
impact-response approach 30
imperialism 30–1, 33, 52, 163
improvisation 92, 94, 97–9, 126, 162, 171, 177
in-between space 8, 81
indigenous 47, 180, 181
individual freedom 38, 51, 53, 57, 58, 89
individualism 38, 53
individuality 7, 12, 14, 63, 67, 156, 161, 166–7, 177
individuation 14, 63, 96, 176
inequality 76, 94
inner work 13–14
insider 32, 35, 59, 94, 153
insight 26, 90, 96, 97, 99, 101, 116, 135, 140, 141, 143, 146, 161, 164, 172, 173
instrumental 54, 97, 101, 133, 169–70, 173, 182, 183; non- 167, 169–70; rationality 89, 103
integration 2, 4, 5, 7, 14, 50, 63, 91, 96, 114, 122, 134, 146, 147, 158, 168
intellectual engagement 11, 29, 43, 49, 55, 84, 139, 148, 161, 173
intellectual freedom 51–3, 54, 170; *see also* academic freedom

intellectual history 48, 72, 91, 97, 138
interbeing 7, 39, 147
inter-space 8
interconnectedness 4, 12–15, 36, 71, 88, 113, 126, 145, 147, 161, 169, 177, 179
intercultural 5, 9, 19, 26, 28, 72, 89, 118, 153, 165, 173; conversation 6; creativity 150; education 2, 14, 22, 29, 39, 69, 159; learning 166; relationship 35, 41; understanding 179
interdependence 3, 4, 13, 99, 138, 185n2
international education 14, 183
international studies 182
interplay 4, 14, 62, 124, 132, 166, 169, 176, 181
intersection 7, 12, 35, 72, 97, 138, 156, 160, 165, 179
intra-cultural 148, 165
intuition 74, 127, 134, 145, 146, 147, 149
intuitive understanding 138, 145, 147

jagodzinski, jan 41, 121, 125
Ji, Xianlin 61
Johnson, Allan G. 175
Jung, Carl 14, 29, 63, 96, 127–8, 156, 161, 166, 176, 184n1
justice 26, 86, 138, 155, 174; popular 98; restorative 180; social 37, 88, 90, 115, 116, 174, 182
juxtaposition 11, 66, 71–2, 120, 142, 156

Kahane, David 174, 179
Kaneda, Takuya 111, 177
Kang, Youwei 50
King, Jr., Martin Luther 1, 184
Knight, Louise 115, 116, 158, 180
Kristeva, Julia 20, 36, 40, 41, 57, 93, 126, 177, 179, 183
Kundalini awakening 87, 97, 104n7, 169

Ladson-Billings, Gloria 128
Langmann, Ellen Condiffe 141
language 3, 38, 42, 74, 80, 88, 99, 121, 125, 134, 138, 148, 150, 153, 158, 166, 167, 172; Chinese 19, 24, 25, 27, 29, 41n2, 97, 102, 139, 148, 149; and culture 19, 27, 81, 146; English 12, 42, 114, 124, 149; reform 41n2, 53; vernacular 53; Western 31
Laozi 22, 87, 98, 104n10
learning 6, 19; active 118, 124; cross-cultural 22, 38, 106, 120, 123, 139, 157, 163, 170, 178; deep 24, 124, 165, 182; by doing 109, 110, 114, 120; experientially-based 19,

67, 119, 120; global 6, 7, 180; mutual 16, 38–9, 123; from the other 6, 39, 164, 173; unintentional 74
Lee, Leo Ou-Fan 54
Levinas, Emmanuel 27, 132
Li, Dazhao 52
Li, Xin 6, 35, 93, 94, 100, 178
Liang, Qichao 50, 51
Liang, Shuming 51
liberal thought 2, 50, 51, 159
life and thought 55, 56, 161
Lin, Jing 14, 92, 123, 177
Lin, Xiaoqing 46, 52
literary criticism 8, 43, 46–8, 65, 159
literary revolution 50, 51, 53
lived experience 7, 14, 25, 37, 91, 114, 161, 164, 165, 172–4
living conditions 18, 20–2, 73, 75, 76
locality 9, 84, 114, 129; and the global 7, 114, 160, 180
Loewen, James W. 181
logocentrism 139
loss 23, 35, 38, 73, 83, 89, 91, 120, 158, 184
love 4, 14, 90, 107, 118, 138, 155, 184; and education 83; -hate 118; romantic 10, 53, 108; *see also* universal
Loy, David 5, 99, 138
Lu, Xun 53, 57, 63, 70
Luce-Kapler, Rebecca 113
lucid dreaming 89

Macdonald, James B. 125
Mandela, Nelson 180
Mann, Susan 58
market 6, 76
Marxism 47, 48, 50–2; Chinese 48, 52, 62; Western 45, 48
maternal 175, 183, 185n2
May Fourth 22, 53; era 47, 48; generation 22, 47, 159; legacy 53; literature 53, 59; movement 22, 51–4, 57
Mayes, Clifford 14, 63, 96, 127, 161, 185n2
meditation 6, 10, 71, 86–8, 96, 98, 99, 101, 122, 158, 174
memory 36, 37, 72, 83, 154, 178
metanarrative 48, 52
Metteyya, Ananda 18
militarism 116, 118
Miller, Janet 5, 55, 56, 71, 72, 98, 133n3, 139, 142, 150, 164, 177, 178
Miller, Jeffrey C. 166
mindfulness 91, 115, 141, 179
modern-indigenity 47

modernity 30–2, 46, 48, 50, 54
modernization 31, 82, 88, 89, 98, 101, 158
moment of research 134; defensive 135–6; disruptive 136–8; deconstructive 138–9; dialogic 139–41
Moon, Seungho 130
Mother Teresa 88
Muller, Jean-Marie 177
multicultural education 2, 83, 115
Munro, Petra 141, 142, 145, 150, 151
mutuality 6, 34, 150, 151, 152
mysticism 86

Nagler, Michael 12, 14, 66, 114
Nakagawa, Yoshiharu 172
national college entrance exam 43, 77
national salvation 49, 50
nationalism 6, 52, 88, 178–80
neo-traditionalism 50
New Culture Movement 4, 22, 49–51; *see also* May Fourth
New Youth 51, 53
Ng-A-Fook, Nicholas 150
Noddings, Nel 182
nonattachment 88, 89, 97, 99, 140, 167
non-bridge bridge 8, 26, 89, 150
non-dualistic 3, 13, 99, 101, 171, 177
non-duality 72, 97, 99, 101, 179
Nonlinear 72, 124, 135, 157, 171, 174
non-sense 40, 93
nonviolence 1–3, 13–15, 34–6, 66, 71, 103, 119, 143, 151, 154, 156, 163, 181–4; curriculum dynamics of 174, 176; curriculum of 155, 156, 181, 184; definition of 114; education 2, 13, 36, 38, 72, 101, 157, 174, 176–80; message of 12, 143, 155, 180, 181; and non-violence 12; as truth 91; and violence 12, 38, 181, 182; a zero space of 155, 166–74
nonviolent relationship 35, 40, 41, 91, 159, 163, 171, 177; with the other 13, 36, 40, 91, 132, 162, 167, 177; with the self 13, 40, 91, 162, 167; with temporality 159
no-self 3

objectivity 48, 141, 142
Olson, Nadine 115, 132, 133
online university 6
open-mindedness 21, 129, 177
Opium Wars 29, 31, 33, 49,
organic relationality 13, 40, 55, 161, 164, 167–9, 172, 184
Orientalism 27

otherness 7, 20, 27, 132, 162, 179
outsider 31, 32, 35, 82, 117, 153

Palmer, Parker J. 28
peace 2, 3, 36, 45, 50, 71, 75, 81, 86, 89, 90, 107, 115, 134, 155, 165, 171; definition of 116; education 106, 114–15; indigenous 180; inner 3, 13, 14, 97, 98, 99, 101, 123, 177, 178; movement 116, 163; negative 114; outer peace 13, 103, 114, 177; positive 114; studies 114, 118, 181; world 107
pedagogical 39, 67, 122, 130, 161, 163, 170; condition 125, 173; intuition 127; patience 39, 157; relationship 40, 122, 123, 125, 127; situation 14, 125, 130; thoughtfulness 39; tradition 122
pedagogy 2, 8, 11, 68, 123, 132, 159, 164, 180; contemplative 174; culturally relevant 129–30; distance 170; of mutual engagement 16, 35, 38–41; of nonviolence 14, 106, 119–28, 132; of play 125–8; *see also* teaching
Penn, William 12
persona and shadow 128
personal cultivation 15n1, 63, 164, 170, 173
personhood 7, 15, 50, 58, 86, 142, 169; authentic 54; cross-cultural 2, 8, 15, 39, 134, 158, 165; ontology of 53; site of 137, 164, 165; situated 7, 8
philosophy 5, 8, 43, 44–6, 55, 95, 135, 174; Chinese 4, 29, 43, 49–51, 54, 57, 62–3, 65, 87, 90, 135, 149; educational 8; empiricist 48, 81; Enlightenment 29, 48, 50, 63, 172; Greek 49, 62; liberal 2, 48; Western 4, 48–51, 81, 84, 86, 90, 138
Pinar, William F. 2, 5, 6, 7, 14, 36, 47, 115, 133n3, 154, 157, 160, 162, 164, 170, 180
Pitt, Alice 170
play 3, 4, 14, 43, 60, 90, 93, 148, 159, 166, 171, 176, 181; with boundary 60, 182, 184; Derridian 139; with ideas 68; and learning 68; linguistic 3, 148, 149; and reason 4, 102; with relations 184; serendipitous 170–1; Taoist 101; and teaching 68, 111, 122, 125; as transcendent 14, 85, 156
Pohl, Karl-Heinz 29, 160
popular culture 45, 63, 65
Porche-Frilot, Donna 20
postcolonial 33, 47, 58, 65, 95
postmodern 33; condition 48; discourse 32, 47; society 89, 95; theory 45, 48, 54, 65

postmodernism 32, 42, 48
post-structural 27, 33, 56, 58, 132, 138, 162, 178
power 25; abuse of 93; authoritarian 66; game 46, 77, 163; masculine 96; persuasive 65, 78; political 51, 79; postmodern notion of 162; relationships 20, 32–3; state 34; structure 97; struggle 60, 93, 162, 163
pragmatism 50
prejudice 27, 28, 34, 165
progress 3, 49–51, 57, 161
public intellectual 13, 28–9, 64–5

racism 20, 117, 119, 130
Raphals, Lisa 62
reason 4, 89, 95, 146; and emotion 146; instrumental 89, 90, 91, 102, 173; moral 4, 90; scientific 4, 5, 51, 158
reciprocity 6
relational dynamics 13, 14, 39, 66, 163, 177
relationality 14, 55, 86, 103, 123, 156, 177, 183; compassionate 182; cross-cultural 169; nonviolent 12, 176, 180; research 134; *see also* organic relationality
religious 34, 86, 166; culture 119; dogma 172, 173; education 172; faith 10, 113, 158, 171; freedom 76, 100, 103n3; knowledge 144
research 2, 28, 47, 65, 113, 121, 134, 145–50, 159; educational 141; journal 10, 72, 145; methodology 96, 145, 147; organic 8, 145; qualitative 134, 141–7, 150–1; relationship 143, 151–2, 154; scientific 141
resilience 22
resistance 64, 94, 100, 130, 173
resonance 14, 63, 71, 140, 156
revelation 1, 134, 143, 145, 146, 147
Rosen, David 156
Rosenblatt, Paul C. 142, 144

sage 62, 64, 101
Said, Edward 27
Sawyer, Richard 113
Schoeberlein, Deborah 179
science 14, 30, 51, 113, 163; and democracy 22, 51; educational 96, 141; natural 2, 49; political 8, 10, 25, 80, 96; social 2, 81, 86, 96, 141, 181; and technology 86, 91, 172
Schweitzer, Albert 107
scholar-official 49, 64

Index 207

self 2, 5, 13, 27, 32, 36, 40, 49, 62, 88–90, 94, 115, 123, 161, 165, 169, 177, 179; American 33; and the other 2, 13, 20, 27, 33, 35, 39, 83, 91, 119, 132, 153, 161, 162, 168; -centered 38, 84, 85, 96, 111; -creation 177; definition of 15n1; -education 11, 173; -image 33, 57; -interest 38; sense of 21, 93; -transcendence 69; -understanding 98, 127, 128, 137, 184n1
serendipity 105, 106–9, 113, 141, 143, 156, 165, 176; and nonviolence 113; notion of 112; in pedagogical relationship 127–8; spiritual 112, 125; and teaching 113–14, 119, 125–6, 170
service learning 105, 106, 109–12, 114–17, 123
Shen, Heyong 96
Sheth, Suki 179
Sikes, Pat 142, 143, 145
Smith, David Geoffrey 5, 6, 7, 29, 30, 159, 179
Smith-Christopher, Daniel L., 12, 180
Smythe, Jon 56, 130, 157
Social Darwinism 50, 51
social justice 37, 115, 174, 182
socialist 3, 33, 37, 52, 116, 117
solitude 45, 73, 182
Spence, Jonathan D. 33, 92, 93, 98
spirituality 1, 4, 5, 36, 85, 125, 126, 134, 145, 171–3, 184; definition of 4, 144, 172
stereotype 19, 91, 173
stillness 3–5, 71, 96–9, 122–23, 134–5, 144, 146, 158, 169, 173, 179, 184
storytelling 43, 64, 72, 142, 152, 153, 178
stranger 19, 20, 59, 81, 105, 126, 154, 166, 176, 182
subjective positioning 61, 68, 129, 148, 150, 153
subjectivity 6, 8, 15, 55, 59, 145, 166; research 150, 153
surprise 1–3, 5, 16, 18, 108, 112, 119, 125, 129, 134, 144, 170, 184
sustainable 7, 15, 122, 166, 180

Taiji 4, 87, 94, 167
Tan, Sitong 50
Tao 4, 73, 87, 90, 96, 145, 146, 149, 167
Tao Te Ching 4, 35, 40, 90, 98, 104, 132, 167
Taoism 3, 29, 30, 47, 63, 91, 96, 104n10, 130, 138, 160, 166
Taubman, Peter 170
Taylor, Jeremy 14, 36

teacher education 8, 86, 87, 108, 133n3, 137, 178, 182
teaching 2, 10–11, 26, 60, 79, 89, 102, 114, 131, 142, 148, 169, 175, 183; beyond the category 66–9; college 67, 125, 130, 137, 163–6, 171, 172, 182; content 11, 35, 84, 124, 137, 165, 181; culturally relevant 2, 119, 128; feminist 131; method 26, 35, 67, 75, 84, 109, 137; orientation 9, 67, 119, 166; as phenomenological 137; philosophy 9; position of 173; style 120, 124, 129; as translation 27; as a vocation 28
temporality 72, 135, 144, 154, 157–9, 167, 184
Teng, Jinhua Emma 58
tensionality 8, 66, 101, 126, 132, 143, 150, 171
Thich, Nhat Hanh 7
third space 4, 126, 166
thought reform 26, 38
Todd, Sharon 6, 27, 39, 132
Tolle, Eckhart 3, 4, 87
tradition 12, 17, 48, 49, 51, 65, 81, 92, 115; American 118; Chinese 4, 37, 47, 50, 64, 66, 117, 125, 131, 144; Christian 158; Eastern 5; educational 180; European 160; native 47, 48, 180; research 45, 134, 142, 144, 146–8, 152, 154; scholarly 82, 134, 136, 138, 146–8; Western 46
tradition and modernity 46, 30–1
traditional versus radical 56–8
transcendence 20, 53, 54, 85, 90, 98, 101, 140; and education 20, 68; and immanence 2, 63–4; self- 69
transformation 24, 49, 66, 98, 146, 149, 150, 162, 172, 181; cultural 51–3; global 7; internal 49, 180; personal 7, 166, 182; political 64; social 165
translation 12, 27, 42, 49, 67, 148, 150, 151
transnational 2, 5–6, 11, 27, 35, 150, 148, 178
trauma 22, 35, 36, 41, 83, 88, 89, 93, 140, 152, 157–8, 166, 169, 179
truth 47, 48, 49, 74, 79, 86, 88, 91, 95, 139, 151, 162; and concept 86; and meditation 86, 90; women's 151; *see also* universal
Tu Wei-ming 5
Tung, May Paomay 177
Tutu, Desmond 180

unconscious 38, 63, 89, 146; collective 127, 179
uniformity 7, 92, 93, 169

United Nations 106, 107, 114
unity 7, 64, 101, 178, 179
universal 119, 132, 158, 159, 160, 177, 180; love 119, 131, 161, 163; time 158; truth 47–8, 48, 49
unlearning 13, 19, 102–3, 116, 130, 138, 161, 173
US countercultural movement 17

vernacular literature 49–50
violence 1, 4, 12, 34, 36, 38, 41, 73, 83, 86, 97–100, 114, 118, 132, 166, 177, 181, 184; intellectual 102; passive 83; and revolution 36, 92–3, 155; state 34, 37, 41n4; social 174; structural
Vokey, Daniel 99
voice 3, 36, 71, 83, 87, 131, 142, 150, 151, 179; autobiographical 5, 9, 143; inner 2, 84, 183; of nonviolence 3, 38, 182

Wang, Guowei 91, 104n9
Watts, Alan 17, 18, 160
Wells, Ida B. 116
Western culture 9, 20, 44, 46, 57
Western intellectual 29, 46, 54, 65–6, 160
Western learning 49, 51, 65, 159
Western rationalism 81, 90, 91, 94–7

Western scholarship 96
Western thought 2, 9, 42–4, 46–8, 52, 63, 87, 159–61
Whitlock, Reta Ugena 171
whole-being experience 144, 145, 146, 122, 126
wholeness 7, 14, 100, 126, 132, 156, 166, 167, 176, 184
Wisdom 26, 96, 100, 108, 125, 146, 149, 158, 160, 165, 171, 172
Women's International League for Peace and Freedom 116
Wuwei 125, 132n2, 175

Xu, Yuzhen 47

Yin and *yang* 3, 4, 83, 86, 87, 90, 166–7, 185
Yuanfen (chance/fate) 60–2

Zen 29
Zero 3–4, 15, 73, 87–90, 99, 139–40, 147, 149, 150–1, 155, 166–8, 174, 184
Zha, Qiang 66
Zhuangzi 87, 98, 101, 104n10
Zhuangzi (*Chuang Tzu*) 98, 101, 104n10
Ziarek, Ewa Płonowska 177